Culturally Relevant Teaching

Culturally Relevant Teaching

Making Space for Indigenous Peoples in the Schoolhouse

Beverly J. Klug

ROWMAN & LITTLEFIELD
Lanham • Boulder • New York • London

Published by Rowman & Littlefield
An imprint of The Rowman & Littlefield Publishing Group, Inc.
4501 Forbes Boulevard, Suite 200, Lanham, Maryland 20706
www.rowman.com

6 Tinworth Street, London SE11 5AL, United Kingdom

Copyright © 2021 by Beverly J. Klug

All rights reserved. No part of this book may be reproduced in any form or by any electronic or mechanical means, including information storage and retrieval systems, without written permission from the publisher, except by a reviewer who may quote passages in a review.

British Library Cataloguing in Publication Information Available

Library of Congress Cataloging-in-Publication Data
Names: Klug, Beverly J., author.
Title: Culturally relevant teaching : making space for indigenous peoples in the schoolhouse / Beverly J. Klug.
Description: Lanham, Maryland : Rowman & Littlefield Publishing Group, 2021. | Includes bibliographical references and index. | Summary: "The purpose of this book is to provide insights into effective teaching of Native American students in our schools"-- Provided by publisher.
Identifiers: LCCN 2020057496 (print) | LCCN 2020057497 (ebook) | ISBN 9781475853315 (cloth) | ISBN 9781475853322 (paperback) | ISBN 9781475853339 (epub)
Subjects: LCSH: Indian children--Education--United States. | Indian students--United States. | Culturally relevant pedagogy--United States.
Classification: LCC E97 .K569 2021 (print) | LCC E97 (ebook) | DDC 370.1170973--dc23
LC record available at https://lccn.loc.gov/2020057496
LC ebook record available at https://lccn.loc.gov/2020057497

This book is dedicated to the following individuals:
Delbert Farmer (deceased, Shoshone-Bannock), champion of education for youth of the Shoshone-Bannock Tribes of Fort Hall, Idaho.
The children, teachers, Shoshone-Bannock community and schools, and my American Indian relatives and friends who have taught me so much.
Indigenous students, teachers, and communities throughout the country and members of educational communities that support all of our students.
Finally, the late Robert J. and Joan L. Klug, parents who not only supported me on my journey but provided role models throughout their lives of working for social justice.

Contents

About the Title	ix
Preface	xi
Acknowledgments	xvii
Introduction	xix
Organization of This Book	xxv

Part I: The Roots of Who We Are in America — **1**

1 Unraveling the Puzzle of How Humans Came to Be — 3
2 Humans' Continuing Development and the Americas — 17
3 Who Were These Europeans? — 45
4 The Clash of Cultures and *Doctrine of Discovery*: The Rise of Racism in the Americas — 69

Part II: Past and Present Education of Indigenous Students in This Country — **87**

5 Racism, Stereotypes, and Education for Assimilation — 93
6 Twentieth-Century Change and Rising Native American Voices — 113
7 Indigenous Families, Communities, and Ways of Learning: The Heart of Resiliency for Native Students — 133

Part III: Designing Schools in Partnership: Educators, Schools, Native American and Non-Native Communities — **155**

8 Creating Resilient Students: Secrets to Success for Native American Children — 161

9 Educational Collaborations with Native American Communities	183
10 Celebrations: Shared Success Is Success for All	205
Short Biographies of Those Providing Quotations	227
Appendix A: Important Legislation for Indigenous Education	231
Appendix B: Resources for Teachers	233
Index	239
About the Author	249

About the Title

The term "making space" as used in this title is not the same as making a physical place or counting spaces held by Indigenous students for school attendance purposes. The term refers to opening our minds, curricula, schools, and society to the inclusion of Indigenous societies and histories that have been closed previously to this possibility.

By making space for Indigenous peoples in our everyday lives, we are countering the Colonial mindset. This thinking promotes the false narrative that everything Western European is superior and everything Indigenous is inferior.

Postcolonial theory advances arguments for inclusivity of all peoples in the Americas and other areas of European domination. It calls for acknowledgment of the wrongs perpetrated against Aboriginal peoples in the name of God and European countries. Postcolonial theory carries the concepts of equality for all ethnic groups and sharing power within schools and other cultural institutions with our non-European constituents.

Thus, "making space" reflects the postcolonial position that the ideology of white European superiority is a false narrative. This chronicle lasted for over five hundred years and was devised to legitimatize the taking of Indigenous lands and their riches for the profit of the conquerors.

It is time to recognize these pretentions have no place in our twenty-first century America. We must divest ourselves of a system that rewards only those in power and reinvest in a system of equity distribution throughout our diverse populations.

Preface

Throughout more than forty years of teaching students of all ethnicities, abilities, and ages from preschool through middle-aged adults, I have found that one of the key components to working with them has been that of understanding who they are and from where they have come. This has been true whether my students were from suburban Midwestern areas, Appalachia, rural Midwestern farm country, the dust-bowl areas of the West, inner-city urban areas, reservations, or living in areas of the western Rocky Mountains.

Due to being able to relate to my students, I could tailor my teaching to their interests and needs. My message to my university preservice and inservice teachers has always been the same. We need to understand who our students are, what their interests and desires are, what their goals are for becoming adults in our society, and not pay sole attention to what labels may have been applied to them. In turn, I have been educated by my students, acting in shared partnership with them as they taught me what they knew about their home areas and interests.

I believe this is a characteristic of what all good teachers do: We focus on our students. In this process, I have learned many things from how to birth pigs, hunt 'coons, play Skittles, how railroads work, the way to braid hair in several cultural styles, what "playing the dozens" really entails, and how to observe nature with reverence—topics far from my upbringing. While many of my students may have experienced difficulty with book learning, they had a wealth of information about the world in which they lived. Capitalizing on students' cultural knowledge has made a difference in their learning. Most of all, I have learned to listen and read between the lines.

In teaching Indigenous students in urban, rural, and reservation settings, I have also been exposed to some of the worst prejudices against groups of color in our country. These prejudices have not abated following the civil rights movement of the 1960s. Say the word "Indian" and a host of stereotypes and prejudices come to mind. Due to these experiences, I began talking with educators around the country concerning the lack of information about Indigenous peoples in school curricula. I then began to research and write about Aboriginal education and what needed to be done to change the status quo for our Native American students.

The history of physical and cultural genocides of Native Americans across this hemisphere is almost totally ignored in American schools. Occasionally, a few pages of history from dominant cultural views about Indigenous peoples may be included in state or U.S. histories. These generally concern the Indian Wars but not the dominant-culture infractions as causes of these hostilities.

Outside of these instances, rarely do American Indians/Alaska Natives make an appearance in our textbooks. They are not included in the history of this great nation. Even accounts of fighting for freedom from the British do not include the different Tribes who fought alongside the colonial forces. Thus, a false impression is created of Indigenous absence from this country and consequently, their perceived unimportance.

This lack of information has led to questions from others about whether or not Native Americans still exist, and the next question, "Do they still live in teepees?" These questions are not asked by ignorant people, but by those who are uninformed about the past and current states of Indian country.

Lately, our collective conscious recognition of American Indigenous nations has been aroused by the protests against the Dakota Access pipeline and the refusal of the current administration to grant long overdue CARES monies to Tribal nations during the COVID-19 pandemic (finally required by order of a judge in mid-July 2020). The recent ruling that one-half of the state of Oklahoma is still an American Indian reservation reconfirmed Indigenous treaty rights in this country.

During the last century and a half, it is as though a total mist of collective amnesia has descended on our nation regarding Indigenous peoples and their treaties with the U.S. government. Perhaps this is a way to try to expurgate the sins of the past. There appears to be fear that our children will not respect their elders or the people declared as heroes of the nation if the wrongs of their decisions are unmasked in our schools. Deep in our hearts and consciences, we know that this land did not belong to Europeans. Perhaps with collective denial of the past, somehow the population of the dominant culture thought issues regarding sanctity of the land and cultural worldviews would never prevail on twenty-first-century discussions concerning wealth and power in this country.

We must be willing to acknowledge that this land was *not* European land. Many times it was acquired through unethical and immoral practices by those in power. This was true in this country even before its inception in 1776 with the Declaration of Independence. The acquisition of territory occurred at great expense to the Indigenous peoples in this hemisphere to whom it belonged. There are many areas in the country where treaties with Native tribes went to Congress but were not passed for one reason or another. However, that did not prevent non-Natives from staking out claims and settling in those places, especially in the western part of our country.

One of the ways we could correct these wrongs is to make space for our Indigenous peoples in our schools. In doing so, we recognize the need to be honest about the American Indian/Alaska Native saga which took place in these lands, as well as in the areas of the world where lands became territories of the United States. We must do this to correct misperceptions of Native peoples in this region of the world before the coming of Europeans. Then we must elevate in our minds the advances and achievements of Indigenous peoples in the last five hundred years. Finally, we must acknowledge contemporary Aboriginal peoples and their contributions to our world.

VALUING OUR INDIGENOUS STUDENTS AND THEIR COMMUNITIES

Far too many of our Tribal youth give up on themselves. Due to systemic racism that has been part of our dominant culture society, many of these students fall victim in the face of this prejudice and do not understand or appreciate their own value as human beings. On the other hand, Indigenous children who grow up learning about their cultural heritages and values oftentimes can surmount these challenges to their identities. Educators need to be aware of this and assure Aboriginal students that not only are they worthy of our attention, but that their ancestors were intelligent, powerful, and spiritual people.

We build pride in children's heritages by reinforcing these messages through bulletin boards, images, and objects in classrooms representing Native American peoples and cultures positively. We already do this with regard to the dominant culture in our classrooms. Doing so for our Indigenous students provides opportunities to share information with and among students which can lead to valuable discussions.

An important message to share with Native American students is to "follow the Red Road," or as in the Navajo prayer, to "Walk in Beauty." Both of these precepts reinforce the importance of following the cultural teachings of elders; staying away from harmful behaviors and substances; working for the betterment of one's family and community; and keeping the spiritual, mental, emotional, and physical aspects of one's being in balance. In other words, they are callings to be one's best and to become healthy contributors to one's family, community, and society. They exhort students to utilize their talents and abilities whatever they may be. They are reminders to treat one's life and all life as sacred and be thankful for the gifts from the Creator. We don't just endure life, but celebrate it and the lives of all that surround us.

In Western terms, these messages can be translated into the Judeo-Christian teaching that "the body is the temple of the soul," and therefore sacred. Other world religions have similar sayings. Therefore, we must treat our lives, and the lives of others around us, in such a way that reflects our respect for the sacred. Unfortunately, the message of man's dominion over the earth has obscured the notion of the earth being a sacred habitation for the people who live on this planet, as it is a gift from Creator to us. However, this message is obvious in many of the prayers that are said thanking God for the gifts we have received.

In this age of secularism, it is very easy to dismiss these messages as unimportant and unscientific. Joseph Campbell researched many of the mythologies and religions of the world. He found that they are all connected with similar messages to people wherever their origins. These messages reflect the deep respect fostered over millennia that all life is sacred.

In Aboriginal societies, there is no hierarchy of life forms: man is not given dominion over other life forms or considered superior. Man is a partner in a relationship with all of life on this earth and the universe. Stated this way, we understand the importance of all life and life-givers, and we are thankful for the gifts of all. We take care of and nourish each other.

If we can understand this message, we can begin to understand the importance of the land in nourishing the spirits, foundations, and identities of Native Americans. Religious practices take place as always in nature, in areas considered to have special potential for connecting with the Creator and the spirit world. Native American peoples have worshipped in these places for millennia, and just as we would not destroy temples, cathedrals, churches, or mosques, we need to respect these sacred places.

As stated eloquently by Jaimie A. Pinkham (Nez Perce):

> America's diverse environment fashioned a mixture of cultures. Each tribe across the landscape maintained an autonomy that could be heard in the distinct

languages, observed by independent movements across exclusive homelands and distinguished by individual styles of customs and governance.

Then and today the natural world is a mainstay of tribal existence and identity: from the Keepers of the Forests in the northern hardwoods of Wisconsin, to the coastal rain forests of Washington where the canoe builders still practice their craft; from the snowcapped Sierra Blanca, birthplace of the Mescalero Apache in New Mexico, to the spruce forests that wrap life-sustaining resources around the village of Galena in the Alaska Yukon. . . .

Over those ten thousand [plus] years, our ancestors maintained a special relationship with the land, acknowledging that our livelihood depended on bounty provided by the seas, rivers, prairies, tundra, and forests. Land offered up foods to nourish us and medicines to heal us. It provided materials and places that were essential to our education, spiritual connectivity, and recreation. (2015, p. 256)

FOSTERING INDIGENOUS VALUES AS EQUAL VALUES IN OUR SCHOOLS

In today's world, school knowledge is needed to be able to flourish in society. As Indigenous peoples' economies are growing, new opportunities for employment on reservations are becoming available. To heal our relations with Native American peoples, we need to understand the complexities of Indigenous societies and their cultures. We need to teach about how their practices and products positively influenced life for Europeans and other people around the world. Foodstuffs, pharmaceuticals and medical practices, modes of transportation such as canoes and snowshoes, and even some of the games played around the world today had origins in the Americas. All of these enhanced the lives of Europeans, not the other way around.

We also need to be clear that—due to cultural and physical genocides—Native Americans were deliberately relegated into poverty status by those European and European Americans making decisions at the top levels of government, not that Aboriginals have claimed this position for themselves. Dominant-culture beneficiaries of these decisions made in our country's past need to acknowledge this as the first step towards making a difference in the lives of all of our students, Indigenous or not.

Educators need to find ways to build bridges between home and school for our Indigenous students. Our non-Native students and colleagues will not shatter when we share Aboriginal histories with them. Instead, I have seen appreciation in colleagues and students when they begin to learn about Native American peoples. Attitudes begin to change. They are more apt to reach out to Indigenous students/

classmates when they learn to put aside their fear of "the other," much of that fear created and fed by media stereotypes.

As educators we can be sociocultural mediators in our schools. We can work in concert with Aboriginal families and communities in ways that are respectful to all. Thus we are fulfilling our promises to meet the needs of all of our students, enhance their interests, and assist them in fulfilling their dreams for their futures. We attest to our students that they are important. We validate their cultural teachings and understandings. We reinforce that following the Red Road provides them a good life emotionally, spiritually, physically, and mentally. Our future as a nation requires nothing less.

For this reason, I have added to information about culturally relevant teaching, oftentimes referred to as Culturally Relevant Pedagogy or Culturally Responsive Pedagogy, by including important information in this book about Indigenous peoples and historical events affecting them in this country. I fully acknowledge that there is much more information available. I hope that this book will stimulate you as readers to continue on your journeys to learn more about Native America and Indigenous peoples. Most importantly, I am hoping for the development of strong relations among Native Americans, school administrators, teachers, counselors, and the general public as a result of this book that will, in turn, enhance the education and learning opportunities of Indigenous students in our nations' schools, making education an enriching experience for all.

Thank you for taking this journey to learn more about Indigenous peoples and how we can work together coequally in our educational institutions. As with my other books on Indigenous education, any royalties realized by the sale of this book will go toward scholarships for Aboriginal students who want to be teachers.

Beverly J. Klug, EdD

REFERENCE

Pinkham, J. A. (2015). Native endurance: A connection to place. In M. Jaffe & R. Wandschneider (Eds.), *The longest trail: Writings on American Indian history, culture, and politics*, A. M. Josephy Jr. New York, NY: Vintage Books.

Acknowledgments

I would like to thank Thomas F. Koerner, PhD, Vice President/Publisher of Education at Rowman & Littlefield Publishing, without whose encouragement this book may have continued to be just an idea. I appreciate and thank Carlie Wall, Managing Editor at Education, Rowman & Littlefield, for her assistance with the production of this book.

I would also like to thank my readers in alphabetical order who provided valuable feedback to me concerning the writing, information, and ideas presented in this manuscript: Cydney Crue, PhD Sociology; certification in Educational Leadership; Sherice Gould (Shoshone-Bannock), MA Anthropology; Verlon Gould, (Shoshone-Bannock), Elder; Barbara Griggs, BA, Elementary, Early Childhood, & Special Education; James Liday, MEd, Educational Administration; Judy Liday, MEd, Early Childhood Education; Donna Houtz McArthur (Shoshone-Bannock), BA Secondary Education; Marvin McCall, BA Speech and Communications; certified Secondary Education; Sandy Rainey (Shoshone-Bannock), BA Elementary Education; Suzanne Klug Thum, MS Audiology; Caleb Tinsley, AA in Criminology; and Patricia T. Whitfield, PhD Education, Professor Emerita Lyons College.

In addition, I would also like to thank the university students, many teachers, many colleagues, and members of the Association of Teacher Educators and the American Indian Education Association, who have supported my work throughout the years. I appreciate the generosity of those who have allowed me to use their voices in parts of this manuscript to create better understandings of Indigenous peoples and their challenges in our country. Their short biographies appear at the end of chapter 10.

I take responsibility for any errors that may appear in the final book.

Introduction

The purpose of this book is to provide insights into effective teaching of Native American[1] students in our schools. In doing so, it is imperative to raise awareness of the latest scientific information concerning the origins of humankind made available through the Human Genome Project (HGP; NIH, n.d.). This knowledge provides new understandings of the development of our species that impacts the relationships between Indigenous peoples and Western Europeans; indeed, with all ethnic groups (Mukherjee, 2016; Wells, 2002).

Technology for shipbuilding and information about navigation had reached a significant point before the coming of Europeans into the Americas. There were some recorded meetings with Native peoples and Greenlanders in the far north. Vikings were visitors in what is now Newfoundland, Canada; records show Basque fishermen from Europe also went there (Barnes, 2010; Marshall, 1997). These groups were not looking for settlements in the Americas and generally were not in conflict at the time with the Native populations. All of this changed with the sailing expeditions of Christóbal Colón (Christopher Columbus; Mann, 2011).

> For millennia, almost all Europeans were found in Europe, few Africans existed outside of Africa, and Asians lived, without exception, in Asia alone. No one in the Eastern Hemisphere in 1492, so far as is known [in the general population], had ever seen an American native.... Colón's voyages inaugurated an unprecedented reshuffling of *Homo sapiens*: the human wing of the Colombian Exchange.[2] People shot around the world like dice flung on a gaming table. Europeans became the majority in Argentina and Australia, Africans were found from São Paulo to Seattle and Chinatowns sprang up all over the globe. (Mann, 2011, p. 366)

Eltis and Halbert (2009; cited by Mann, 2011) headed a study team of multiple researchers of the African slave trade which led the way in this process. According to documents from around the world, there were thirty-five thousand slave voyages with approximately 11.7 million captive Africans headed to the Americas. There were tens of millions of Indians in the Americas at the time of Colón, not the little-settled lands as has been stated previously (Mann, 2011).

The impact on the Americas was unfathomable. Thus began five hundred years of history that included enslaving thousands of Indigenous peoples who were shipped to Europe and/or used as slaves in the Americas (American Indian Histories and Cultures, 2019; Wilson, 1998). Hence the theft of lands from Native peoples by Europeans and their governments, including the newly formed United States and Canadian governments, began (Wilson, 1998).

The creation of reservations (or reserves in Canada) in North America (Deloria, 1974) expelled thousands from their homelands. Missionaries forced conversions to Christianity (Sowell, 1998). Physical and cultural genocides were committed against Native peoples (Adams, 1999; Churchill, 1994; Stannard, 1992). In all, this began a period of immense cultural mixing.

CURRENT POPULATIONS OF AMERICAN INDIANS AND ALASKA NATIVES IN THE UNITED STATES

There are currently 5.2 million American Indians and Alaska Natives in the United States, or 2 percent of the population as of 2010 (Norris, Vines, & Hoeffel, 2012). This information was compiled after the 2010 Census. The number is believed to be an undercount since many American Indians refused to take part in the census. According to a study by Jim, Arias, Seneca, Hoopes, Jim, Johnson, and Wiggins (2014), American Indians and Alaska Natives have a high rate of misclassification of their identities as that of other races by the Indian Health Services, which also leads to undercounting of Aboriginal people.

As of January 30, 2020, there are now 574 Tribal Nations recognized by the federal government (Sweeney, 2020). This number may increase as Tribal entities that were previously terminated are restored to their rightful place as Native Nations. Eleven states recognize sixty-three Tribal entities that may or may not also be federally recognized (National Conference of State Legislators, n.d.). In addition, there are some states which do not have a formal process for recognizing Tribal entities but still adopt resolutions to support and honor Tribes that have not gained federal recognition (Salazar, 2016).

As educators, we are more aware of the populations of Euro-Americans, African Americans, and Asian Americans than of Native Americans in our schools. Yet, Indigenous populations are part of active student populations in most of the United States. For various reasons, their presence has been largely ignored in programs as we prepare students for careers as professional educators. As a result, there are many false perceptions or biases against Aboriginals in our schools, prejudices that have been perpetuated over the last several centuries in the European quest to control all of the Americas.

Areas of the United States annexed from Mexico carry histories of the Native American and Latinx populations which are not well represented or taught in the Western European hegemonic curriculum presented in today's schools. Instead, curricula is presented primarily from the conquerors' viewpoints, exalting the roles that Europeans played in making the Americas resemble European cities and cultures.

Currently, we are experiencing a great influx of refugees who are coming from the areas of Central and South America seeking asylum in the United States. The majority are Mestizos—Latinx combined with Indian heritages—or who have only Indian identities. There were no political boundaries in the Americas before the conquest, and Indigenous peoples traveled throughout the hemisphere. Their histories are part of the Aboriginal history of all of the Americas.

We can no longer afford to present only the European view of history in our schools. Our Indigenous populations deserve to be represented as they are the original peoples in this land. As teachers, we need to know the truths of their lived realities, and celebrate the great strengths and gifts that all of our Aboriginal students bring with them to our halls of learning.

Due to the actions against Native Americans, Latinx, and African populations and their descendants, we encounter many students in our schools who are suffering from the legacies of colonization (Mukherjee, 2016). Intergenerational trauma is a real concept, stemming from the historical trauma (HT) inflicted on these populations. HT manifests itself in the behaviors of affected students in our schools, challenging the abilities of teachers to reach these children. This has rarely been addressed in our teacher preparation programs but needs to have a focus so that teachers are prepared to work constructively with all students.

Racism, prejudice, name-calling, bullying, and bias in teaching curriculum materials are all indicted when it comes to teaching in schools with Native American populations, whether Indigenous students are majority or minority populations. The racism perpetuated for over five hundred years has not automatically gone away in schools or the public since the civil rights era of the 1960s. Educators need to know how these biases and prejudices came to be to address them in their classrooms. Therefore we need to also understand accounts of European and American histories that allowed attitudes of superiority and exploitation of others to become legitimized.

As educators in the twenty-first century, we know that many of the practices recently legislated are not working well for Indigenous students. The high rates of school dropout and suicides for Indigenous youth cannot continue to be ignored. In the end, we are all family and want what is best for all of our family members. We need the tools and abilities to change teaching practices to become more effective with Indigenous students.

REFERENCES

Adams, H. (1999). *Tortured people: The politics of colonization* (Rev. ed.). Penticton, BC: Theytus Books Ltd.

American Indian Histories and Cultures. (2019). *History*. Adam Matthew Digital. Thousand Oaks, CA: Sage Publishing. Retrieved from http://resources.amdigital.co.uk.libpublic3.library.isu.edu/aihc/time/.

Barnes, I. (2010). *The historical atlas of Native Americans*. New York, NY: Chartwell Books.

Churchill, W. (1994). *Indians r us?* Monroe, MN: Common Courage Press.

Deloria, V., Jr. (1974). *Behind the trail of broken treaties: An Indian declaration of independence*. New York, NY: Delta Books.

Jim, M., Arias, E., Seneca, D., Hoopes, M., Jim, C., Johnson, N., & Wiggins, C. (2014). Racial Misclassification of American Indians and Alaska Natives by Indian Health Service Contract Health Service Delivery Area. *American Journal of Public Health*, 104 (3). Retrieved from: https://www.researchgate.net/publication/261799829_Racial_Misclassification_of_American_Indians_and_Alaska_Natives_by_Indian_Health_Service_Contract_Health_Service_Delivery_Area.

Mann, C. C. (2011). *1493: Uncovering the New World Columbus created*. New York, NY: Albert A. Knopf.

Marshall, I. (1997). *A history and ethnography of the Beothuk*. Montreal & Kingston: McGill-Queen's University Press.

Mukherjee, S. (2016). *The gene: An intimate history*. New York, NY: Scribner.

National Conference of State Legislators. (n.d.). State recognition of American Indian tribes. http://www.ncsl.org/research/state-tribal-institute/state-recognition-of-american-indian-tribes.aspx.

National Institutes of Health. (n.d.). *National Human Genome Research Institute*. Bethesda, MD: Author. Retrieved from https://www.genome.gov/about-genomics.

Norris, T., Vines, P. L., & Hoeffel, E. M. (2012, January). *The American Indian and Alaska Native Population: 2010, C2010BR-10. 2010 Census Briefs*. Washington, DC: U.S. Census Bureau, U.S. Department of Commerce Economics and Statistics Administration. Retrieved from https://www.census.gov/history/pdf/c2010br-10.pdf.

Salazar, M. (2016, October). State recognition of American Indian Tribes. *NCSL News, 24* (39). Retrieved from https://www.ncsl.org/research/state-tribal-institute/state-recognition-of-american-indian-tribes.aspx.

Sowell, T. (1998). *Conquests and cultures: An international history*. New York, NY: Basic Books.

Stannard, D. E. (1992). *American holocaust: The conquest of the New World.* New York, NY: Oxford University Press.

Sweeney, T. (2020). Indian Entities recognized by and eligible to receive services from the United States Bureau of Indian Affairs. *Federal Register, 85 FR 5462,* 5462–5467. Washington, DC: Bureau of Indian Affairs, Interior. Document Number: 2020-01707. Retrieved from https://www.federalregister.gov/documents/2020/01/30/2020-01707/.

Wells, S. (2002). *The journey of man: A genetic odyssey.* Princeton, NJ: Princeton University Press.

Wilson, J. (1998). *The earth shall weep: A history of Native America.* New York, NY: Grove Press.

NOTES

1. The terms Native American, American Indian/Alaska Native, Indigenous, and Aboriginal are used interchangeably. All refer to populations native to the Americas. Hawaiian, Pacific Islanders, and Caribbean Islanders are also considered Indigenous or Aboriginal peoples.

2. This was a term coined by Alfred S. Crosby (cited in Mann, 2011).

Organization of This Book

This book is divided into three parts:

Part I: The Roots of Who We Are in America
Part II: Past and Present Education of Indigenous Students in This Country
Part III: Designing Schools in Partnership: Educators, Schools, Native American, and Non-Native Communities

WHO WILL BENEFIT FROM READING THIS BOOK?

This book is meant to be read by those involved in the field of education, especially those who are engaged with Indigenous populations. This community includes teachers, teachers-in-preparation, administrators, counselors, coaches, school nurses, and members of school boards of education. It also includes members of the public that we serve in our schools.

Our American education is based in Western European values and culture.

Nevertheless, intelligence is not owned by one group of people but is a shared quantity with anyone who is of the human race. Ethnic groups of color have developed their ways of viewing the world and socializing their members. In many instances, these ways—or "mores"—are different from the Western European ways of learning and doing.

Culture, values, and the way people view others who are "different" are learned from those who came before us. These cultural attributes evolved over thousands of years across different areas of the world. Consequently, we need to interrogate the information that we have learned over our lifetimes as to its accurate perceptions of others in our human family.

As educators and policymakers, we need to understand how our values and cultural practices impact our teaching of students from other cultural groups. Otherwise, we will continue to produce a system of haves and have nots that rewards those who think like Western Europeans and punishes those who do not. This means that one set of values or cultural practices should not be privileged over others within our ethnically diverse country.

While the American Indian and Alaska Native populations in particular will be discussed, many similarities are shared with other Indigenous populations living in this country. These are primarily Latinx and multiethnic populations living in areas of the southern United States annexed from Mexico, as well as Puerto Rican and other Caribbean Islands; Hawaiian and Pacific Islands; members of Canadian First Nations and Métis populations; and Indigenous Asians and Australasians.

Numerous members of these populations reside now in the contiguous lower forty-eight states and share characteristics with Aboriginal North American populations. Others may be in schools that are under the auspices of the U.S. Department of Education in their home territories. The largest percentage of Indigenous peoples in the United States are living in urban areas of the country. Their schools are, indeed, multicultural and multiethnic.

While I am not a member of an Indigenous community, I have been active in Native American education for more than forty years. Most importantly, I believe that teachers can become "bicultural" themselves, understanding Indigenous cultures and ways of being so they can effectively teach all Native American students, whether they are assimilated to the dominant culture, are bicultural, or are traditional. By learning more about Aboriginal cultures in communities where we teach, mistakes and misunderstandings can be avoided that may damage our relationships with them.

Readers will be excited to learn many new concepts about Indigenous peoples in this hemisphere that have been kept buried for the last five hundred years. Sharing this knowledge with all of our Native American and non-Native students can make a tremendous positive change in the way Aboriginal students are viewed in our schools. In turn, our Indigenous students can become co-equals with their peers in activities that utilize school knowledge while engaging Indigenous students' cultural capital. By so doing, Native American students respond more enthusiastically to their educational environments. Some of these activities will be shared with readers in the second half of the book, as well as resources available for teachers for curriculum inclusion.

Many blessings to you, the readers of this book, and to those who have contributed in numerous ways to the information contained in this book.

Part I

The Roots of Who We Are in America

In this section, we will be examining the way humans developed and came to occupy different parts of the world. Once areas became peopled in these different regions, humans continued to evolve in their abilities to utilize materials in their locales to meet their needs for food, clothing, and shelter. Huge steps were made from there throughout thousands of years to learn about plant life and cultivation, which led to being able to support larger groups of people.

While the sciences have taken different parts of the mystery to examine, the parts are now coming together to confirm what we are learning about our ancestors and their societal values.

Cultural values and beliefs do not usually disappear from one generation to the next without having a reason to discard them. Many of our beliefs and values served people well in the past and will continue to do so. For this reason, it is difficult for humans to examine their own ethnically diverse groups' belief systems, including attitudes toward other diverse populations. As noted, the Indigenous populations are continuing to grow in numbers and as teachers, we need to spend time "unlearning" old beliefs promulgated by the media and in our textbooks that are inaccurate concerning Native peoples.

As educators, we cannot afford to let negative attitudes and stereotypes toward Indigenous students influence our teaching of them. This is why we need to examine our roots, to question beliefs and cultural value systems. Those that no longer serve us well or have relevance in this century need acknowledgment as such. These must be replaced with those beliefs/values that will enhance our abilities to reach all our students, maximizing their growth and development.

When we teach, we not only convey information to our students, but also our values, feelings, dispositions, morals, mores, and views about the world. This is because we are humans, not robots who are just distributing knowledge collected in textbooks. When we are ignorant of our students' cultures and histories, we nonverbally convey to them that they and their communities are unimportant to us. This is especially true of Native and commingled populations.

What happened in the past in Europe and the Americas has left us a legacy that lingers on today in our conscious and unconscious worlds. Native communities pass on their histories through oral language, and for those of us who expect that anything important needs to be written down—a perception of Western European cultures—it may be difficult to realize that much of what happened in the Americas before and after colonization has been deliberately hidden from view.

Much new information has been gained over the last forty to fifty years about the human genome, how people evolved in different areas of the world, and the Americas before colonization. This is why the information on the growth of civilizations, and then European and Indigenous histories before the coming of Spanish conquistadors are included in this book. This material is not readily available in our textbooks but can be utilized to augment our curricula and perceptions of Native populations, teaching Indigenous students and their peers this essential information.

We also explore the beginnings and rise of racism in this country as millions of Native Americans and Africans were forced unwilling into slavery with its consequent horrors. Unfortunately, we are again experiencing a rise in racism in this country since 2016. Many of the people involved in these movements claim they are the victims in the stories of America and Europe; obviously they are unaware of the true histories of these countries.

Chapter One

Unraveling the Puzzle of How Humans Came to Be

In the last six hundred years, the world of science has continued to steadily evolve and separate into subspecialties such as astronomy, archaeology, anthropology, chemistry, biology, biochemistry, geology, ecology, genetics, climatology, and many others in response to specific societal needs. For example, the field of anthropology evolved in response to a concern that American Indians were becoming a vanishing race in North America (Berkhofer, 1978).

During this process of specialization, much has been discovered about planet earth, the forces that act on this planet, and the entities making up the life-forms of the planet. Scientists are still making discoveries every day, and as they do so, information about these findings have changed the ways people view life on our planet.

SCIENTIFIC FINDINGS CONCERNING THE HUMAN GENOME

What is the human genome? This is a question that would have been unanswerable before the last half of the twentieth century. Students learned about Gregor Mendel's experiments with peas in the mid-1800s in biology classes, and how inherited traits produced in peas are called "genes," a word coined by Wilhelm Johannsen in 1909.

Students learned that genes hold the mystery about the color of their eyes and skin, their straight or curly hair, their tall or short builds. The thought that the whole human genome—what makes us who we are—could be examined and the makeup of our genes and chromosomes discovered was out of the realm of most people's thinking.

The period between 1990 and 2003 of the Human Genome Project (HGP) proved to be exciting in the relatively new field of genetics. With advances in biotechnology, biogeneticists identified all of the thirty thousand genes that make up each person and the chemical compositions of genes. In solving this puzzle, scientists have been able to use this information to further examine the origins of our species.

The ramifications of these findings have changed the way we can now look at who we are and that of who our future generations may be. For the general public, it has provided understandings of the human species and where we have come from to populate the world. Many of us know people who have submitted genetic material to be analyzed and now know more about their ancestors than ever before possible.

Regrettably, stories of conflict among ethnically diverse populations or of the inferiority of other ethnic groups have been handed down through our cultural institutions, including religious institutions. These are used to justify long-held hatreds and prejudices believed about those who appear physically unlike ourselves. The following information is provided to begin to erase some of the myths about different ethnic groups perpetuated over the centuries by those in power, allowing people to work against other diverse groups for their purposes.

Finding the Composition of DNA

The deoxyribonucleic acid (DNA) molecule is located in the nucleus of almost all living cells for those organisms with nuclei, and in the cell itself for those without nuclei. The DNA molecule holds our genetic information and allows it to be passed on to future generations (Ghannam & Arif, 2019).

We commonly think that it is the work of James Watson and Francis Crick which marked a milestone on the road to understanding the composition of DNA. However, Watson and Crick's work was built on that of Rosalind Franklin, a researcher at a lab at King's College in London. She took a photograph of the DNA molecule by x-ray diffraction. This famous photograph is known as Photograph 51 (Borman, 2017).

The photograph was shown to Watson by Franklin's laboratory partner, Maurice Wilkins, without her permission. From the photo, Watson and Crick—working at the Cavendish Laboratory in England—were able to determine important information as the photo contained the necessary data to determine the double helix nature of DNA. Since that time, James Watson has been known as the father of DNA, not acknowledging the work of Franklin which made this discovery possible (Lloyd, 2010).

After publishing their results in 1953, Watson, Crick, and Wilkins received great acclaim for their work. They shared the Nobel Prize in 1962 for their discovery of the chemical structure of the DNA double helix molecule. I hope that Rosalind Franklin will someday receive the recognition she so rightly deserves for her contribution to the discovery of DNA.

DNA is a very long molecule found in the nucleus of all human cells. It consists of twenty-three pairs of chromosomes in a ladder-like structure. The chromosomes contain our genes which are made up of long chains of nucleotide submolecules (Ghannam & Arif, 2019). Genes, or traits, were first discovered in 1869 by Frederich Miescher, a Swiss doctor treating soldiers. Gene submolecules are composed of four nucleotides—Adenine, Cytosine, Thymine, and Guanine—usually referred to as A, C, T, and G. Different genes are made through the multiplicity of combinations of these nucleotides (Ghannam & Arif, 2019).

The Search for Human Origins on the Planet

Biogeneticists involved in the HGP determined that with studying the changes or mutations of genes through time, the oldest human genes could be determined (Wells, 2002). In turn this would lead to a rediscovery of the history of humankind. To appreciate how monumental this process was, we need to know that the first sequencing of the six billion base pairs that make up humans' twenty-three chromosomes took the work of many scientists over a decade and cost $3 billion (Wells, 2002).

Searching for the First Woman and the First Man

We can readjust our ideas about the origins of humanity by examining a summary of the initial findings of the HGP and more findings to date. The major findings of those working on the human genome reveal information about all human populations (Wells, 2002). While it is impossible to delve completely into the HGP here, we can touch on the most important aspects that will influence our understandings of how humans populated the earth within the relatively short time our world has been in existence.

Biogeneticists determined that to find the oldest female and male genes, they would focus on genes passed on from mother to daughter and father to son unchanged. The mitochondrion from women around the world was studied to find the first woman. The mitochondrion is a complete cell with its genome found elsewhere in the cell of the DNA molecule, and it passes unchanged from mother to daughter (Wells, 2002).

Since the mitochondrion does not make a copy, it is passed down completely, along with polymorphisms (mutations or mistakes on chromosomes) which occur about once in one hundred times of being passed down to the next generation (see Wells, 2002, for more thorough explanations of this cell). Mitochondrial Eve, as she is known, was discovered first from relics found in Africa. Her age was determined to be roughly two hundred thousand years old through an examination of the mitochondrion genome by Cann, Stoneking, and Wilson in 1987 (cited in Wells, 2002).

It is important to note that she was not the only woman at that time in Africa, but the only one whose lineage developed into our Homo sapiens line. To find the first man, "Adam," biogeneticists determined to follow the male Y chromosome. This chromosome undergoes very little change as it is passed down from father to son because the Y sex chromosome does not recombine the way other chromosomes do when new offspring are being formed. Consequently it was ideal for this purpose (Wells, 2002).

Scientists worked backward by tracing these genes and the mutations on chromosomes from examining human genome cells of contemporary humans around the world. Through this process, it was determined that the earliest male genes belonged to the San population (formerly called Bushmen) in Africa, and are thought to be approximately two hundred thousand years old, around the same age as Mitochondrial Eve.

HUMANS' JOURNEY OUT OF AFRICA TO POPULATE THE WORLD

One of the most important findings of the HGP is that humans all belong to the same species, not separate species as speculated by Coons (Wells, 2002). Homo sapiens comprise one human race to which we all belong. The idea of different human "races" has a relatively recent history and differences in human characteristics are only seen in the fossil records of the last thirty thousand years. These differences are now thought to be due to the consequences of populations being separated for a prolonged period during the last Great Ice Age or what is referred to as the Last Glacial Maximus (LGM; Wells, 2002), which began about 110,000 years ago and ended approximately 12,500 years ago (Briney, 2019).

By examining Figure 1.1, we can see how humans sojourned from one place to another. This was an artifact of humans being hunter-gatherers and/or fishermen, following their food sources and taking advantage of the plant life around them.

Years Ago	Geographical Area Migrations	Chromosomal Gene Mutations (Markers) DNA Polymorphisms
200,000	None: In Africa San people (formerly Bushmen) Eastern and Southern Africa	All have the same Y Chromosome construction
100,000*	From Africa	To Australasia; traces of original Y chromosome found in Papua New Guinea population.
60,000	Migration out of Africa Along Australasia Coast	First genetic mutation » Eurasian Man (M_{168})
60-50,000	Migration out of Africa To Middle East via Sahara	Upper Palaeolithic Humans » NE Africa and Middle East (M_{89})
40,000	From Eurasian steppes of central Asia or plains of Iran Dispersion into Central Europe (Germany and France), Korea, and China; to the interiors of Asia and India	Homo sapiens, modern humans » Eurasian Clan (M_{168}, M_{89}, M_9) »Eurasian Clan (M_9)» Asian Clan (M_{45}) » Eurasian Clan (M_9)»Indian Clan (M_{20})
35,000	From west to east Asia And inland from south to north Asia	»East Asian Clan (M_9, M_{45}, M_{175}) (China, Korea and Japan) » Australia Coastal Clan (M_{168}, M_{130}) (also found in Indonesia, Melanesia, and Polynesia; North America)
30,000	Continuation in Western Europe	Eurasian Clan » Asian Clan » European Clan (M_9, M_{45}, M_{173})
10,000-7,000	Neolithic Period	Development of Agriculture »Neolithic farmers (M_{172})
Between 34,000 and 6,000	Genetics determined there were at least two waves of migration to the Americas: one group settling both North and South America; other settling only North America	Asian Clan » Siberian Clan (M_{168}, M_{89}, M_9, M_{45}, M_{242}, M_3) ~ Amerind Languages in North & South America Coastal Marker » (M_{130}) Present only in N. America and Na-Dené populations. Sino-Tibetan languages include Chinese and other Eastern Asian languages; shows unique genetic link between East Asians and Native Americans.
15,000	Meadowcroft, PA and other sites	Carbon dating of teeth found at site showed Native Americans had been here at this point in time; crossed Bering Strait when Ice Age most intense. People in Americas at least 15,000 years ago.

» read as "leads to"

Figure 1.1. Inheritance of Genes on the Male Y Chromosome. Adapted from *The journey of man: A genetic odyssey*, by S. Wells, Princeton, New Jersey: Princeton University Press, 2002.* New information from 2017 Preface. The Cooper's Ferry site in western Idaho is dated at approximately 16,000 years old and points to Hokkaido, Japan, as a possible origin of migration. This migration may have followed south along Pacific Coast from Beringia (Davis, 2019).

We must remember that before the LGM the world appeared to be different than it does today.

With the effects of the LGM, warming and drying of regions on different continents, and the movement of the tectonic plates impacting continents and where they lay, the whole earth was beginning to become colder. This may have been a catalyst for those who made migrations out of Africa. There is also mitochondrial DNA evidence of a population explosion taking place simultaneously (Wells, 2002). Because of the LGM, much of Europe, North America, and parts of South America were covered with thick sheets of ice. While these areas were experiencing extreme cold, other areas were experiencing warm, drier weather, which may have impacted regional food sources.

Eurasian Man

The first migration out of Africa occurred approximately sixty thousand years ago.[1] This is verified through the earliest mutation—called a "polymorphism"—on the male Y chromosome (Wells, 2002). Mutations occur when gene nucleotides are not copied exactly to the next generation due to conditions that interfere in this process, such as hardships created during migrations. All populations living outside of Africa have this polymorphism referred to as M_{168}, considered the Eurasian marker (see Figure 1.1); it is not present in populations living exclusively in Africa (Wells, 2002).

Through using information from female mitochondrion DNA and other sciences such as archaeology, geology, and climatology, findings concerning human population growth and migrations can be substantiated to a high degree. The making of symbolic representations by Homo sapiens such as paintings of animals and people—plus learning speech communication—is referred to by some researchers as the "Great Leap Forward" for humankind. This process possibly started as early as seventy thousand years ago, aiding in the process of migration (Wells, 2002).

Onto Australasia

After the migration of Eurasian man (M_{168}), we find the next chromosomal polymorphism with the Indigenous peoples of Australia and the region (see Figure 1.1). This mutation, M_{130}, is found in the Coastal Clan ($M_{168} + M_{130}$). Biogeneticists believe this polymorphism was acquired sometime during the journey around the coasts that separate Africa from Australasia in a period when sea levels fluctuated due to the Ice Age. While the M_{130} marker is indicated as possibly thirty-five thousand years old, it could be older. In fact, the Mungo Lake site in Australia has yielded a skeleton whose remains have been continuously pushed back from

35,000 years to much earlier as it was found atop human artifacts that may be 60,000 years old (Wells, 2002).

Next Stop: The Sahara and the Middle East

Not all of those leaving Africa traveled by the same route, but diverged into different areas (see Figure 1.1). When modern humans entered the Upper Palaeolithic period 50,000–70,000 years ago (Wells, 2002, p. 85), they were still hunter-gatherers and relied on their skills and the bounty of nature for survival in all geographical ranges they inhabited (Wells, 2002).

As humans traveled in a second migration out of Africa to the Middle East via the Sahara, a new chromosomal marker, M_{89}, was added to their genomes. From here it appears that modern humans ($M_{168} + M_{89}$) spread out from the steppes of central Asia or the plains of present-day Iran into new areas approximately forty thousand years ago (Wells, 2002). They dispersed into central Asia, Iran, Central Europe, East Asia, the Asian interior, and India. In doing so, three new clans developed: The Eurasian Clan, M_9, which then splits into (a) the Asian Clan, $M_9 + M_{45}$; and (b) the Indian Clan, $M_9 + M_{20}$ (Wells, 2002).

Dispersals to Parts of Asia and America

Researchers know that a portion of the Coastal Clan ($M_{168} + M_{130}$) moved inland from south to north Asia, as their polymorphism is now found in Indonesia, Melanesia, and Polynesia (see Figure 1.1). Note the absences of the M_{89} and M_9 markers in the Coastal Clan that appear in other Asian populations. One theory is that some of the original M_{168} group leaving Africa by way of the coasts (and then adding M_{130}) became expert sailors during the period when agriculture exploded. This Coastal Clan stayed awhile in Southern Asia before moving on to other areas. Linguistic data support these inferences, as languages in the Austronesian family are all connected (Wells, 2002).

This evidence suggests that at least two waves of human beings migrated to the Americas (see Figure 1.1). The Coastal Clan M_{130} polymorphism appears in some Native American populations in western North America, but it is not found in Central or South American Indigenous communities. New archaeological findings in western Idaho at Cooper's Ferry along the confluence of the Columbia and Snake Rivers support the theory of at least one additional wave of migration that was not through the Bering Strait (Davis, 2019).

Archaeologist Loren Davis from Oregon State University has worked on the Cooper's Ferry site for many years. He and his crew found stemmed points like those made in Hokkaido, Japan at this site, providing a link with the ancient people of Japan (Ross, 2019). Antiquated fire pits and tools in Cooper's Ferry indicate an active community lived there. The Nimiipuu (Nez Perce)—some of whom accompanied the latest expedition—know the site as a village called Nipéhe or "Nip" (Smith, 2019).

The Cooper's Ferry site is dated to at least 16,500 years old, almost one thousand years before any of the other occupied land sites found in North America (Smith, 2019). While we can't say for sure which clan lived there, the assumption is that it would be the Coastal Clan since the land bridge did not exist when these people journeyed to what is now Idaho. This finding supports the theory of a journey made by island hopping along the coasts, sailing around the coasts to the coasts of North America by water instead of crossing a land bridge.

Approximately thirty-five thousand years ago, the Asian Clan moved from west to East Asia, becoming the East Asian Clan ($M_{168} + M_{89} + M_9 + M_{45} + M_{175}$) found in China, Korea, and Japan (see Figure 1.1). Then it appears that another group from the Asian Clan traveled to what is now Siberia and made two more polymorphisms while occupying the area of the Siberian steppes and/or progressing across the Bering Strait: $M_{242} + M_3$. They are known as the Siberian Clan. They carry the early Eurasian and Asian migration markers which are found throughout the Americas. It is believed that members of the Siberian Clan crossed into the Americas using the northern route of the Bering Strait over the land bridge—Beringia—made when the ice impacted sea levels by lowering them (Wells, 2002). Today, the Indigenous Chuckchi (or Chuckchee) people inhabit the Russian area of the Chuckchi Peninsula, on the shores of Chuckchi Sea and the Bering Sea (Maltby, 2003).

Today, multiple theories are articulated about settlement in the Americas. A new proposal is the possibility of a linked coastline between Asia and North America that would have allowed humans to gradually migrate to these areas (Montaigne, 2020). A different theory states that people could have come by way of boats, using the "Kelp Highway," allowing them to take advantage of the rich resources available. A third theory is the Beringian Standstill hypothesis which suggests that humans could have "settled" for some time in Beringia before moving further on (Montaigne, 2020). Still, others speculate that there may have been a southern route followed by the Coastal Clan as early as fifty thousand years ago (Wells, 2002).

The oral histories of Native Americans themselves have a variety of explanations for their presence in the Americas varying from Tribal nation to nation. Some support the Bearing Strait migration; some support the theories of traveling the oceans by boat; some support creation in place; and others speak of arriving from other planets (Deloria, 1995). It seems probable that there were multiple migrations to the Americas, not just one main means of travel here.

Into Europe

Meanwhile, other members of the Asian Clan continued on their migration, this time into Western Europe (see Figure 1.1). As the genetics tell their story, the European Clan evolved from the Asian Clan: $M_{168} + M_{89} + M_9 + M_{45}$, adding M_{173}, the genetic polymorphism, or marker, which Europeans carry. From this we can conclude that Europeans are descended from the Asian Clan, one of the last of the clans to evolve as shown in Figure 1.1. We can also conclude that Europeans and members of Native American tribes dispersed throughout the Americas are genetically "cousins," both emerging from the Asian Clan.

We can now state from following the genetic trail outlined above that all humans are from the same species, Homo sapiens. Therefore, we are all related. There are no separate "races"—a social construct put forward beginning in the 1500s—only the human race.

DEVELOPMENT OF AGRICULTURE

The beginning of agriculture is estimated to have begun twenty-three thousand years ago (see Figure 1.1) with experiments in growing proto-weeds on the shores of Galilee (Smirk, Nadel, Groman-Yaroslavski, et al., 2015). It was previously thought that agriculture developed at the beginning of the Neolithic period between 10,000 and 7,000 BCE. Scientists now agree that agriculture may have begun in several places in the Mideast Fertile Crescent and around the world as people were transitioning from hunter-gatherers/fishermen to deliberately propagating preferred foods as shown with the agricultural chromosomal polymorphism M_{172} that humans carry (Wells, 2002).

With the development of agriculture, larger populations of people could be supported and the chances of survival to adulthood and beyond enhanced (Chatterjee, 2016). This would provide time and opportunity for a greater emphasis on the development of culture and cultural artifacts (Wells, 2002). Emphasis on toolmaking, artistic expression, pottery making for utility and aesthetics, experiments in cloth-making, and other areas such as musical instruments, could all have been accomplished with longer settlement periods in particular areas. Animal husbandry as well began to develop through the centuries.

Wells (2002) and others conjecture that unexpected, negative results arose with agriculture in this period. These consisted of higher density populations; more focus on smaller entities instead of the community; less cooperation than is needed in hunter-gatherer societies; and the presence of disease. In other words, a recipe for competition among groups of people for fertile, arable land that would support larger populations followed by possible health disasters.

This would have led to a rise of other divisions among groups plus social stratification and wealth production that privileged some people over others (Barnes, 2010; Jones & Sidwell, 1997; Phillips, 2017; Wells, 2002). Territories needed defense; fields needed cultivation; and development needed expertise in many areas of this population's contemporary life. At the same time, people began living longer and were able to teach skills to new generations, in addition to providing more care to younger and older than ever before (Wells, 2002).

CONCLUSIONS MADE POSSIBLE BY THE HGP

Over the decade when the majority of work was completed on sequencing the human genome, the HGP research involved biogeneticists from six countries who made contributions to its findings: the United States, the United Kingdom, Germany, France, Japan, and China (Jones, Ankeny, & Cook-Deegan, 2018). While we knew previously that certain problems were caused by chromosomal polymorphisms, such as Down syndrome (Chromosome 21; Mukherjee, 2016), the fact that there was now the ability to access all of our genetic histories was astounding.

Ethical and moral considerations had to be addressed during the whole period of the project, such as "Should human genes be allowed to be patented? If so, by whom?" (Jones, Ankeny, & Cook-Deegan, 2018). When the sequencing of the human genome was completed in 2003, information was freely shared within the international community so that no one country could keep all of the information, try to paten human genes, or give corporations information without consent from the consortium (Jones, Ankeny, & Cook-Deegan, 2018; National Institutes of Health, n.d.).

By the year 2004, a more sophisticated map of the human genome was made available to the public in pieces, necessary because of its great size (Jones, Ankeny, & Cook-Deegan, 2018). Access by corporations was possible after this release.

Some of the major conclusions reached by biogeneticists include the following:

- the oldest human genes are from the San (formerly Bushmen) in Africa, who bear characteristics of all people on earth;
- there is only one human species, not different "races," though the term race has become ingrained in our collective cultures;
- changes in the physical appearance of humans can probably be accounted for by the separation of human populations from each other during the LGM;
- the greatest amount of human variations occur on the African continent while other groups—Europeans, Asians, and Native Americans—represent only a small sample of those variations;
- Homo sapiens are all descendants of a woman ("Mitochondrial Eve") who lived around 150,000–200,000 years ago;
- the estimation for "Adam" is within the 200,000 year period; and
- it is possible that the human species is older than that estimate since the chromosomes studied only show *mutations*, not telling scientists when these chromosomes originally evolved (Wells, 2002).

There Is Much Still to Be Done

There is a great deal of research in related fields that support the results of the HGP. These include the studies in anthropology, linguistics, archaeology, biology, climatology, geology, and other sciences that coincide with information gained about human beings, our genetic makeups, and the approximate timelines of the appearance of different human clans as shown by the HGP. There will continue to be new findings related to our genealogy.

As stated by Barnes (2010), most anthropologists, archaeologists, and historical linguists agree that some American Indian Nations descended from Northern Asians. Though physical artifacts are still lacking, there is also agreement at this writing concerning the high probability of at least three separate waves of migrations into the continent. Corrections to the record are occurring quickly as new findings are uncovered all the time.

The Aboriginal Maori populations of Australia and New Zealand have oral histories of migrations to different lands including Asia, the Polynesian islands, Hawaii, and North America. Their oral histories are kept by tribal Elders, told by memory, and then are taught to their tribal members. Oral histories are also told by Native Americans and passed through generations, which were largely ignored in the past by Western historians. Thanks to the work of anthropologists and ethnographers, some of these oral histories are now being acknowledged by academic and research communities.

Additionally, with the U.S. passage of the Native American Graves Protection and Repatriation Act of 1990 (NAGPRA) and similar legislation passed in other countries around the world, museums and private collectors are returning samples of ancient human remains that have been found and kept by collectors, their family members, and others. Because of this, more information is coming to light about human populations as these materials are actively being examined now instead of being kept in storage (Perrottet, 2019).

Consequently, we are continuing to learn about our ancient relatives. One thing we do know is that when humans migrated, they took their cultures with them, including their languages. While languages, too, have changed over sixty thousand years, there is evidence of two European/Asian "super families" of languages containing both living and extinct languages.

One super-language is the Indo-European language family which contains many "living" and "extinct" East Indian and European languages. The other super language is the Dene-Caucasian super-family, which contains Basque, Caucasian, and Sumerian. From this family, the Sino-Tibetan and the American Na-Dene languages are found and speakers are also linked by the M_{130} polymorphism, showing a genetic link between these languages and American Indian Dene languages such as Navajo (Wells, 2002).

Our understandings of humanity are still at the elementary stage. We will continue to learn more about our histories waiting to be discovered within the human genome. In drawing this chapter to a close, we want to share the prophetic words of *Nokus Feke Ematha Tustanaki* (Bear Heart), a traditionally trained Choctaw medicine man born in 1918 whose English name was Marcellus Williams. Bear Heart combines his knowledge of Western psychology and other sciences he studied with his traditional wisdom in assisting people around the world:

> The number 4 is very significant to Native people—it is a number of completeness. The white, black, yellow, and red races represent all humanity. At one time there might even have been a common race of people who divided and became different colors with different backgrounds. Maybe this was a preparation for each of these races to learn all they could among their own people and then in time we will combine the red, black, yellow, and white into one big culture. And if the Spirit is one, we may not change colors, but instead change our attitudes into the spirit of oneness with all living things on this planet, not only the two-leggeds, but the four-leggeds, the wingeds, those that are in the water, and those that crawl. *It's time to stress the things we have in common with one another, to show how much alike we are. We might be surprised to find that we are truly brothers and sisters in this universe, and most important, that we have to maintain that relationship in order to survive.* (Bear Heart, 1996, p. 162)

What we do know is that when European boat-making and sailing technologies advanced, a chance meeting between peoples of the Americas and those of Europe erupted in such a way that the two hemispheres of the world would never be the same. While there had been meetings with the Vikings previously, and possibly lost sailors, none of these previous encounters led to permanent changes in the Americas for those involved (Marshall, 1996). Our next chapter explores the influential civilizations created in the world with a special focus on the Americas.

REFERENCES

Barnes, I. (2010). *The historical atlas of Native Americans*. New York, NY: Chartwell Books.

Bear Heart (with Molly Larken). (1996). *The wind is my mother: The life and teachings of a Native American Shaman*. New York, NY: Berkley Books.

Berkhofer, R. F. (1978). *The White man's Indian: Images of the American Indian from Columbus to the present*. New York, NY: Random House.

Borman, S. (2017). These female scientists should have won the Nobel. *Chemical & Engineering News, 95* (36), 22–24. Retrieved from https://cen.acs.org/articles/95/i36/female-scientists-should-won-Nobel.html.

Briney, A. (2019, July 27). *An overview of the last global glaciation*. ThoughtCo. Retrieved from https://thoughtco.com/the-last-glaciation-1434433.

Chatterjee, R. (2016). Where did agriculture begin? Oh boy, it's complicated. *The Salt*. U.S.: National Public Radio. Retrieved from https://www.npr.org/sections/thesalt/07/15/485722228/where-did-agriculture-begin-oh-boy-its-complicated.

Davis, L. (2019, September 10). Idaho artifacts suggest Pacific entry for first Americans. *Idaho State Journal*. New York, NY: Associated Press.

Deloria, V., Jr. (1995). *Red earth, White lies: Native Americans and the myth of scientific fact*. New York, NY: Scribner.

Ghannam, J. Y., & Arif, J. (February 28, 2019). Biochemistry, DNA Structure. In *StatPearls*. Treasure Island, FL: StatPearls. Retrieved from https://www.ncbi.nlm.nih.gov/books/NBK430685/.

Jones, K. M., Ankeny, R. A., & Cook-Deegan, R. (2018). The Bermuda Triangle: The pragmatics, policies, and principles for data sharing in the history of the Human Genome Project. *Journal of the History of Biology, 51,* 693–805. Retrieved from https://doi.org/10.1007/s10739-018-9538-7.

Jones, P. V., & Sidwell, K. C., Eds. (1997). *The World of Rome: An Introduction to Roman Culture*. New York, NY: Cambridge University Press.

Lloyd, R. (2010, November 3). *Scientific American*. Blog. Retrieved from https://blogs.scientificamerican.com/observations/rosalind-franklin-and-dna-how-wronged-was-she/.

Maltby, C. (2003). *The Journey of man: A genetic odyssey. Hosted by Spencer Wells*. Documentary video.

Marshall, I. (1996). *A history and ethnography of the Beothuk*. Montreal & Kingston: McGill-Queens University Press. (Originally published 1929).

Montaigne, F. (2020). The fertile shore. *Smithsonian: Tracking the first Americans, 50* (9), 30–41.

Mukherjee, S. (2016). *The gene: An intimate history*. New York, NY: Scribner.

National Institutes of Health (NIH). (n.d.). *National Human Genome Research Institute*. Bethesda, MD: Author. Retrieved from https://www.genome.gov/about-genomics.

Native American Graves Protection and Repatriation Act of 1990, 25 U.S.C. § 3001 *et. seq* (U.S.C., 2000).

Perrottet, T. (2019, September). A 42,000-year-old man finally goes home. *Smithsonian*. Retrieved from https://www.smithsonianmag.com/history/mungo-man-finally-goes-home-180972835/.

Phillips, C. (2017). *The illustrated encyclopedia of Aztec and Maya: The greatest civilizations of ancient Central America with 1000 photographs, painting and maps*. London, UK: Anness Publishing, Ltd.

Ross, E. (2019, September 3). *North America's oldest human artifacts found in Idaho*. Oregon Public Radio. Retrieved from: https://www.opb.org/news/article/oregon-state-university-oldest-human-artifacts-idaho-north-america/.

Smirk, A., Nadel, D., Groman-Yaroslavski, I., Melamed, Y., Sternberg, M., Bar-Yosef, O., Weiss, E. (2015). The origin of cultivation and proto-weeds, long before neolithic farming. *PLOS ONE*, *10*(7): e0131422 DOI: 10.1371/journal.pone.0131422. Retrieved from https://www.researchgate.net/publication/280298835_The_Origin_of_Cultivation_and_Proto-Weeds_Long_Before_Neolithic_Farming.

Smith, K. N. (2019, August 29). Stone tools suggest the first Americans came from Japan. ARS Technica/Science. Retrieved from: https://arstechnica.com/science/2019/08/16000-year-old-site-in-idaho-indicates-people-sailed-around-the-ice-sheet/.

Wells, S. (2002). *The journey of man: A genetic odyssey*. Princeton, NJ: Princeton University Press.

NOTE

1. The dates are constantly being readjusted as new knowledge emerges.

Chapter Two

Humans' Continuing Development and the Americas

To review from the previous chapter, biogeneticists' research on the HGP showed that Homo sapiens, the group of which modern humans are all a part, evolved from Eurasian Man. This group developed into modern humans and became the Eurasian clan, which later split into the Asian Clan and the Indian Clan (East India), during their migrations to different parts of the world. From the Asian Clan, a portion of the population journeyed to Europe, becoming the European Clan (Wells, 2002). For a review of this information, see Figure 1.1.

Other members of the Asian Clan went on a different route across the far eastern steppes of Europe becoming the Siberian Clan. Many are still found in Russia (the Chuckchi), while others appear to have crossed the Bering Strait into the Americas. They became the ancestors of some of the Native Americans that are found throughout North, Central, and South America and developed Amerind languages (Wells, 2002).

It appears that there are at least one or more other groups of migrants from the Australasian Coastal Clan, with whom we share very ancient genes from Africa and polymorphisms from the migration out of Africa. This group appears to have arrived in the Americas during a different period in time, and members employ languages from the Na-Dené group spoken in the southwestern U.S. and western Canada (NIH, n.d.; Wells, 2002). Linguists also recognize another group of languages, the Eskimo-Aleut family, spoken in Greenland, eastern Siberia, Alaska, and northern Canada, which may represent another migration (Wells, 2002). In addition, we are now finding archaeological sites that may indicate even more migrations, as shown by the Cooper's Ferry site in Idaho (Davis, 2019).

In other words, Native American tribal members and Europeans share genetics from distant ancestors. At the time of contact in the Americas between these two groups of people, they had developed different cultures over at least the last thirty thousand years. This separation occurred with the Ice Age that left thick ice sheets covering the European continent, North America, and parts of South America. The Ice Age may well be responsible for changes in skin color and physical characteristics of humans in the affected areas (Wells, 2002).

As members of the same species, the Human Clan, we have more in common with each other than not. One of the messages that is heard throughout Indian country is that "We are all related," meaning that all living things on this planet, animate and inanimate, have a shared history on our earth. Knowing this is important for us as educators as it changes our views of where we fit into the course of the history of humankind. We may have evolved in different cultural respects, but in doing so, the ingenuity of the human species can be seen at play in our struggles for survival and overcoming adversities in different areas of the world.

With the onset of agriculture, people could settle into different places around the world. There they would persist in developing intellectually, growing bigger brains in the process. It is thought that languages in their earliest forms were used during migrations and possibly hundreds or thousands of years before, and they continued to evolve.

Languages are important cultural tools. The ability to pass on information from Elders to younger group members would have been essential for continued existence. As groups migrated and then remained in different regions, languages began to evolve from the original super-families into separate distinct languages (Barnes, 2010; Wells, 2002). Two thousand different languages were manifest in the Americas at the time of meeting the first Europeans.

As we look at the different civilizations around the world immediately before the conquest of the Americas, it is important to note that cultural information traveled in two directions: throughout Africa and Asia, into Europe, India, and the Middle East on the one hand; and the Americas on the other. Due to the great distances between these landmasses, contact does not appear to have taken place between these peoples until the relevantly recent history of humankind inhabiting these two large regions of the world (Heather, 2009; Jones & Sidwell, 1997; Mann, 2005/2011; Sowell, 1998).

We need to examine the way people learned to come together to form groups or societies. While groups developed different cultures around the world, we know that these were partially a result of acclimating to new environments. We also know from the research being done in the area of linguistics that there may be both language and cultural overlaps throughout the world, probably as a result of migrations of different groups throughout several areas of the world. What is "culture," and how does it function in our lives and the lives of our students?

> Culture [is] a repertoire of socially transmitted and intra-generationally generated ideas about how to live and make judgments, both in general terms and in regard to specific domains of life. It is an information system with varying levels of specificity: on one level it is as broad as a set of ideas about styles of self-presentation; on another level, it is the micro-information system prescribing the best way to make bagels, curried chicken, or Jamaican jerk pork. (Patterson, 2000, p. 208)

Food, clothing, and cultural practices may have been different in the two regions of the world, but they were effectively adapted to the environments in which people lived. While religious practices were varied in different areas, there was a common acknowledgement of a single superior supernatural being or many superior beings.

We know that the accomplishments of today are built upon previous foundations. Through ongoing work and advancements in the fields of anthropology and archaeology, we are continually discovering what it was like for those who came before us, including their legacies to us.

CIVILIZATIONS[1] AROUND THE WORLD

There are common cultural foundations found in countries throughout the world today that emerged in pre-modern times. Four areas with these characteristic cultural foundations are the South Asian and East Asian civilizations located in South Asia; the Islamic civilization arising in the Middle East; and the Western civilization established in Europe and its colonial territories (Global Civilizations, 2019).

We can further classify nine historic global civilizations by the art and culture produced in each of them. These areas are Mesopotamia in the Middle East—which evolved into Persia and then into the Islamic civilization—along with the Egyptian civilization; South Asian civilization in South Asia; East Asian civilization in East Asia; Western civilization in Europe and colonial regions of the world; plus Mesoamerican and Andean civilizations in Meso/South America (Global Civilizations, 2019).

The regions of sub-Saharan Africa, North America, Oceania, and the Steppe are seen as having many groups of limited populations with their own cultures rather than any urban centers (Global Civilizations, 2019). This view may be challenged with regard to North America as we are learning more about the great pre-Columbian civilizations, including the Mississippian culture that extended throughout the Americas (Global Civilizations, 2019; Mann, 2005/2011).

We need to take up the story begun in the previous chapter to understand the sustained progression of the human race occurring on both sides of the oceans.

THE NEOLITHIC PERIOD IN EURASIA

Archaeologists have found evidence of many different types of tools being developed and used during the Neolithic era (c. 10,000 BCE–7000 BCE). It appears that as humans migrated to different regions they shared their knowledge and cultural developments with others they encountered. Artifacts such as tools show advances in how they were made and used for many different purposes in the daily lives of Homo sapiens.

Different types of tools were needed for humans to work the land successfully for agriculture in distinct regions. Various types of fishing methods were experimented with in the same way. Shelters could be found in caves or manufactured from the natural materials surrounding groups. Evidence indicates a wide variety of assorted shelters were utilized in different parts of the world suited to particular climates. Weapons for protection or to procure animals for consumption steadily improved as did the materials from which they were made.

Animals were first domesticated on a large scale, and the art of husbandry was born. Other group or family members may have experimented with creating different types of cloth, again sourcing the materials in nature. Eventually, groups would create ways of distinguishing themselves as members. Importantly, societies and their cultures began to flourish.

THE LAST THREE STAGES OF DEVELOPMENT: THE COPPER AGE, BRONZE AGE, AND IRON AGE

Toward the end of the Neolithic period, the stage was set for future development of Homo sapiens with the beginning of urban civilizations (Stone, Bronze, and Iron Ages, 2019). The Mesopotamian civilization appears to be the oldest on record, arising in c. 3500 BCE during the Copper Age of 5000 BCE–3000 BCE in the Middle East and Mediterranean (Western civilization, 2002). The Copper Age (also estimated at 4500 BCE–3500 BCE) is referred to as the Chalcolithic Period. It is receiving new attention with the recent discovery in Iraq of the oldest copper ornament, dated at 8700 BCE (Copper Age, n.d.).

Copper pipes were used to carry water in 2700 BCE, and used for making weapons as well as tools and armor. This was done approximately three thousand years before Greek and Roman civilizations as evidenced by artifacts found in many places around the European/Middle Eastern world (Copper Age, n.d.). The Copper Age is considered as a transition period for early European use of metal tools and the development of complex societies and trade routes. Human hierarchies were being developed between the rich and the poor at this time, as well as rulers and the ruled (Copper Age, n.d.).

The Cuneiform script used to represent the Sumerian language appeared in c. 3000 BCE, mostly in conjunction with keeping records. Mesopotamia was a multilingual society, and writing became an important record-keeping tool (Sumerian language, n.d.). The first evidence of literature—the art of recording tales told orally and writing new stories for larger audiences—appears in 2500 BCE (Sumerian language, n.d.).

The Egyptian civilization appears in approximately 3000 BCE during the Bronze Age c. 3000 BCE–1000 BCE (Stone, Bronze, and Iron Ages, 2019). The climate in this area was warmer in comparison to other regions of the world, making a difference in cultural practices and what could be manufactured or grown in these areas.

The Bronze Age started in Southwest Asia and then radiated outward in all directions and into Eurasia (Stone, Bronze, and Iron Ages, 2019). Smelting, the process of hammering or casting metals, began first with copper, and eventually with a combination of copper and tin to make a harder metal for weapons: Bronze. Bronze had a distinct advantage over stone due to its malleability and strength (Stone, Bronze, and Iron Ages, 2019).

The Indus civilization began in approximately 2500 BCE, followed by the Chinese civilization in 2000 BCE, the Aegean civilization in 2000 BCE, and then the Greek Age in 1200 BCE (Stone, Bronze, and Iron Ages, 2019). Throughout these periods people continued to refine their tool-making, cultures, arts, philosophies, and religious practices.

Once modern humans in Southwest Asia discovered how to create higher temperatures in their smelting pits to melt iron ore, the Iron Age began which persists into our present era. It, too, radiated outward from its origins across the Eurasian world by 500 BCE, but this time also included North Africa and across the sub-Saharan desert by 0 BCE. Because iron ore is readily more available than copper or tin, it was used in making stronger implements for agriculture. Weapons then began to be mass-produced due to the abundance of iron ore (Stone, Bronze, and Iron Ages, 2019).

EARLY CIVILIZATIONS IN THE AMERICAS

At this point, there is a wide variation in estimates of when Native peoples first appeared on the American continent, the most common estimates are that they were present as early as 40,000 years ago; others as late as 21,000 years ago (Barnes, 2010; Stannard, 1992; Wells, 2002). Ongoing research may confirm or set new dates for their migrations in the future.

The Native peoples in Mesoamerica and the Andes carry the Eurasian marker (M_{45}) and additional polymorphisms of their journey over the Bering Strait and down through the Americas. This gives credibility to the approximate date of twenty-one thousand years ago for the first migration (Wells, 2002). The Australasia polymorphism M_{130} is only seen in North America (Wells, 2002), providing evidence of at least two migrations.

Some believe that there were three or more migrations (Barnes, 2010). Reasons for this include that the physical features of Native peoples in the regions of the Northwest Coast in North America are more Asian than anywhere else on the continent. Many use this information to conjecture that those living in the area now known as Japan could have reached North America using the Japanese current or Hawaii. The recent findings in Cooper's Ferry Idaho in 2019 discussed previously may support this theory (Davis, 2019).

Civilizations developed on a different plane in the regions of the Gulf of Mexico, seven thousand years ago; Mexico, five thousand years ago; and South America, two thousand years ago. While the Copper Age and Iron Age appeared in Egypt, Mesopotamia, and Asian areas, the Andean Inca of South America experienced only the Bronze Age. Metals such as gold, silver, and copper were utilized in creating art in North America before colonization (Smelting in China and India, n.d.; Stone, Bronze, and Iron Ages, 2019). These civilizations represent a New World counterpart to the Old World civilizations of the ancients (Mann, 2005/2011; Editors, n.d.).

Holmberg's Mistake

Fortunately, we are now learning more about the Native peoples of the Americas, a view that contradicts what was perpetrated by one of the early anthropologists to enter Beni in Bolivia (Mann, 2005/2011). Allan R. Holmberg lived among the Native groups in Beni and concluded that the Aboriginals in these areas were the most culturally backward people on earth. He spread his beliefs in publications that before 1492 the Indians had no histories or cultures.

New archaeological work in the area has shown just the opposite: While the Sirionó Indians were neglected due to epidemics of diseases that caused a loss of 95 percent of their population in one generation, they were also fighting cattle ranchers who wanted to take over their region, and the Bolivian military who were putting them in prisons. They did not have an established base and had to keep moving because of these forces (Mann, 2005/2011).

Holmberg's conclusions about Native peoples in the Americas were wrong, but they became popularized by people who wanted to believe that the Americas, especially North America, were largely empty spaces occupied by people who were inferior in terms of cultural growth and development. We can now correct these impressions as much new knowledge from the fields of archaeology, linguistics, anthropology, and geography have confirmed the existence in all of the Americas of vibrant Native societies existing thousands of years ago.

As noted by Mann (2005/2011),

> One way to sum up the new scholarship is to say that it has begun, at last, to fill in one of the biggest blanks in history: the Western Hemisphere before 1492. It was, in the current view, a thriving, stunningly diverse place, a tumult of languages, trade and culture, a region where tens of millions of people loved and hated and worshipped as people do everywhere. Much of this world vanished after Columbus, swept away by disease and subjugation. So thorough was the erasure that within a few generations neither conqueror nor conquered knew that this world had existed. Now, though, it is returning to view. (p. 31)

This newer information coming to light since the later part of the twentieth century is providing substantiation that peoples have existed in the Americas for a very long time. Current knowledge contradicts former notions that the Americas were relatively devoid of populations until the last several hundred years. Understanding the data, we can confirm that the peoples of the Americas were not just occupying the land through default, but had a claim to the land in the same way that early peoples in the "Old World" civilizations did.

Peru

We know now that Peru hosted the first technologically complex societies in the Americas, estimated at 3200 BCE–2500 BCE. In Peru, the people of Norte Chico built cities and one great urban complex, Sumer. These areas had long-lasting cultural traditions. There was little interaction with other areas in Mesoamerica, as the great mountains kept information from flowing between these areas.

Peru's first inhabitants seem to have appeared about 10,000 BCE (Mann, 2005/2011). They mummified their dead around 5000 BCE and held beliefs that the dead could have impacts on the living. At least twenty-five sites have been found in the region where people lived and held ceremonies. They also built mounds of approximately fifteen feet tall with platforms for ceremonies (Mann, 2005/2011).

Other sites have been found that show evidence of occupation as early as 9210 BCE with several urban complexes including Caral and Pativilca; plus Huaricanga, dated to 3500 BCE (Mann, 2005/2011). Recently, archaeologists discovered six sites with platform mounds built around a huge platform in Caral (established c. 2600 BCE). Stairs, rooms, and courtyards were found, and it appears that Caral was a great trading center. Much of Caral is still being excavated, and there is a possibility of its founding date being pushed back (Barnes, 2017).

While Peruvians acquired most of what was needed from the ocean, agriculture also developed. Irrigation ditches have been located, and it appears that cotton was their most important crop. Cotton once grew wild along the shores of both the Pacific and Atlantic coasts (Mann, 2005/2011). Evidence of a spiritual tradition that began in approximately 2280 BCE was confirmed with the discovery of a gourd painted with the image of the fanged Staff God, a center of the area's religions (Mann, 2005/2011).

Mesoamerica

From Norte Chico, it seems that others in Mesoamerica came and then took cultural traditions back to their areas. New societies and cities were built in the wake of tragedies—such as volcanic actions—on the remains of the old societies and traditions. There is evidence of hunting 11,500 years ago for deer, horse, antelope, jackrabbit, and giant turtles. Maize was raised; and seeds, cactus leaves, agave plants, acorns, and wild squash flowers were part of native diets. Squash, beans, melons, tomatoes, chilies, sweet potato, jicama, amaranth, and mucuna also entered the agricultural landscape (Mann, 2005/2011).

It is estimated that some agriculture arose in different regions in this area where people migrated c. 6500 BCE to 1500 BCE, with ongoing hunting, fishing, and gathering taking place before, during, and after this development. These regions then entered into their formative period up to the early classic period of 100 BCE.

As the people in this region built causeways and canals, it is estimated that the Mesoamerican and Andean regions could have supported as many as four hundred thousand people (Mann, 2005/2011). This implies that there would have been many languages, much trade, and many cultures in the region that sustained these Indigenous peoples.

Due to relatively recent archaeological discoveries in the area of Mesoamerica, we now know that the Aboriginals here experienced a second, independent Neolithic period approximately ten thousand years ago, not long after the Neolithic period on the other side of the world (Mann, 2005/2011). There is an indication of a third Neolithic period at the foot of the Andes. The most prominent crop in Mesoamerica, maize, would have developed during this time, along with squash and beans (Mann, 2005/2011).

In a region of what is now Mexico, the Olmecs became the first highly developed civilization around 1800 BCE, developing complex religious rites (including human sacrifice to appease the gods) with cities and towns built on temple mounds (Mann, 2005/2011). Their art included huge stone carvings of male heads, some six feet tall, with frowning visages. The Olmec were involved in scientific and economic activities, creating a 365-day calendar and establishing trade routes across a wide area. Several writing systems were utilized, and their histories were recorded in Codices or books consisting of folding pages of fig tree bark (King, 2012; Mann, 2005/2011).

Olmec mathematicians discovered the concept of zero, hundreds of years before the Visigoths and the Arabs—to which this discovery used to be attributed. This breakthrough led to a turning point in science and technology before any other recorded civilization. The Olmec were great astrologists along with the Mayan and other Mesoamerican societies (Mann, 2005/2011).

The Maya and Aztecs used a numbering system based on twenty instead of ten, as in Europe. Some attribute the concept of zero to the Maya, using a stylized shell to represent zero in a written number recording system using dots and bars. The Aztecs also used a similar system to record numbers, and some scholars believe that this system heralds back to a shared Mesoamerican tradition begun with the Olmecs (Phillips, 2017).

The wheel was used for children's toys, but not for other purposes that are currently known, in all probability because there were no draft animals to use in agriculture production due to rugged terrain. Instead, porters hauled fifty pounds of goods to market securing a load around their heads with a rope or by using chest ropes and traveling in convoys. The Maya built some roads, but due to the terrain, they weren't always necessary and people could choose their own paths to the marketplaces (Mann, 2005/2011; Phillips, 2017).

While the Aztecs had a special class of people called *pochteca* who did all the trading, including that of slaves to be used in ritual sacrifices, the Maya did not.

Mayan rulers and nobility carried out long-distance trading. Local small-scale peddlers and entrepreneurs carried out the short-distance trade. Long-distance "trade was the lifeblood of development: because they traded in elite goods such as feathers, jaguar skins and sacrificial knives that were needed for religious ceremony, traders began to enjoy religious prestige" (Phillips, 2017, p. 319).

Trade was carried on throughout the areas of South America, Mesoamerica, and there was a northern Mexican trade network with the city of La Quemada that thrived throughout the Classic Period until c. 850 CE. Turquois from New Mexico was a major import. Casas Grande, part of Chihauahua, was a major trading center linked to the Southwest in what is now the United States (Phillips, 2017). Trading posts were also established among the coastal communities as well as other waterways throughout the region. Canoes were commonly utilized to transport goods in these areas.

The Caribbean coast as well as islands were involved in sea trade for hundreds of years and made many wealthy in the Yucatán peninsula. The *Strombus gigas*—a type of conch shell used for religious ceremonies—came from Tancah, a fortified town on the eastern coast in northern Yucatán. Obsidian, pyrite, jade, granite and slate vessels also came through Tancah (Phillips, 2017).

In the Mesoamerican regions, the plumed serpent god was worshiped by peoples and the different cultures under the names of Quetzalcóatl, Kukulcán, and Gucumatz (Phillips, 2017). The sacred *Popol Vuh* book of the Maya of Quiché bears the stories of the creator gods making the earth, animals, and people. The people believed that many gods resided in the heavens. Planting and harvesting were done in accordance with where some of these gods were in the night skies in different areas of Mesoamerica (Phillips, 2017).

The artwork in Mesoamerica and the Aztec regions was distinctive with its stylized characterizations of Indigenous mythologies, family lives, and histories which were incorporated in paintings and sculptures. They also made clay figurines. Glyphs and hieroglyphs were used in many of their creations. While some artwork was on small pieces in the Codices, other artwork adorned temples and public spaces within cities (Phillips, 2017).

The marketplaces attracted thousands of people, traders, and buyers. They were places where religious processions were held, people gathered to chat, sing, and dance. Goods were sold by their size, never their weight, and customers bartered with sellers. Feathers, cocoa beans, gold dust, and copper ax blades were used as currency for purchasing goods (Phillips, 2017).

Peoples in Mesoamerican and Aztec societies did not fear death. It was believed that slaves who were sacrificed to certain deities then became the deity.

Consequently, slaves were treated well before their loss of life. For those not given up to ritual sacrifice, it was important to be remembered by one's descendants. The celebration of the Mexican Day of the Dead is believed to be an extension of the Aztec ceremonies honoring the dead (Phillips, 2017).

Ball courts are a common feature found in Mesoamerican and Aztec cities, with some places having several courts located usually in the cities' sacred districts. The ball game was played both for honoring deities and for divination of future events. There is speculation that the ball itself may have represented the sun or other heavenly bodies. Unfortunately, there were many times when the losers of the games also lost their heads (Phillips, 2017).

The oldest known ball court was discovered in 1998 by archaeologists in Paso de la Amada, Chiapas, dated at c. 1400 BCE (Phillips, 2017). "In Mesoamerican mythology the game is an important element in the story of the Maya gods Hun & [sic] Vucub Hunahpú," two brothers who were tricked into going to the underworld (Cartwright, 2013). The game was played with 8 cm to 25 cm latex balls, and begun in 2500 BCE and played through the Classical Period and eventually was exported to other areas in the region.

The collapse of the Maya capital of Mayapán between 1441 and 1461 CE cast a shadow across Mesoamerican communities. The community of Progresso Lagoon was one of these that suffered political uncertainties and eventually moved from its original setting on the island of Caye Coco to the west shore of the lagoon. Economic uncertainty, combined with trying to maintain their prestige as a community, took a toll on residents before the coming of the Spanish as they were reorganizing themselves politically (Oland, 2012).

The Aztecs

The Aztec city-state of Xaltocan, thirty-five kilometers away from Mexico City, provides an excellent example of how the Aztec Empire—or the *Triple Alliance* as contemporary historians now refer to it (Mann, 2011)—was formed and operated. This city initially was founded on an island in Lake Xaltocan c. 900 CE as a rural Indigenous community and eventually became part of the core of the Empire (Rodríguez-Algería, 2012).

The people of Xaltocan lived in a regional capital. They utilized the gifts from the lake for their needs (fish, waterfowl, and other vegetable and animal foods), hunted, and made cloth, salt, and tools. Maize was a staple crop; they produced chipped stone tools and were involved in thread production. The Aztecs carried out elaborate religious practices as reflected in their ceramic artifacts. They were involved with the solar ideologies, the cosmos, warfare, and sacrifice when needed. Xaltocans were a prosperous part of the Aztec Empire (Rodríguez-Algería, 2012).

Then in 1395 CE, after one hundred years of war, the city of Xaltocan was conquered by the nearby city-state of Cuauhtitlan. Xaltocan was then deserted for thirty years before being reconquered by the Aztecs in 1428 CE. This was a time of independence and prosperity during which they received tribute from forty-nine nearby towns over which they had control (Rodríguez-Algería, 2012).

When the Triple Alliance took over again, the economy of the region plummeted as the Xaltocan community was now expected to pay tribute to the now-centralized Aztec government. Xaltocans were no longer able to hold onto much of their wealth. They continued in their production of maize and ceramics, salt and thread; they also continued with ceremonial feasts as evidenced by different types of ceramics produced for celebrations (Rodríguez-Algería, 2012).

The Xaltocan community produced varied types of ceramics according to time and politics (Rodríguez-Algería, 2012). Early images of ceramic objects portrayed cultural interest in the cosmos and solar entities, warrior ideology, conquest, and human sacrifice. Production was reduced when the citizens came under the central control of the Aztec government. It is apparent from artifacts that not all citizens were unified in their traditional beliefs.

The Andes

The Andean city of Chiripa may date from 900 BCE and was built around a Norte Chico–style with a sunken plaza. Chiripa and other similar small political entities surrounded Lake Titicaca where the people used raised flat platforms for agriculture.

By 750 BCE, two other cities were prominent: Pukara on the northern edge of Lake Titicaca, and Tiwanaku opposite on the Bolivian side. Tiwanaku was occupied since 800 BCE and was the highest city in the ancient world at 12,600 feet (Mann, 2011). Tiwanaku had religious prominence, and other local leaders submitted themselves to members of the priesthood who controlled these powers.

The temple Akapana in Tiwanaku was laid out in the form of the Andean cross and was seven stories high with a moat surrounding it. Water was channeled through a cistern-like well down the sides of the temple (Mann, 2005/2011). The monumental Gateway of the Sun was constructed from a single block of stone with reliefs carved on the lintel forming an astronomical calendar.

While Tiwanaku did not have markets as can be found in other cities and civilizations, it did have relationships built on kinship and the government, which controlled the flow of goods, including agricultural and clothing goods. Goods could also be picked up at the government warehouses (Mann, 2005/2011).

Eventually, a cultural group referred to as the Wari moved into the same region as Tiwanaku. It is apparent that these two groups kept themselves apart from each other, spoke separate languages, and had different cultural traditions. They did not intermarry and kept their distance from each other. The fall of both the Wari and Tiwanaku civilizations occurred around 800 CE, with the successors of both going on to establish other civilizations (Mann, 2011).

One of those cities—Chimor—became the greatest Empire in Peru. The people there grew cotton and maize on fifty thousand acres around the Moche River through irrigation practices (Mann, 2005/2011). Following a major destructive El Niño episode, elite rulers forced captive laborers into chain gangs to build a masonry-lined channel that would bring water from the Chicama River fifty-three miles away to irrigate the fields. However, the canal failed to fulfill its function (Mann, 2005/2011).

A new city needed to be found which would provide for the needs of this large population. Armies were sent to look for possibilities, and the city of Chan Chan became the new capital of the Chimor Empire. There were a good number of palaces and only the elite could travel on the city streets. Each succession of rulers built their own palaces for postmortem occupation there as gods, and the city offered a place where the distinctions between the upper class and others were always apparent (Mann, 2005/2011).

Chan Chan is considered as one of the wonders of the fifteenth century (Mann, 2005/2011). The élite employed gold, silver, and gem workers and were surrounded by beauty in their city. Nevertheless, Chan Chan fell to a new invading group in c. 1450 CE: the Inca. The initial wave of Inca was at first not considered to be a threat. When future waves of Inca warriors came to Chan Chan, they threatened to cut off the water supply to the city and thereby overcame the Chan Chan armies (Mann, 2005/2011).

Qosqo

The Inca were relatively new on the scene before the Spanish conquered the city of Qosqo one hundred years later. Pachakuti was the reigning ruler who commanded troops to conquer as much territory as possible. When other cities were subjugated, their rulers became vassals to the Inca; even so, they were allowed to continue to control their own cities (Mann, 2005/2011). These same cities were forced to export thousands of their workers to perform the labor for Qosqo, and everything produced in their cities was ultimately for the Empire. Eventually, Pachakuti turned over the military to his son, Thumpa Inca (Mann, 2005/2011).

Qosqo was transformed when Thumpa Inka found all of the glories of the city of Chan Chan after his victory over the people there (Mann, 2005/2011). The gold, silver, and gem workers, along with other craftsmen, were forced to go to Qosqo and told to make the city into another magnificent Chan Chan. All of this transportation of goods and peoples was by foot since the Native peoples had no horses, requiring a great deal of travel time (Mann, 2005/2011).

Amazonia

Formerly, Amazonia was thought of as a place where primitive Native tribes dwelled. There is now evidence that "a fully operational forest civilization [existed] on the Brazilian Amazon. . . . [a civilization which] lasted some 8,000 years and ended after the Europeans arrived in the sixteenth century" (Barnes, 2010, p. 24). There are estimates that some five to seven million people lived in Amazonia alone, and this helps us understand how heavily populated the region was in pre-Columbian times (Stannard, 1992).

There have been new discoveries of Huanca de la Luna, in the heart of the Moche Empire, Caral in the Supe valley north of Lima and several other sites that have been dated back as far as 2670 BCE (Barnes, 2010). Caral is as large as other sites at that time in Egypt and Sumer and is comprised of six platform mounds surrounding a huge plaza. The current thought is that it was a great trading center for the time, and that class societies were beginning to emerge from tribal societies (Barnes, 2010).

The Moche Empire was constructed in the desert on Peru's northern coast and appears to be advanced with adobe structures, terraced fields, and irrigation canals. The Pyramid of the Sun stands at 130 feet and is 1,148 feet long. Some uncovered gravesites demonstrate that many warriors stood at six feet tall, much more than the average person in the region. The Moche were fine craftsmen and craftswomen, and they left behind ornamented artifacts, much of which remains still to be exposed to view (Barnes, 2010).

The third site discussed by Barnes (2010) is that of Llanos de Mojos, also built on a series of mounds on which cities were built and from which radiated a series of causeways. Thousands of miles of artificial walls and canals supported sophisticated farming systems and fish weirs. Aboriginals' pottery was sophisticated and their fields were laid out in a north-south direction.

Early Portuguese accounts tell of large villages with many inhabitants and civilizations with developed social orders and leadership roles (Barnes, 2010). These accounts confirm what recent archaeological sites are revealing. The use of recent technologies, including air flyovers that reveal landscapes, tell the stories of many civilizations that are only now being uncovered which changes our perceptions of these highly developed peoples (Mann, 2005/2011).

Much to Be Learned

There is still much to be learned about Central and South America, as well as Amazonia. As additional archaeological studies are being conducted of these regions, more has come to light with uncovering sites of great cities and smaller communities in these regions. Indeed, we are acquiring more information about Indigenous peoples, such as the reason that many individuals in South America and Mesoamerica acquired gold: The Indians believed that they needed this metal for the afterlife, and so were buried with as much gold as possible. Gold was also used as tribute for the kings in various societies (Hill, 1994).

As new knowledge of the Southern and Central Americas is learned, misperceptions are being corrected. Indigenous peoples across the Americas are being listened to by the experts as they supply alternate worldviews about their ancestors' pasts. As teachers, we can develop more understandings and respect for our students who are descendants of these great peoples, knowing that they indeed are part of rich legacies.

Aboriginal Societies in North America before Conquest

Traditions dictated how affairs were taken care of throughout Native America:

> Children are born within circles of tradition that define the world views of their communities. For example, an Iroquoian child's first moccasins are punctured to keep the relationship between the child `and the earth intact. Traditional birth, with the mother squatting down to deliver her baby, symbolically pulled the child to the earth. (Hill & Hill, 1994, p. 23)

In North America, there is much evidence of a region that was well-occupied for thousands of years before the coming of Europeans. While population estimates vary from one to eighteen million for the continent, it is believed that two million Native Americans lived in what is now the United States and Canada

(Barnes, 2010). However, Stannard (1992) states that many of the earlier figures are too low and that the pre-Columbian Americas may have been populated by 145,000,000 in the hemisphere and 18,000,000 in North America.

In many tribal communities, the Bering Strait theory of migration is considered to be faulty in comparison to their own Creation stories (Truer et al., 2010). We do know that the Coastal marker M_{130} is only found in Western North America (Wells, 2002) and of the recent discovery of an ancient community in Idaho whose tools are similar to those of the ancients of Hokkaido, Japan (Davis, 2019). Both of these findings indicate that there were more than one way of reaching the Americas for Indigenous peoples, and perhaps there are more of which we are currently not aware.

Tribal Nations

The exact number of Tribal nations in North America before encountering Europeans is still unknown. While there are estimates of over two thousand languages that were being used in American Indian/Alaska Native communities, we are still finding more information as technology increases our abilities to examine the northern lands to learn about Tribal nations which may have become extinct due to the epidemics which proceeded actual European presence.

In general, Tribal nations lived in smaller groups than those in Mesoamerica and South America. Indigenous people were very independent and protected their members and their borders. While gentle with their families, especially their children, Aboriginals could be ferocious when it came to their enemies, just as soldiers are today in the midst of wars.

Slavery occurred generally when one group defeated another and those left could be taken by the victors. At times, children were adopted into tribes when a family member had died and the child was to replace that individual. In many instances, leaving children on their own would have resulted in death within a short time due to the distant regions between settlements.

Some Tribal nations were patrilocal with the father in charge of the family and children belonging to the father and his family. Some of the nations were matrilocal, with everything belonging to the mother and her side of the family, including the children. Some nations, linked through language and locale but living in smaller groups, could be a mixture of both matrilineal and patrilineal, dependent upon the particular group and circumstances (Barnes, 2010; Mann, 2005/2011). In all, though, the extended family was very important and being part of this family gave one his or her identity.

In general, the raising of children was not left just to the parents. Children were considered a responsibility of the entire community, and they could be taught by different members who had expertise in various areas. Children often stayed with different members of the extended family, in particular, grandparents. In many ways, Native Americans had the first childcare and educational systems on the continent.

In many instances, a grandparent had a dream which included a vision of what each child should become. Parents and children respected these visions and children received schooling to support their future Tribal roles. Children were allowed to practice alone what they were learning until they became proficient. At that point, they would then demonstrate to a "teacher" what they had learned. Discipline, when necessary, was not carried out by parents, but by an uncle or in public gatherings, the "Whipman." This was done to preserve the sacred bond between parents and children (personal communications with Tribal members over thirty years).

Agriculture

Hunter-gatherer societies began to gather wild plants during the Archaic period of c. 7000 BCE to 2000 BCE (Barnes, 2010). By 7000 BCE, there is evidence that Mesoamerican hunters were growing squash and chilies, beans, pumpkins, and gourds. Maize was added to the mix c. 3000 BCE. While dates are not specifically known for when Mesoamerican plants were first introduced to Northern neighbors, various dates from 3500 BCE to 1500 BCE have been deduced from archaeological sites (Barnes, 2010; Mann, 2005/2011).

There is evidence that by 3000 BCE, gourds, squash, sunflower, maygrass, pigweed, knotweed, goosefoot, and marsh elder were grown and eaten in the Northeast. Propagation of plants soon followed and supplemented a diet of meat provided by hunters (Barnes, 2010).

In the Southwest, maize, squash, and more than one variety of beans from Mexico were being cultivated. In addition, cotton and amaranth were being grown, as were agave, tobacco, dropseed, lamb's quarters, cholla, barley, and panic grasses. Baskets were made for storage from devil's claws cactus. Native Americans developed different irrigation techniques for their needs dependent on the area of the country and the amount of rain received (Barnes, 2010; Mann, 2005/2011).

In the Great Lakes region, fish and waterfowl were predominant foodstuffs, along with wild rice that was gathered. People gathered the rice while in canoes, using beating sticks to make the heads fall off into special baskets made for the rice (Barnes, 2010). Different types of nuts were eaten in the lower forty-eight states. Farther north, in what is now Alaska and Canada, seal, whales, salmon, and crustaceans were taken from rivers and the ocean, many times dried for storage and eaten later. In coastal communities in the North American Northwest, Aboriginals also pursued these animals. Additionally in both regions, large game such as moose, deer, and bear, added to their diets, as well as many different types of berries (Barnes, 2010).

Forty-seven known varieties of berries have been found in the United States (Weatherford, 1988). Blueberries make up twenty different types and gooseberries as many as twelve varieties. In the Northwest regions, huckleberries and chokecherries are culturally important to Native peoples. Some of the additional wild and cultivated plants used by Native peoples included the following: dandelion, pokeweed, milkweed, mustard, watercress, and dock. The Navajo developed different varieties of red, blue, yellow, black, and white corn. Wild honey and maple syrup were collected in some areas of the country. Numerous types of seeds and nuts were collected and added to the store of available nutritional goods (Barnes, 2010).

In California, nuts and berries grew in abundance. Native American women learned how to make acorns edible by grinding and leaching out tannins to take away the bitter taste. Acorn flour was used to make bread, added to soups and other foods. Special baskets were made to gather foodstuffs and others to store them, such as the ones used to store acorn flour. Women made a phenomenal number of different types of baskets in this area, as well as in Nevada, Arizona, and New Mexico (Basha's Western Museum, n.d.; Margolin, 1981/1993).

Storage of foodstuffs by California Indians took place in a pit in the dwellings where the earth kept the temperatures cooler. Baskets with flour, dried berries, nuts, and other edibles were kept on a shelf above the pit (Margolin, 1981/1993). Surrounding dwellings for some of the Native people, such as the Hupa, had calendar rocks that served also as markers for weather and festivals. Invitations to neighbors were given for Spring dances by means of a rope with knots tied to indicate in how many days the dances would be held (Margolin, 1981/1993).

Bags made from cornhusks were used to gather and store plants in areas of the Pacific Northwest. As with all things, these were not just utilitarian items but were covered with special designs and artistry. Most often, the designs utilized had spiritual importance for their makers. Always, prayer was used while making these objects.

The same was true in the areas of the Southwest where pottery and earthenware goods were used for storage. Some of the designs were used for hundreds of years and represented family designs, as even now. For Navajos, the designs used for making woven goods such as rugs and bags are owned by the family making these items.

Of course, some of the plants originating in Mesoamerica and Peru made their way to North America, considering the trading network that was well developed and the areas of Mexico that are now part of the United States. The potato, while originating in South America in its many varieties, manioc (cassava), and cocoa probably came north that way, though we can only speculate about when they may have begun to be planted in the northern climes. The tomato caused consternation with non-Natives until they were convinced it was not poisonous and now it is used and grown around the world.

From Weatherford (1988), we know that wild berries became a staple for many when they were mashed and mixed with fat. *Pemmican* became the perfect carry-all snack when parties went out to gather, hunt, and fish, giving needed calorie boosts to travelers. Natives also used teas made of wintergreen, peppermint, and other plants, many times to aid in healing someone who was sick. Spices were also added to the European diet from the Americas.

Large animals, such as buffalo, deer, elk, and moose, were hunted for food and clothing across the northern areas of the United States and Canada. Additional animals used for food were rabbits, squirrels, rock chuck (marmots), and dogs (in some groups); snakes (in some areas); wild turkey and geese; cod, shellfish, salmon, halibut, and other types of seafood; and whales, again dependent on the areas where people lived. Daily eating or feasting was accompanied by giving thanks for the food that had been provided to them.

Pharmaceuticals and Healing

"Medicine" did not mean what we think of today as medicine. The term comes from a similar native word used to describe a variety of ways used to keep people healthy. In particular, Native American healers relied on spiritual power from the Creator as well as numerous plants, such as cocoa, quinine, willow bark, and sometimes alcohol to heal the sick. The idea was to prevent sickness by keeping a balance in one's life in terms of the physical, mental, emotional, and spiritual areas that make up the whole of one's being. Over two hundred pharmaceuticals have been added to the *United States Pharmacopoeia* which were first used by Native Americans (Vogel, 1991).

Surgeries were performed by healers, as well as amputations. Steam was used to cure illnesses, to help with the aftereffects of giving birth, and to relieve sore muscles with people going into sweat lodges (Weatherford, 1988). Many of these activities were carried out throughout the Americas, with some peoples more skilled than others, but always with the spiritual connections of the Medicine Men and Women asking for sacred assistance.

Spirituality

Moreover, spiritual ceremonies were an intricate part of daily life for Native Americans in North America. Ceremonies were developed to ensure success in gathering, planting, and harvesting, as well as in fishing and hunting rituals (Barnes, 2010). Indigenous peoples recognized supreme beings in their creation stories and legends and were respectful toward them, no matter the groups to whom the supreme beings belonged. Ceremonies and special prayers were also held before and after any group activity to gather or hunt for food.

Spirituality was not only for observation on the weekends: Every day was to be begin and end with prayers thanking supreme beings, Mother Earth, and the Sun or Father Sky for all of the blessings the people received. Performing daily ablutions—sometimes completed by jumping into rivers, even if frozen—was an important ritual in making oneself clean before the spirits.

Cleanliness, not necessarily valued by all Europeans, was considered a requirement for health for body, mind, and soul. "The widespread and persistent use of steambaths and of water baths by the Indians paralleled the practices of ancient Mediterranean cultures . . . [and] probably served to reduce diseases among the Indians prior to European arrival and thereby partly accounted for the general freedom from epidemic diseases" (Weatherford, 1988).

Settlements

The rise of agriculture in North America influenced Indigenous groups to build settlements and raise plant foods in the Eastern Woodlands, where women were responsible for most of the farming. Contrary to building large cities, Native Americans in the north lived in smaller groups, sometimes referred to as "towns." There were many more distinct groups of Indian people than found in Mesoamerica and South America.

The Hohokam may have been established by 300 BCE, the Anasazi by 185 BCE, and the Mogollon by 700 CE. The Hohokam lived in what is now Arizona and the northern part of the Sonoran Desert (Barnes, 2010). They built plazas and homes of adobe; the élite building homes on top of mounds. Indications are that as many as two thousand Hohokam lived in the Casa Grande Pueblo in Arizona. These people used irrigation systems to grow their crops. They also participated in a wide trading network, receiving mosaic mirrors, copper bells, parrots, and latex balls (Barnes, 2010).

The number of ballcourts found in the area around Casa Grande demonstrates that playing this game was a widespread activity. Games also provided opportunities for social mixing, politics, and completing business. By 1150 CE, there were two hundred ballcourts in this area. We don't know if changing climate conditions affected the world of the Hohokam, but they appear to have disappeared by 1450 CE. One cause may have been overpopulation. Their descendants are thought to be members of the O'Odham (formerly known as Pima and Papago) and possibly other communities (Barnes, 2010).

Rock art is found throughout the Americas and was used as a way to depict ceremonies, belief structures, important animals in the areas, and historical information. Glyphs and hieroglyphs, or rock pictures called petroglyphs, portray much information to those who read them. These "newspaper rocks" are found throughout the Americas, as well as in other countries, and portray active, vibrant communities with strong spiritual belief systems (Paterson, 2012).

The Mississippi Mound Builders

The Mississippian Mound Builder culture is estimated to have begun by 750 CE and flourished until c.1500 CE. They were known by the huge mounds along both sides of the Mississippi River and its tributaries, upon which they built their cities and held their ceremonies. They grew maize, squash, and beans, again relying on women to grow their produce. The best-known sites are "Cahokia in Illinois; Etowah and Ocmulgee in Georgia; Moundville in Alabama, Spiro in Oklahoma, SunWatch in Ohio; and Nanih Waiya in Mississippi" (Barnes, 2010, p. 48).

The waterways were common means of transportation of people and goods by canoe in the Mound Builder culture. The Mississippi River was essential in terms of trade routes along its intersecting rivers, carrying freshwater pearls, copper, silver, obsidian, soapstone pipes, chert, galena, mica, bears' teeth, shells, shell beads, alligators' teeth, turtle shells, and pottery, as well as tools needed for everyday living (Barnes, 2010).

The estimated population of Cahokia was between twenty and forty thousand people. This mound community contained smaller mounds, which may have been for subcommunities. Bows and arrows as well as the *atlatl* were used to keep away invaders and were probably used in other Mound Builder cities. Some of these cities flourished after the arrival of the Spanish, having survived initial conflicts with them. However, many were deserted prior to that time, perhaps due to disease or overpopulation (Barnes, 2010). Their residents may have become the ancestors of other Tribal nations, or have joined other Native American tribes.

The Northeast

Water correspondingly played an important role throughout the Northeast, providing transportation by canoe for trade, diplomacy, and war. There were three mother groups from which all tribes in the region were descended: the Algonquian (or Algic), Iroquoian, and Siouan, eventually becoming twenty-seven separate Nations (Truer et al., 2010).

This was the area of the League of Five Nations (a.k.a. the Iroquois League, or Five Nations of the Longhouse) consisting of Mohawk, Onondaga, Oneida, Cayuga, and Seneca. The League—referred to as the *Haudenosaunee*, or the Great League of Peace—was formed as a way of resolving differences in the region among tribes and to make decisions for the good of everyone in an area heavily populated at the time (Barnes, 2010). It is considered to be one of the greatest polities north of the Rio Grande for the two centuries before Columbus and the two centuries after (Mann, 2005/2011).

The League and their constitution, the Great Law of Peace, was proposed by Deganawidah, a Shaman, and Ayanwatha, a great orator of the Onondaga who vowed no one else would ever lose their children to war. Members of the groups forming the Haudenosaunee stated that it began before the coming of the Europeans. Through the examinations of astronomical calculations, oral traditions, and the Condolence Canes—a system of pegs and carved images used to record council members—the age of the League is indicated to have come into existence between 1090 BCE and 1150 BCE (Mann, 2005/2011). "The Haudenosaunee thus would have the second oldest continuously existing representative parliaments on earth" (Mann, 2005/2011, p. 383).

The Great Law of Peace also includes women's rights regarding which men were chosen as sachems by clan mothers to represent their clans at councils. Members of the league could be forced out by matrilineal clan mothers if they had cause. All sachems had to agree to any decision made unanimously before it could take effect. It is believed that The Long House was comprised of twenty thousand people before European contact.

Many others were living in this region, including the Abenaki, and the Hurons who were enemies of the Iroquois. They and others had developed similar ways of living with depending upon agriculture as well as hunting and fishing. Life in Aboriginal communities throughout the region was distinguished by personal freedom and social equality, a concept not accepted in Europe. There were no hierarchies which determined what those below them would do: the belief that all men were equal comes from our Native American relatives. Because this belief was broadcast through writings of Europeans, many Europeans who came to the Americas deserted colonial communities and joined Indigenous ones (Mann, 2005/ 2011).

Pacific Coastal Region

This area of North America is thought to have been the most populous with an estimated number of at least 130,000 people in 1492. Three main groups of Native Americans occupied the land: the Salish-speaking group, Tlingit, and Haida speakers. The range of peoples in this area included Southeast Alaska, British Columbia, Washington, and Montana.

Even with a wide range of languages being spoken, the Aboriginals here developed close-knit communities, practiced important ceremonies, and used the abundance of available wood in building their homes, canoes, and totem or house poles that marked the beings that were sacred to each family. Artistic expression was very important, and kin groups owned songs and dances. Clothing and other objects were decorated with important family symbols. Totem poles do not represent hierarchical arrangements of figures. This form of crest art gave the family's mythic origins (Macnair, Hoover, & Neary, 1984), as do other crests around the world.

The potlatch was a way for Native peoples in this area to redistribute wealth within communities. The cultural misunderstanding of Native peoples as "Indian givers," with the ability to walk away and take back initial trade items, came from early observations by religious figures. Many times potlatches were given by leaders in the groups. As leaders, they would have acquired wealth; to keep all of this would have been dangerous spiritually for them. Native people were honored when the community came to their potlatches to carry away some of these riches (Macnair, Hoover, & Neary, 1984).

In other areas throughout the country, people held "giveaways" as a means of redistributing wealth. It was important to help other members of the community who were not as fortunate as oneself. The circle is an important symbol for many reasons, and the idea that when you give to others the giving comes back to you was specifically taught to community members (Allen, 1989).

The Plains

Before the coming of European fur traders and explorers, Indigenous peoples lived in the areas between the Rocky Mountains on the west and the Mississippi River to the east, all the way north and south from Canada to Mexico. A few of these were speakers of Siouan, Uto-Aztecan, Athabaskan Algonquian, and Caddoan languages. Some of these people were settled and were farmers and hunters. They lived in settlements year-round in teepees made from bison skins, and are known for their feathered bonnets (History.com Editors, n.d.).

Others were nomadic and followed the trail of the buffalo herds. They only killed bison when they needed food, and then all parts of the buffalo were used. Hides were used to make teepees; the tails became whips; stomachs carried liquids; bones were used to make spoons and needles. These people also ate deer and antelope. Travois were used to carry their possessions. They were made from three poles from sturdy trees woven together with strips of leather then covered by teepee hides and pulled by dogs (Great Plains Indians, n.d.).

The Great Basin

The area between the Rocky Mountains to the east and the Cascades to the West is referred to as the Great Basin. It extends to the Columbian Plateau in the North and the South. This is an area of deserts, including the high-altitude deserts of Idaho and Utah. Shoshonian and Ute speakers lived in these areas and were hunters of bison, elk, bear, and occasionally, mountain lions; fishers, especially of salmon; and gatherers of wild plants and nuts, such as piñon pine nuts and camas bulbs.

Some of the people here lived in wiki-ups, conical shelters built from the plants and tree branches in the areas occupied by them (History.com. Editors, n.d.). These were mainly Bannock and Paiute shelters. Others, such as the Shoshone, lived in teepees similar to those on the Plains.

The Southeast

According to Truer et al. (2010), the Southeast has been occupied by American Indians for eighteen thousand years.[2] In the Southeast, there were several fishing and farming communities, some of whom were related, others who stood on their own. A sample of these were the Meherrin, Tuscarora, and Nottaway of Iroquoian lineages. The Cherokee (Tsalagi) were related to them but distinct from them and with their large numbers, stood apart from the others (Barnes, 2010).

The Powhatan Confederacy was composed of the Powhatan, Weapemeoc, and Secotan. They had joined together for protection and making important decisions regarding their communities. Muskogee speakers were divided into the Chickasaw, Choctaw, Apalachee, and Creek. Their ancestors had been part of the previous Mound Culture in that region (Barnes, 2010). The Cherokee, Choctaw, Chickasaw, Creek, and Seminole of what is now Florida later formed what Europeans named the Five Civilized Tribes. Along with those, there were the Caddo, Natchez, and Atakapa who were unrelated to others. In Florida, the Timucua, Calusa, and Tekesta also resided.

Basketmaking was important in these areas, as was making pottery. Turtle shells were used upon which engravings were made. Fish, deer, squirrel, and other animals comprised Indigenous diets along with corn, beans, squash, and berries. Native clothing was largely made from deerskin and woven fibers.

The Native American World Writ Large

What is written here is only a small portion of the entire story of Native America before colonization. Many books written about Aboriginal peoples after colonization do not reflect the diversity of Indigenous people in the Americas. Recent writings have given a more accurate view of what the Americas were like before the devastation that was wrought through terrible epidemics of diseases; conquering of Native peoples by the Spanish, followed by other European powers; wars with Europeans; greed for Indian lands; and cultural as well as physical genocides against the ancestors of today's American Indians/Alaska Natives.

We know that musical instruments were an important part of Indigenous lives in all regions. Aboriginals were intelligent, creative, and diligent as seen in the art they produced, including the clothing they wore. They were original thinkers, scientists, astronomers, and ecologists. They were people who laughed, played, and had a strong spiritual connection to the earth, all of creation, and to the Creator, called by many names throughout the Americas.

At the first meeting, Colón described these people as gentle, trusting, and welcoming (Mann, 2005/2011). What happened in history to turn this image into something brutal appears to be the result of economic greed for the wealth of the Americas. In the next chapter, an examination of European development in history holds some clues about the creation of a narrative that cruelly defames the Indigenous peoples of this country, leading to false conclusions about Native peoples' intelligence, abilities, cultures, and cultural values.

REFERENCES

Allen, D. (1989). *Indians of the Northwest Coast*. Seattle, WA: Hancock House.
Barnes, I. (2010). *The historical atlas of Native Americans*. New York, NY: Chartwell Books.
Basha's Western Museum. (n.d.). The Zelma Basha Salmeri Gallery of Western American and American Indian Art. Chandler, AZ: The Eddie Basha Collection.
Cartwright, M. (2013, September 13). The Ball Game of Mesoamerica. *Ancient History*. Retrieved from https://www.ancient.eu/article/604/the-ball-game-of-mesoamerica/.
Davis, L. (2019, September 10). Idaho artifacts suggest Pacific entry for first Americans. *Idaho State Journal*. New York, NY: Associated Press.
Editors. (n.d.). Mesoamerica. *Encyclopaedia Britannia*. Retrieved from https://www.britannica.com/topic/Mesoamerican-civilization.
Global Civilizations. (2019). *Essential humanities*. Retrieved from http://www.essential-humanities.net./history-overview/global-civilizations/22019.
Great Plains Indians. (n.d.). *Native American Indian facts*. Retrieved from https://native-american-indian-facts.com/Great-Plains-American-Indian-Facts/Great-Plains-American-Indian-Facts.shtml.
Hill, R. W., Sr. (1994). Native gold, Spanish gold. In T. Hill & R. W. Hill, Sr. (Eds.), *Creation's journey: Native American identity and belief* (pp. 220–32). Washington, DC: Smithsonian Institution Press.
Hill, T., & Hill, R. W., Sr. (1994). Growing up Indian. In T. Hill & R. W. Hill, Sr. (Eds.), *Creation's journey: Native American identity and belief* (pp. 23–31). Washington, DC: Smithsonian Institution Press.
History.com Editors. (n.d.). The Plains. *Native American Cultures*. Retrieved from https://www.history.com/topics/native-american-history/native-american-cultures#section_5.
History.com Editors. (n.d.). Native American Cultures. *Native American History*. Retrieved from https://www.history.com/topics/native-american-history/native-american-cultures#section_5.
Jones, P., & Sidwell, K. (Eds.). (1997). *The world of Rome: An introduction to Roman culture*. New York, NY: Cambridge University Press.
King, S. M. (2012). Hidden transcripts, contested landscapes, and long-term Indigenous history in Oaxaca, Mexico. In M. Oland, S. M. Hart, & L. Frink (Eds.), *Decolonizing Indigenous histories: Exploring prehistoric colonial transitions in Archaeology* (pp. 230–63). Tucson: University of Arizona Press.
Macnair, P. L., Hoover, A. L., & Neary, K. (1984). *Tradition and innovation in Northwest Coast Indian art*. Seattle: University of Washington Press.
Mann, C. C. (2005/2011). *1491: New revelations of the Americas before Columbus*. New York, NY: Random House.
Mann, C. C. (2011). *1493: Uncovering the New World Columbus created*. New York, NY: Albert A. Knopf.
Margolin, M., Ed. (1981/1993). *The way we lived: California Indian stories, songs, and reminiscences*. Berkeley, CA: Heyday.
National Institutes of Health (NIH). (n.d.). *National Human Genome Research Institute*. Bethesda, MD: Author. Retrieved from https://www.genome.gov/about-genetics.
Oland, M. (2012). Maya history at Progresso Lagoon, Belize. In M. Oland, S. M. Hart, & L. Frink (Eds.), *Decolonizing Indigenous histories: Exploring prehistoric colonial transitions in Archaeology* (pp. 178–200). Tucson: University of Arizona Press.

Paterson, A. (2012). Rock art as historical sources in colonial contexts. In M. Oland, S. M. Hart, & L. Frink (Eds.), *Decolonizing Indigenous histories: Exploring prehistoric colonial transitions in Archaeology* (pp. 66–85). Tucson: University of Arizona Press.

Phillips, C. (2017). *The illustrated encyclopedia of Aztec & Maya: The greatest civilizations of ancient Central America with 1000 photographs, painting & maps*. London, UK: Anness.

Rodríguez-Algería, E. (2012). Discovery and decolonization of Xaltocan. In M. Oland, S. M. Hart, and L. Frink (Eds.), *Decolonizing Indigenous histories: Exploring prehistoric colonial transitions in Archaeology* (pp. 45–65). Tucson: University of Arizona.

Smelting in China and India. (n.d.). *Copper Age*. Retrieved from http://www.factsanddetails / copper.com.

Stannard, D. E. (1992). *American holocaust: The conquest of the New World*. New York, NY: Oxford University Press.

Sumerian language. (n.d.). *Ancient history encyclopedia*. Retrieved from https://www.ancient.eu/Sumerian_Language/.

Stone, Bronze, and Iron Ages. (2019). *Essential Humanities*. Retrieved from http://www.essential-humanities.net/history-overview/stone-bronze-iron-ages/.

Truer, A., Wood, K., Fitzhugh, W., Horse Capture, Sr., G. P., Fraizer, T., Miller, M. R., Belarde-Lewis, M., & Norwood, J. (2010). *Indian Nations of North America*. Washington, DC: National Geographic Society.

Vogel, V. J. (1991). What has Native American medicine given to Us? *National Forum, 71* (2), 28–30.

Weatherford, J. M. (1988). *Indian givers: How the Indians of the Americas transformed the world*. New York, NY: FawcetteColumbine.

Wells. S. (2002). *The journey of man: A genetic odyssey*. Princeton, NJ: Princeton University Press.

NOTE

1. A "civilization" here means at least one major urban center with a cultural presence encountered.
2. This date differs from others given.

Chapter Three

Who Were These Europeans?

> Conquest is a major part of [our] past and a major shaper of the cultures of the world today. Wars of conquest have changed the language, the economy, and the moral universe of whole peoples. As a result of conquests, the Western Hemisphere is today a region of European civilization larger than Europe itself. Even those who hate European civilization express that hatred in a European language and denounce it as immoral by European standards of morality. The history of conquests is not just about the past, it is very much about the present and how we came to be where we are economically, intellectually, and morally. (Sowell, 1998, p. 3)

While we may never understand the European mind of the fifteenth century, we do know that cultures carry on practices that may or may not be beneficial to their members or other human beings. Our contemporary understanding of the histories of different countries can best be explained as an analogy to visiting a foreign country for the first time: Depending on the country visited, practices may seem familiar to first-time visitors or may seem very strange or abhorrent depending on our cultural backgrounds.

Human beings were and are very diverse in their traditions around the world. We need to analyze these differences to explain them to ourselves and others, even if we disagree with certain ideas or practices. This doesn't mean that the actions that we would now declare violations of human rights should be condoned, only placed within their historical contexts.

SLAVERY: AN EQUAL OPPORTUNITY PROFESSION FOR THOSE FORCED INTO IT

After the great Ice Age, people began to make contact with other groups around the world and while they noted their differences, this was not a matter of concern. Each group felt they were superior to the other groups with which they made contact (Kendi, 2016).

Slavery is an ancient convention. It became a fact of life for people, usually as a result of warfare with other groups or of raids where those who were gathered up were sold to traders, going to owners geographically far away. Some people even sold themselves into slavery if they were trying to pay off debts, usually until their debts were paid off.

Either way, the foundations for racism and racist ideas were laid in the ancient world. Many later generations would point to the Greek philosopher Plato as the reason they supported slavery. Plato felt that the system was not good, but that slavery was a natural state for some people. Since Aristotle, Socrates, and Plato did not express any moral objection to the use of slaves, but accepted slavery as the only way to be able to run the households in Greece, no one felt they should object to the institution which served owners well (Sanders, 1978/2015).

When there were shortages of Slavs or other white groups to take up this position, justifications were made for the enslavement of Negroes from Africa, who had been captured or sold to the Arabs. A very early argument to enslave these people was that their color was a mark of Cain, and therefore slavery a result of religious punishment from God (Kendi, 2016).

We do not tolerate slavery in this era, though it has existed around the world for thousands of years (Kendi, 2016; Sowell, 1998). We do not tolerate people physically abusing other people or killing others without cause. Nevertheless, through learning about different European historical cultural systems, we can use that knowledge to question European past practices in relation to America's Indigenous populations. By interrogating the past, we can make links to our present and understand the concept of intergenerational trauma which has affected so many in our nation, especially Native Americans and African Americans.

EARLY EUROPEAN HISTORY

From chapter 1, we can acknowledge that those groups who migrated to Europe were originally Asian traveling from mostly northern areas of Asia. At some point, there was a change in their DNA that is now associated with Europeans, the M_{173} polymorphism.

Civilization as we know it today did not exist during the early recorded history of Europe up through the 1700s. The earliest cave paintings found in Europe are dated to 41,000 to 42,000 years ago in Grotte Chauvet, France, and were made by modern humans. Recently, a cave painting of a red disc found in El Castillo, Spain was re-dated to 40,600 years ago, and a hand stencil to 37,300 years ago. However, the question of whether the paintings were made by Neanderthals or by modern humans is unknown (Thompson, 2012). We don't know exactly what Europe was like after the Great Ice Age, referred to as the Last Glacial Maximus (LGM), and there is still work being completed to answer questions about that period for humans.

We do know from early European recorded history that it was primarily a continent of many individual tribes, some more intent on raiding and warring with their neighbors. Others were determined to harass those who lived great distances from their homes. The many rivalries among differing tribes resulted in battles, with the victors taking all including slaves that they sold, many times to people in the Middle East.

> Slavery was not unique to Africa or Africans, but was in fact common on every inhabited continent for thousands of years. As recently as the eighteenth century, it existed in Eastern Europe, and it continued to exist in the Middle East after the Second World War. What was unusual about Africa was the magnitude of the trade in human beings within recent centuries. (Sowell, 1998, p. 109)

In all early civilizations in the European, Mesopotamian, Middle Eastern, and African worlds, it was considered the legitimate right of the conquerors to capture and keep or sell vanquished peoples as slaves. As early as the Mycenaean civilization in Greece, existing from 1600 BCE–1100 BCE, there are depictions of the taking of slaves from those defeated and using them in Greek households. While women were considered legitimate plunder, it was dishonorable for warriors to be taken as slaves, preferring death instead (Sanders, 1978/2015).

During the seventh and sixth centuries BCE, there were approximately eighty thousand slaves in Athens alone. In the sixth century BCE, Athens became the first city with an organized slave trade. Slaves did the work to keep households running; fields plowed, planted, and harvested; and they tended to the animals raised for food and work. This freed the Greeks to develop deep thoughts about philosophy and to develop the arts (Sanders, 1978/2015).

Thus began the civilization that greatly influenced the development of Europe and European ideals of democracy. With Greek religion consisting of worshipping gods and goddesses, the Greeks developed temples, ritual worship practices, and epic stories of the deeds of these deities. The Greeks also ventured to lands further across the sea to plunder goods and human bounty. Many of their deeds were later related in the epic poetry of Homer. The Greeks were heralded as great warriors, philosophers, scientists, and creators of the arts.

Rome began with the founding of the city in 753 BCE on the Tiber River in what is now Italy. Eventually, Romans from the West traded with the Greeks. They spoke each other's languages, and the two had exchanged many ideas by the sixth century BCE. Rome and Greece differed in the way they treated conquered peoples. While Rome allowed those who had been vanquished the opportunity to eventually become citizens, Greece, consisting of city-states, did not (Grant, 2003). Greek common citizens had rights to own property, punish slaves, marry, and inherit wealth.

The Etruscans controlled the region which is now Italy from the ancient Italian city of Etruria (Tuscany) north of Rome from the period of c. 575 BCE to c. 450 BCE (Grant, 2003; Wellard, 1973). The Romans were under the control of the more developed Etruscans, who were considered "the most advanced sanitary and civil engineers in the ancient world" (Wellard, 1973, p. 130).

While the Etruscans were influenced by Greece, they developed a more sophisticated sense of the mystical in their religion than did either Greece or Rome. In the fourth century BCE, Rome was not content to be under the control of the Etruscans. Consequently, the Etruscans lost their political control of the area but left their influence on all facets of Roman life (Grant, 2003; Richard, 2010; Wellard, 1973).

Over the years of contact between the Greeks and the Romans, they became almost indistinguishable. While the Romans were known for their military prowess, the Greeks were known for their intellectual prowess. The Romans had their equivalents of the Greek gods and goddesses, and the two cultures shared common values. The arts flourished in both regions as citizens could commit their energies to enhancing their lives and the lives of those around them through painting, ceramic works, stone carving, theater, and rhetoric, while slaves performed the hard work required for agriculture and other forced labor.

Rome eventually became a republic by 509 BCE. This was accomplished by continually warring with its neighbors near and far, therefore accumulating new territories. Romans repelled those tribal peoples whom they considered savages: those undesirables unworthy of Roman citizenship. Walls were built by slaves to keep the savages out, and those same walls were guarded by the military, scores of whom came from other lands conquered by the Romans (Heather, 2009; Lafferty, 1971).

Roman Accomplishments

During this period until Rome became an Empire, Roman law advanced the idea of fairness in the application of the law, though the people themselves were not considered equal under the law. The second idea advanced was that prosecutors had to prove the guilt of defendants (Richard, 2010). Circa 450 BCE, civil law began with the Law of the Twelve Tables, which applied to Roman citizens. Later, international law was used in faraway lands based on the mercantile laws that had long been in existence among nations (Richard, 2010).

Engineering, art, and architecture flourished in Rome. The aqueducts were built in 310 BCE; the use of concrete began in 193 BCE; and many other improvements occurred in the territories held by Rome. Basilicas—large, roofed rectangular buildings with Greek Columns and interior business spaces—were built, along with theatres and amphitheaters (Richard, 2010).

Prose and poetry were written by many upper-class citizens, including Roman women, and some slaves. Greek comedies and tragedies were translated into Latin. Cicero's *On Duties*, a tome written about the duties of physicians, statesmen, and others, was produced in 44 BCE. Cicero's works influenced future generations of Romans and non-Romans alike, including Christian leaders such as Petrarch, Father of the Renaissance; Erasmus, a Catholic reformer; Martin Luther, leader of the Protestant revolution; as well as affecting several of the founding fathers of the United States such as John Adams (Richard, 2010).

Of all writings, those on agriculture had the greatest impact on all members of the Roman Empire. Cato the Elder's *On Agriculture*, c. 160 BCE, was consulted as a manual on how to run a large estate with the labor of dozens of slaves while Virgil's *Georgics* catered to the small farmer who did not have additional help in the fields. Cato admonished masters to ensure that "servants" were well-provided for and never cold or hungry, and that the various gods be respected through the prescribed rituals and prayers required for appeasement (Richard, 2010).

Women with means were allowed to accompany their brothers to elementary school. In general, they did not go on to advanced educations as they married while still young. They were allowed to learn mathematics and how to read and write (Heather, 2010; Jones & Sidwell, 2007).

Speeches, letters, comedies, and satire were all consumed by literate members of Roman society. Statuary, murals, and mosaics graced the open spaces of Rome and in some of its provinces (Richard, 2010).

Thus, the Romans and Greeks made great contributions upon which the Western world today has been built. It is important to remember that much of what was done was not completed only by original Romans from the land in modern Italy, but also by Romanized citizens and slaves bringing their knowledge from all regions where Rome held sway.

Unrest in Rome

While the previous section gives an idea of the many diverse accomplishments in the early half of Roman history, it does not tell the story of Roman turbulence. The Romans were harsh with their slaves, which led to several slave revolts beginning in Sicily in 135 BCE (Richard, 2010). The largest of all slave revolts was that of 73 BCE to 71 BCE which was led by Spartacus, a Thracian gladiator who led seventy thousand slaves to revolt. The slave army defeated several of the Roman legions before they were stopped. Six thousand slaves were crucified and their bodies were left on display in the Apian Way as a lesson for others wishing to revolt (Jarvus, 2013).

There was a Civil War from 49 BCE to 46 BCE due to inequities among the elite and the poor citizens in Rome. Tiberius and Gaius Gracchus tried to have laws passed that would limit land given to the wealthy to restore plots to the landless poor who could work them. However, the Senate blocked these proposals, so that the inequities continued (Richard, 2010).

ROME BECOMES AN EMPIRE

In 27 BCE, Rome became an Empire when it added more countries to its ever-expanding girth. The nations of the empire included Syria, Galacia, Palestine, and Armenia; Greece, Thrace, and Macedonia; Numidia, Gaul, and Britain; the wandering nations of the Western Goths; Libya and Egypt. In all, there were two hundred nations encompassed in the empire (Richard, 2010).

Augustus, great-nephew of Julius Caesar, became the sole ruler of the empire in 27 BCE, beginning a two-hundred year plus long period of peace referred to as "Pax Romana," from 27 BCE to 180 CE. Augustus was born under the sign of Capricorn which then became an imperial symbol (Jones & Sidwell, 1997). During this period, the various Roman values of peace (pax), harmony (concordia), duty (pietas), decency (humanitas), and wealth (copia) were emphasized and reinforced ("Pax Romana," n.d.).

Whereas the wealthy aristocrats could retire to their villas on the weekends, the commoners in the city and countryside had harder lives. Nonetheless, workers or plebeians:

> formed social clubs called *collegia*. The collegia involved themselves in feasting, celebrating, and giving decent burials to members. . . . Even these clubs reflected the Roman love of order. . . . [with] new members [advised] to read the club's rules, which were couched in the formal language of Roman law, and minutes were taken at meetings. (Richard, 2010, p. 28)

Slaves were treated better during the imperial rule and performed such roles as being messengers, doorkeepers, secretaries, teachers, nurses, and financial managers, among others. State-owned slaves were employed at the public baths; to keep street sewers cleaned out; and in general, to be sure the city's roads were kept in good condition (Richard, 2010).

While kings and emperors in conquered territories kept their titles and continued their rule, the Senate in Rome enacted the laws. The ordinary citizens and peasants of Rome took an active part in keeping the city, and later the empire, alive by making their own decisions concerning the work that needed to be done in the various warehouses, wharves and docking areas (Jones & Sidwell, 1997). They controlled the production of agriculture so that there was always enough food—but never too much—produced; thereby, commoners influenced the economics of the republic.

Roman emperors primarily led the military on campaigns to conquer additional new territories. And, a feature of all conquered territories, taxes were applied to all new territories; approximately 80 percent and higher of the taxes regulated on agriculture went to the Gross Imperial Product (Richard, 2010).

One of the areas that distinguished Romans from the Greeks and others of their time was the belief that their Emperors became gods after their deaths. Many temples formerly built to honor the ancient Roman gods and goddesses later served as centers for community gatherings (Jones & Sidwell, 1997). Unfortunately, they eventually became neglected during the Imperial reign, especially as emperors built their palaces (Crossan, 2007).

People accepted and did not question the prowess or desires of the emperors, at least not openly. Behind the scenes, there was constant intrigue that took place with plots of assassinations of emperors. In 44 BCE, one of the first victims of these plots, Julius Caesar, was assassinated. He was certainly not the last (Crossan, 2007).

The Goths of Europe Living beside the Romans

The Visigoths, or Western Goths, were one of the groups of Germanic tribes which included the Eastern Goths and Northern Goths, or Norsemen—more often referred to as Vikings. These groups were outside the boundaries of Roman control. They had coalesced by the third century and had acquired wealth and made their own goods (Heather, 2010).

The Visigoths had been employed for centuries to haul Roman products throughout the empire. They traded with the Romans for the goods they wanted. These people spoke several languages fluently, including Latin and Greek, and translated languages other than German for the Romans (Lafferty, 1971). The Goths were physically different from the Romans and other peoples of the empire: They were very tall—described as giants—and very hairy. Their clothing included wearing animal skins, furs, and some cloth as can be seen in depictions of the northern Goths, the Vikings (Lafferty, 1971).

The Goths had better equipment, furs, linen, huge horses, and made a different style of saddle than the Romans. They developed superior goods needed for daily living. The Goths carved in wood instead of stone, developed a runic system of numbers that included the number zero (later introduced as the Arabian system) and incorporated positional values for numbers (Lafferty, 1971).

The Goth lifestyle was to tour their territories, then establish great farms for two to three years to grow their crops and animals. While the Germanic groups had slaves, their slaves ran their farms on which they grew crops, giving part of the produce to their masters as opposed to supplying labor on someone else's estate (Heather, 2010). After crops had been harvested on the land for that period, Goths would pull up stakes and move to another territory, using a form of crop rotation to keep the soil productive. Visigoths used large carts pulled by their draft horses for moving. These horses were huge compared to Roman horses (Lafferty, 1971).

The Germanic groups had kings by the latter part of the fourth century. None of them had a desire to become part of the Roman Empire, though they had experienced the great inequalities that existed between the Romans and other groups outside of Rome (Heather, 2010). The Romans viewed them as barbarians, pagans, and uncivilized, and wanted to keep them out of the empire. The Goths practiced their ancient religion and were condemned for it (Lafferty, 1971).

In 372 CE, the Visigoths came under Rome's protection while fleeing from attacking Huns (Heather, 2010; Richard, 2010). The Eastern Goths, or Ostrogoths, fled in other directions to escape the Huns. Some of the Eastern Goths wandered further and became cut off from their cousins. A couple of centuries later, they became involved with the Huns of the steppes, earning the name of the white Huns (Lafferty, 1971).

After joining with Rome, the Visigoths played important roles in the military and expansion of Roman territories. They were great warriors and if they joined the Roman military, they could earn Roman citizenship, which many did. Alaric, the king of the Visigoths, was an especially gifted warrior who rose rapidly in the ranks of the Roman military.

However, the Visigoths were never treated as equals by the Romans. They continued to pay tribute to Rome in exchange for its protection, largely provided by the Visigoths themselves (Heather, 2010). It would have been unacceptable if they did not do so.

Christianity Comes to Rome through Paul, a Roman Citizen

The Roman general Pompey led an army into the Middle East to conquer Jerusalem in 63 BCE. Due to the suppression felt by all of the Jewish people, as well as the continual tribute that had to be given to Rome's governors for the Roman government, the Jewish people wanted to escape from the control of Rome. They were looking for a Messiah, a military commander that would lead an army to accomplish this goal. Some of the Jews believed Jesus to be the Messiah.

Through historical research, Richard (2010) and others provide new dates for the birth and death of Jesus of Nazareth at 3 BCE–32 CE, due to a correction of errors in the medieval dating system. The Jewish Pharisees, or high priests, considered him a blasphemer. After declaring that he was king of the Jews, Jesus was turned over to Pontius Pilot for the punishment of crucifixion. After his death, the teachings of Jesus began to be spread by his apostles. Finding his tomb empty, it was proclaimed that Jesus had arisen from the dead (Crossan, 2007).

Many Jews punished Jewish Christians who preached the gospel of Jesus, declaring them to be blasphemers. The apostle Paul was one of those. He eventually converted to Christianity and determined to spread the gospel among the Roman and other non-Jewish, or Gentile, groups. This outraged some Jewish Christians who felt that Christ's messages were for them alone (Richard, 2010).

Thus began almost three hundred years of Roman persecution of Christians in the empire. Paul was eventually beheaded c. 67 CE, followed shortly by the death of Peter the Apostle who was crucified upside down. Nero tried to blame the burning of Rome on the Christians as a way to cast them out of the empire, though this ruse didn't work in his favor (Richard, 2010).

Nevertheless, by the middle of the third century, Christianity was the fastest-growing religion in the empire (Richard, 2010). Its emphasis on love and equality appealed to the poor as well as many of the wealthy. Whole communities of early Christians were attacked, tortured, and died at the hands of the Romans. The fact that Christians were willing to suffer and die for their beliefs added to the attraction for nonbelievers to further investigate their religion (Richard, 2010).

Yet Christianity still attracted converts, including the emperor Constantine. The message of God's love for his people, couched in metaphors Jesus used relating to agriculture and animal husbandry, made a significant difference for listeners—especially those whose livelihoods involved farming and sheep herding. The words of the New Testament were easy to understand when read by literate church members to congregants. "Yet its wisdom was profound enough to dazzle intellectuals like Augustine" (Richard, 2010).

In 313 CE, Constantine issued the *Edict of Milan* which accepted Christianity in the empire and ended the persecutions of Christians, including excluding Christians from being enslaved. When the *Edict of Thessalonica* was issued in 380 CE, the Emperor Theodosius I made Nicene (Catholic) Christianity the official state religion. It was expected that Roman subjects convert to Christianity, which became a particular problem for those who already practiced other religious systems (Richard, 2010).

Christianity was Romanized with many simple changes that made a great difference in formalizing the religion. Instead of informal gatherings of believers, the Latin Mass became established; the Bible was translated into Latin and used in all services, instead of the Greek and Aramaic languages.

Pagan (non-Christian) religions contained pantheons of gods and goddesses, which Christianity did not. Knowing that pagans would not want to abandon their festivals in celebration of their gods and goddesses, numerous pre-Christian festivals were incorporated into Christian celebrations with Christian names, such as Christmas (Mass of Christ). Mary, the mother of Jesus, was selected to fill the need for worshipping goddesses, many times acknowledged as mothers of humanity (Richard, 2010).

Mary is not considered a "goddess," but as an intermediary between people and Jesus/God the Father. She became a part of worship services as Christians prayed for her intercession, even though she was not a subject of note in the Christian testaments. Christian feast days and festivals were merged into the Roman calendar. These efforts imposed an organizational structure on Christianity as a result (Richard, 2010).

Through the initial efforts of Constantine, Christianity became synonymous with Rome. Later, when the empire ended, Christianity became a state of its own with the Pope making all the decisions for "Christendom." Christian missionaries accompanied military excursions into different lands as a way to "spread the Gospel," though as a matter of forced conversion rather than a choice of religion by conquered peoples.

The Roman Empire before the Fall

Romans enjoyed a wonderfully diverse society that incorporated other ethnic cultural practices within their Empire and government. For example, the Roman affinity for wearing the purple-bordered toga came from Etruscan practices; their writing system came by way of the Phoenicians, as well as military might, and gladiatorial contests. Greek philosophy and thought influenced the Romans' thinking, writing, and practices (Forsythe et al., 2019; Jones & Sidwell, 1997).

By being open to the cultures and accomplishments of those incorporated within the empire, Romans became rich in their abilities to showcase great art, in the way of theater, the visual arts, and their architectural achievements, thanks to the labor and skills provided by their many slaves hailing from throughout the empire.

These accomplishments included the building of arches, of which the Triumphal Arch is an example. Romans built the Colosseum for entertainment. Apartment buildings were built to efficiently house citizens; they built public baths which became places for social gatherings, with separation by gender. Some baths had water organ music, a Roman invention; others had steam rooms as well as cold baths; libraries; and exercise areas (Forsythe et al., 2019; Jones & Sidwell, 1997).

Rome became the first successful territorial empire and was able to hold onto those territories when other governments had tried to and failed. Rome's military power came from its twenty-eight (later reduced to twenty-five) legions, many of whom were stationed along the borders of the empire. Soldiers built well-paved roads for travel so they could move their equipment quickly (Crossan, 2007). The Romans had political power through their landholding elite, incorporating those from conquered territories as equals in the Senate once they became Roman citizens (Crossan, 2007).

Romans had ideological power through their military might and belief in the power of their emperors. Because they were so wealthy, they actually hired those they vanquished to fight their wars (Crossan, 2007; Lafferty, 1971). Roman economic power came from tribute (taxes) paid by people in cash or grain who lived in vanquished lands.

In effect, all of the conquered nations supplied much of what was needed for the survival of Rome, especially grain for bread for the common people. Rome required nearly two hundred thousand tons of grain annually for its citizens at the height of its population (Jones & Sidwell, 1997). Because it was not economically feasible for Roman farmers to continue growing grain, many gave up and went on Roman public assistance. Others who were wealthier began to experiment with growing grapes for fine wines while continuing their olive orchards (Heather, 2010).

A few women became physicians, philosophers, and artists recognized in the empire. They were still not allowed political power, even though some women tried to influence their husbands when they were governors of territories or leaders of the military (Heather, 2010).

Bread and Circuses: What to Do When All Needs Are Satisfied by Others

By 180 CE, roughly 15 percent of the populace was unemployed because production of needed goods and services for Roman citizens was supplied by slaves and outsiders (Richard, 2010). To satisfy citizen demands for "bread and circuses," the government set aside 135 "holidays" during the year and organized formal games in various venues. The ever-popular chariot races were held at six different racecourses. The largest of these was the Circus Maximus, which also hosted gladiatorial events. When the Colosseum was built, the gladiators moved to this venue where it was expected that the emperors would be seen (Richard, 2010).

The city of Rome was a marvel to behold with all of its great architecture, statuary, mosaics, wall paintings, and dedicated temples. The wharves that met the ships from other territories brought to its doorstep treasure from imperial lands. Rome operated on a massive scale unlike anything seen in its period of history (Jones & Sidwell, 1997; Richard, 2010).

Toward the end of the fourth century, the Roman authorities desired that the wandering Visigoths settle into one area and establish large slave farms like the Romans. For some of the élite, this was appealing after seeing the riches their Roman counterparts had become accustomed to having. For others, this lifestyle was not productive (Heather, 2010).

Meanwhile, the Goths as well as other Germanic peoples had been steadily increasing in their wealth, beginning with agricultural production. Over the first four centuries of the Common Era, the Germanic peoples contributed a great deal to the wealth not only of their members but in terms of overall economics in Europe (Heather, 2010). This was done through trade in a variety of goods, including pottery, which was eventually made on the wheel; metalsmithing; glassware; and combs, for which many people were needed. These wares also changed the material culture of the Germanic peoples, even to the creation of new hairstyles.

However, the basic inequalities between powerful Rome and the Germanic tribes were still to be found. By the fourth century, Germanic kings had well established and defined rights, and trade with the Romans was firmly established. The Romans demanded additional military support from the Goths in the way of forced military service, which was greatly resented (Heather, 2010).

Also by the fourth century, it was evident that Europe had developed unequally with Roman society, the wealthiest and most prosperous of all (Heather, 2010). This led to a series of conflicts with Rome as the Senate continued to lead without sharing their wealth with the rest of the empire's populations, even as Roman demands of other groups increased (Heather, 2010).

The Culmination of the Roman Empire

By 395, the Roman Empire became very unwieldy and was split into the Western Empire with the capital in Rome, and the Eastern Empire with its capital in Constantinople, each with its own emperor (Crossan, 2007; Heather, 2010; Lafferty, 1971). The leaders of Rome had become corrupt and cruel, used to getting their way without having to do much to attain what they wanted. The populace had lost their abilities to feed themselves and provide for their other needs since they relied on their slaves to do everything.

The Romans made a fatal mistake when they decided to use their powers against the Visigoths to keep them under control. They proceeded to slaughter thousands of Gothic women and children under Roman "protection" to show their might (Grant, 2003; Lafferty, 1971).

Alaric, who up until then had still been loyal to the Romans, made the decision to punish Rome. The sacking of Rome by the Visigoths (or "Goths")—who carried out great wealth and treasures from the city—and the overthrow of the Roman government virtually ended the Western Empire on August 24, 410 CE (Heather, 2010; Lafferty, 1971; "Sack of Rome," n.d.). The Visigoths were blamed for the attack bringing down Rome, however, there is evidence that the Germanic tribes were not so intent on attacking Rome, but on making a first-strike to evade further attacks by Roman legions (Richard, 2010).

The Denouement of the Roman Empire

In effect, the Romans became victims of their own successes and greed (Hölkeskamp, 2010). At the apex of its reign, seventy-five million people belonged to the Roman Empire, plus the Visigoths who had been absorbed, of which two hundred thousand eventually became citizens—even though there was much hatred of Rome by them. While many chaffed under Roman rule and the demand for tribute, the Romans were so successful that eventually the whole of their empire began to resemble them except for religious practices (Richard, 2010).

The Roman world was everywhere, in the form of their appointed governors and ministers throughout the empire. The presence of Roman legions was to guarantee that the laws and mandates emanating from Rome would be obeyed in every corner of the empire. The Romans did not hesitate to destroy any populations they declared their enemies (Crossan, 2007; Forsythe et al., 2019).

The Roman world was falling apart by the end of the Roman Empire. Romans had become apathetic and stopped caring for their great art in the city. They did not provide the labor needed to keep the city sparkling, showing off one of the great marvels of the world. Emotionally, they were not as invested in the idea of unity as Roman citizens or the principles under which Rome operated (Heather, 2010).

Economically, Rome was stretched with having to supply food and weapons to their military to keep the lands they had conquered. Rome benefitted through having slaves of Germanic extraction. Even though wealth was accumulated through trade with Rome, the Goths were tired of the social stratification imposed during the Roman imperial period (Heather, 2010).

From the viewpoint of Germanic non-Romans, four centuries of imperial oppression was enough. There was much resentment across the landscape towards the Romans who were constantly trying to overwhelm them, tell them where they could live, and dictate their lives. While many joined the Roman military, later these trained soldiers gained fame for their resistance against Roman oppression (Heather, 2010; Richard, 2010).

Collapse of the empire on the frontiers could have been due to the alliances that Germanic kings were making, which translated into more manpower to oppose Roman forces. Another argument for the collapse is that by splitting the empire into two, with two different rulers, those who were oppressed were empowered with the idea that they could resist Roman control. A third consideration is the large migration of Gothic allies from East of the Carpathians to the western part of the Empire—possibly due to the movement of the Huns into the eastern regions—that now came within the borders of the Romans (Heather, 2010).

In addition, the Western Empire was beginning to lose its revenues through its taxation of border nations. While the Romans resisted the infiltration of additional Germanic tribes on the border, the taxes they were able to collect from these areas were reduced so border peoples could fight the new invaders. In addition, some of Rome's most prosperous territories had succumbed to the Huns, Vandals, Burgundians, and Alans. The Roman aristocracy refused to pay higher taxes, especially as the landed began to deal directly with the armed immigrants coming into the country (Grant, 2003; Heather, 2010).

The nobility who had served on municipal councils now avoided doing so, as the Roman Senate expected them to make up revenue shortfalls. At the same time, bribes had to be paid to the military to keep them on duty. With no new territories to add to the empire, emperors devalued their monetary system, causing hyperinflation and eventually their coinage lost its worth (Richard, 2010).

> These political, economic, and psychological crises produced a military crisis that proved fatal to the Empire. The absence of that confidence and patriotism that had always formed the foundation of Roman military success forced the emperors to rely increasingly on foreign enlistees and mercenaries, a common sign of a declining power. Indeed, by the fourth century, most barbarian generals in the Roman army retained their Germanic names, rather than adopting Roman names like their predecessors. (Richard, 2010, p. 38)

The constant competition within the aristocracy in the empire added to friction across the territories encompassed (Hölkeskamp, 2010). The only way to gain wealth and power was the acquisition of land and slaves; wealth led to promises of positions within the governing body and the ability to be elected into powerful offices. This, too, took a tremendous impact on the unity within the empire and contributed to its eventual demise (Hölkeskamp, 2010).

The fall of the Roman Empire is dated to 476 CE. The eastern part of the empire continued to survive as the Byzantine Empire with Constantinople as its capital.

THE BEGINNINGS OF FEUDALISM AND OTHER CITY-STATES IN EUROPE

The landless peasants at the fall of the Roman Empire went to live with those who had great estates and needed agricultural workers. Part of the serfs' harvests went to the landowners in payment for living on the land and the protection provided. They also worked in other professions providing the labor that was needed to keep the estates running, such as blacksmithing, cloth making, and furniture making (History.com Editors, n.d.).

As the European continent began to be reshaped into modern Europe, there were still major conflicts and jockeying for power in the lands that are now Great Britain, France, Belgium, Italy, Spain, Portugal, and Germany. Latin, the language of the Roman Empire, evolved into the Romance languages of French, Italian, Spanish, Romanian, Catalan, Romansch, and Portuguese (Wells, 2002). English and its relatives the Frisian, Dutch, and German languages, evolved from a different branch, the Proto-Germanic branch, and then to the West Germanic branch of the Indo-European language tree (McCrumb, MacNeil, & Cran, 2002).

THE MIDDLE AGES AND THE RENAISSANCE

Europe experienced many changes during the Middle Ages, or the Medieval period, from the fall of Rome into the fifteenth century—the period of the Renaissance and Age of Discovery (History.com Editors, n.d.). The Justinian legal code (or Codex Justinian) was developed c. 530 CE, and influenced the laws that were in effect in both the eastern and western parts of the former Roman Empire. This legal code, written by a committee of jurists, reflected the views of the first emperor of the Byzantine Empire, Justinian, and his wife and co-ruler, Theodora. This document included rights for women and rejected prejudices against women in the law. The document still influences Western culture today, though inclusion of women's rights were conveniently ignored (Núñez, 2018).

Universities became established in Europe during this period. They originated from the cathedral or monastic schools for the clergy, or other places of learning not associated with the church throughout what had been the Empire, in the latter part of the first century CE. Eventually universities became places that incorporated both craftsmen and artisan guilds in addition to academic pursuits. Great thinkers, inventors, and creators in the arts were available to students as they taught classes related to their areas of expertise (History.com Editors, n.d.).

The influence of Rome gradually lessened except for some of the institutions that still existed, while the impact of the Catholic Church rose during this period, in the form of the establishment of monasteries throughout Europe and Britain. Here literacy and focus on religious practices were important. Many of the Latin classic tomes were copied by the monks in different monasteries, as well as the Bible. New books were written, such as the *Benedictine Rule* meant to guide the western monasteries. Missionaries from Ireland together with Columba and founders of other monasteries were active in the areas now known as Great Britain (Cahill, 1995).

The fall of the Roman Empire left confusion for common people who tried to find their direction as new communities formed. The period of Medieval Europe was marked by the wealthy acquiring more riches. There were cities and nation-states, but not all areas of the former Roman Empire were united culturally or religiously.

While the peasants continued working as serfs, the nobles, in turn, became knights, fighting for the kings in Europe in return for lands awarded to them. To become a knight required money for expensive horses and armor. Knights were at the beck and call of kings and fought for them in return for grants of land. Sons of knights usually became knights themselves. Knights expected that part of their recompense, or "salaries," would come from ransacking the territories they won and retrieving all that had worth for their use (History.com Editors, n.d.).

The values of loyalty, honor, and courage were promoted, together with keeping family ties. Kings, Lords, and other very rich and powerful families instituted a system of patronage in which they would "sponsor" artists to complete great works for them. Eventually, patronage extended into the sciences (David, 2007; Hollingsworth, 2014).

Secularism arose during this period with an emphasis on the élites hosting great banquets for members of their class, having servants at their beck and call, and having a military that they supported which could be called upon for the kings' defenses. Along with this wealth came changes in clothing styles with élites dressing in fanciful outfits for the day: rich in silks, and for women, encrusted with jewels (David, 2007).

Aristocratic families were very powerful, such as the Medici family, and had great influence on the arts and sciences. In addition, they had political alliances with the Catholic popes. They formed alliances with other aristocrats, and if having differences, usually restored their relationships through monetary means (David, 2007).

Men who became more powerful, especially in the medieval period and into the 1800s, were not wont to listen to those who insisted on freedom and equality for all. For them, to be able to acquire power for their realms and reap the greatest profits, it was an inherent right that they own slaves who would provide their labor and other needs.

Changes in the Roman Catholic Church

Meanwhile, the Roman Catholic Church had become very powerful and acted as its own city-state to unite Europe through Roman Catholic Christianity. The church dominated the western world between 590 CE–1517 CE, from religion to education, art, politics, and morality. The pope and his dependents dictated the ways of the people so much that the church became an organizing force in the lives of many. However, it also became corrupt during this era, resembling less and less the Christianity of its earliest beginnings (Keillor, 1996; Mark, 2019).

From 590 CE, the pope was considered infallible, though a formal declaration of this concept did not occur until 1870 CE. The succession of popes during this period led to the declaration that every human being had to recognize that the pope was God's representative on earth. Those who did not recognize this—or that the Roman Catholic Church was the one true church—were considered damned for eternity (Arnold, 1999). Therefore, salvation in the next world could only be attained through becoming a Roman Catholic in this world.

This began a new cycle where a more militant and less tolerant version of Christianity emerged. While the Visigoths tolerated Jewish people in the fourth century, this tolerance lessened precipitously and was gone during the Middle Ages, as was the tolerance for the Islamic Moors, both of whom inhabited areas of Iberia which stood at the crossroads between Europe and the Middle East and Africa (Sanders, 1978/2015).

The clergy of the church considered themselves holy and above the congregants. Joining the clergy to become priests became an attraction for those of questionable characters. These aspirants were not required to study Latin, Greek, or the Bible, but were told what to preach to their congregants by the Pope and his agents. Because Pope Gregory required celibacy for priests in 1079 CE, many priests at the time had liaisons, visited taverns, and became drunkards (Arnold, 1999).

This was a period when wealthy first sons inherited their fathers' lands and titles, and second sons entered the priesthood and later became wealthy through appointments to church offices. "Simony," or the buying of church offices, abounded; going into the priesthood did not reflect a man's piety or sanctity, commonly required necessary to hold church offices (Arnold, 1999). The church made the salvation of people in the next life dependent upon it, not upon salvation through faith in Christ (Arnold, 1999). Since literacy was primarily gifted in aristocratic families, music and art were used to teach church precepts to the masses during this time. The use of Latin for scholarship was beginning to change as new vernaculars arose in these regions.

There were many scandals in the church during this time, including the buying of indulgences. Persons would be forgiven for their sins if they paid for indulgences. Morality declined as people looked at indulgences as a free path to enter heaven. There were scandals too numerous to address here; the point is that the church permeated all aspects of people's lives, even dictating who could become kings on earth (Arnold, 1999; Mark, 2019). The Roman Catholic pope was concerned with the affairs of Christianity in the Byzantine Empire, and in 1054, the Great Schism between the papacy of Rome and the patriarchy of Constantinople occurred, separating the Roman Catholic Church from the Greek Orthodox Church (Grant, 2003).

Because of heresies or untruths that were being promoted about the role of religion in the lives of people and what was true regarding the faith and what was not, the Inquisition was begun by the Council of Verona in 1184 to root out Roman Catholics accused of promoting heresies. Those accused were beaten and sometimes killed in the process of these hearings (Arnold, 1999).

As can be seen, the church had a part in all the business of the states, nation-states, and the very wealthy. On the surface, this was to protect Christians from temptations and to promote conversions to Catholicism. Nonetheless, the church also benefited economically by being so intertwined in the affairs of states and nations across Europe.

Viking Migrations

Meanwhile, the Vikings—or Northern Goths—from the Scandinavian areas of Norway, Finland, and Sweden began perfecting their sailing ships, as well as knowledge of the various seas around them and of the North Atlantic Ocean. By sailing various routes, they discovered many areas far away from home, and increased their trading, raiding, and settling in these areas to escape from the Danes (Heather, 2010).

The Vikings became the new threat to Europeans. They began raiding the areas of what is now Great Britain, Germany, and France beginning in 793 CE with the sacking of the Lindisfarne, an island monastery off the coast of Northumbria in Britain (Heather, 2010). They would then keep conquered peoples as slaves for themselves or sell them to others, most notably to those in the Middle Eastern Arabian world.

The Vikings began settling into various lands they conquered throughout Europe, including Russia. In that area, they were known as "Rus," which meant "Swedes" in Finnish. Historians now know of these connections both through analyzing languages and word meanings and examining the archaeology of different regions. For instance, in parts of Great Britain, the normal roundhouses and figures of eight that were built for shelter by the Celtics and Pictish were replaced by the rectangular styles favored by the Swedish, Norwegians, and Finnish (Heather, 2010).

There is evidence that the Vikings traveled as far as the Americas c. 900 CE as they explored the Atlantic coastlines. They did not stop there permanently, though remnants from their visit have been found (Assiniwi, 1996/2000). The Norsemen applied the name "Skraelings" to Native Beothuk peoples they encountered in Greenland and then to Inuits in Newfoundland. These Vikings then told stories of their visits when they returned to their homes (Beothuks, n.d.; Marshall, 1996; Skraelings, n.d.).

While the Vikings did not conquer all the territories of the unwieldy Roman Empire, it is clear that they did have an impact on the populations in different areas where they traversed. Their cultural foundations were unlike other Europeans, even though they, too, had nobility in the form of their kingship system. They had migrated to areas like Iceland as a result of trying to avoid being victims of the Danish military, whose kings were anxious to enrich their treasuries (Heather, 2010).

The Migration of Slavs and Conquering by the Islamic World

Alongside the Vikings, the Slavs began migrations to Central and Eastern Europe, first in the form of raids across the eastern border of the Roman Empire. By the middle of the sixth century CE, they had firmly established their presence in those areas. After the collapse of the Hunnic Empire, they made portable wealth through trading and continued their movement deep into European territory where it is supposed that they absorbed the Indigenous populations that had survived the Roman and Germanic conquering groups (Heather, 2010). Some of this migration was by peaceful means; other Slavic groups became more militarized and utilized harsher means, accumulating more wealth and becoming more socially stratified in the process (Heather, 2010).

Meanwhile, the Islamists from Arabian areas began forays into Europe c. 652 CE, followed by more invasions into the Byzantine, Serbian, and Bulgarian Empires. Constantinople was substantially reduced by the incursion of the Arabs. Eventually the Turks conquered it in 1453 CE, and Constantinople became one of the greatest and most learned cities in the world, following in the tradition of the Romans but under Islamic leadership (Richard, 2010).

Spain, Portugal, Sicily, and Malta had large Islamic polities for several centuries before Christian militias began to drive them out during the *Reconquista* when they hoped to reestablish Christianity throughout these areas. These efforts failed in great numbers, and since this time, there have been areas in Europe with large Muslim populations (Richard, 2010).

SUMMARY

The settling of Europe by various groups took place over numerous millennia. Civilizations were built and dissipated, but the Greek and Roman civilizations had great influences on all civilizations to follow. This was perhaps due to the amount of literature written during the time of the empire by citizens, and a focus on the arts that produced cities of wonder that are still considered important to this day.

We owe a great deal of our knowledge of Roman history and thought to the writings of Greek and Jewish historians, scientists, and philosophers. A few are presented here: Josephus ben Matthias wrote of the Jewish insurrection of 66 CE–73 CE recounting the war for posterity. Plutarch (46 CE–120 CE), a Greek, wrote *Parallel Lives*, documenting forty-six historical Roman and Greek figures and their lives. Galen (ca. 129 CE–216 CE), also a Greek, wrote one of the first books for medicine, *Anatomical Procedures*, as well as *The Art of Medicine* and many others. The works of numerous Greek philosophers have influence to this day (Jones & Sidwell, 1997; Richard, 2010).

Competition throughout the ancient European world appears to have played an important part not only in benefits to individual participants but in shaping the culture in general. While competition has been seen in all civilizations, the need to become powerful and rich to gain access to enhanced lifestyles was already in place in the early days of the Roman republic.

The amount of violence that took place within all of these civilizations appears to be taken for granted as part of the need to protect groups from one another and gain advantages that were otherwise impossible to acquire at the time. The role of the peasantry and slave populations in the building of all the ancient civilizations has not been addressed well in the past. Nevertheless, they made Greece and Rome the great civilizations they became.

Technology played an important role in determining which groups had mastery over the others, especially in the next era when Europeans began to set out to "discover" the rest of the world. Regardless, both the positive and negative aspects of European culture, mores, and ethics were determinant factors in the next great clash to come: that of the Europeans and the Native Americans on the other side of the globe. This topic will be covered in the next chapter.

REFERENCES

Arnold, J. L. (1999, March 1–March 7). The Roman Catholic Church of the Middle Ages: Reformation Men and Theology, Lesson 1 of 11. *IIIM Magazine Online*, *1*(1). Retrieved from https://www.thirdmill.org/newfiles/jac_arnold/CH.Arnold.RMT.1.html.

Assiniwi, B. (1996/2000). *The Beothuk Saga* (Trans. by W. Grady). New York, NY: St. Martin's Press.

Beothuks. (n.d.). *Newfoundland: Aboriginal Peoples*. Newfoundland & Labrador Heritage. Retrieved from https://www.heritage.nf.ca/.

Cahill, T. (1995). *How the Irish saved civilization: The untold story of Ireland's heroic role from the fall of Rome to the rise of Medieval Europe*. New York, NY: Random House.

Crossan, J. D. (2007). *God & Empire: Jesus against Rome, then and now*. New York, NY: HarperCollins.

David, P. A. (2007). *The Historical Origins of 'Open Science'. An Essay on Patronage, Reputation and Common Agency Contracting in the Scientific Revolution*. Stanford University & the University of Oxford pad@stanford.edu or paul.david@all-souls.ox.ac.uk. Retrieved from http://www-siepr.stanford.edu/workp/swp06008.pdf.

Forsythe, G. E., Hornblower, S., Saller, R. P., Salmon, E. T., Townsend Vermeule, E., Thomson de Grummond, N., Badian, E., & Ferguson, J. (2019, January 11). Ancient Rome: Ancient state, Europe, Africa, and Asia. *Encyclopedia Britannica*. Retrieved from https://www.britannica.com/place/ancient-Rome.

Grant, M. (2003). *The History of Rome*. London, United Kingdom: Faber.

Heather, P. (2010). *Empires and barbarians: The fall of Rome and the birth of Europe*. New York, NY: Oxford University Press.

History.com Editors. (n.d.). *The Middle Ages*. Retrieved from https://www.history.com/topics/middle-ages/middle-ages.

Hölkeskamp, K.-J. (2010). *Reconstructing the Roman Republic: An ancient political culture and modern research* (H. Heitmann-Gordon, Trans.). Princeton, NJ: Princeton University Press.

Hollingsworth, M. (2014). *Patronage in Renaissance Italy: From 1400 to the Early Sixteenth Century*. London: Thistle.

Jarvus, O. (2013, September 18). *Spartacus: History of Gladiator Revolt*. Live Science. Retrieved from https://www.livescience.com/39730-spartacus.html.

Jones, P., & Sidwell, K. (Eds.). (1997). *The world of Rome: An introduction to Roman culture*. New York, NY: Cambridge University Press.

Kendi, I. X. (2016). *Stamped from the beginning: The definitive history of racist ideas in America*. New York, NY: Nation Books.

Laferty, R. A. (1971). *The fall of Rome*. New York, NY: Doubleday.

Marshall, I. (1996). *A history and ethnography of the Beothuk*. Montreal: McGill-Queens University Press. (Originally published 1929).

McCrumb, R, MacNeil, R., & Cran, W. (2002). *The story of English* (3rd. Rev. Ed.). New York, NY: Penguin.

Núñez, M. I. (2018, May/June). Roman women on the rise. *National Geographic History*, *4* (2), 36–47.

Pax Romana. (n.d.). Ancient History. Retrieved from https://www.ancient.eu/Pax Romana/.

Richard, C. J. (2010). *Why we're all Romans: The Roman contribution to the Western World*. Lanham, MD: Rowman & Littlefield.

Sack of Rome. (n.d.). *Military history encyclopedia on the web*. Retrieved from http://www.historyofwar.org/articles/sack_rome_390bc.html.

Sanders, R. (1978/2015). *Lost tribes and promised lands: The origins of American racism*. Brattleboro, VT: Echo Pointe Books.

Skraelings. (n.d.). *Native American Languages*. Retrieved from http://www.native-languages.org/definitions/skraeling.htm.

Sowell, T. (1998). *Conquests and cultures: An international history*. New York, NY: Basic Books.

Thompson, J. R. (2012, June 14). New dates place Spanish cave art as oldest in Europe. *Earth: The science behind the discoveries*. Retrieved from https://www.earthmagazine.org/article/new-dates-place-spanish-cave-art-oldest-europe.

Wellard, J. H. (1973). *Search for the Etruscans*. New York, NY: Cardinal.

Chapter Four

The Clash of Cultures and *Doctrine of Discovery*

The Rise of Racism in the Americas

From the work on the HGP, we know that there is no basis in reality for using the term "race." Unfortunately, we are saddled with a history and language of racism, permeating human consciousness for over five hundred years in this country and more in European history. Racism can be defined as positioning people in society as superior or inferior according to the color of their skins and/or the ethnic group to which they belong (Kendi, 2016).

Kendi (2016) points to the ancient world of Rome and Greece as the areas where the beginning of ideas of inferior populations based on ethnic, religious, and color prejudices began, though the construction of "races" was not a concept. At the same time, the idea that all people were equal and had their own liberty was also introduced in the ancient world, albeit they were considered for the élite only.

Some, like Alkidamas, Aristotle's philosophical competitor in Greece, were against slavery. The first Roman Emperor Constantine was influenced by his advisor, Lactantius, who pronounced that the god who made men made them all equal. Augustine of Hippo repeated the same message (Kendi, 2016).

Toward the end of the medieval period in 1478, Spanish Christianity took on the task of ridding itself of anyone who was ethnically different—here referring to anyone who was different religiously—as the taint of heresy was considered to be in the blood, not in terms of outward appearance. Indeed, in the 1300s, Jewish citizens had been forced to wear yellow circles on their clothing so they were distinguishable from Spanish Christians as it was hard to tell the difference between them physically (Sanders, 1978/2015).

The deeply religious King and Queen of Spain, Ferdinand and Isabella, took Rome's Inquisition to a new level by forcing their citizens to convert to Christianity. Those who were suspected of being Jewish and did not confess or convert were systematically tortured through horrible contraptions meant to maim or kill if the accused did not renounce Judaism. Those who did convert were called *conversos*, or New Christians, but were still considered lower than Christians. Later, the same fate awaited the Islamic Spanish Moors (Sanders, 1978/2015).

> The idea of race was for better or worse, only a dim and sporadic one to most Europeans during the Middle Ages; its outlines did not begin growing distinct until the fourteen or fifteenth centuries. But when the dawning finally occurred, it shone with particular fury upon the Iberian Peninsula [that was part of Spain], which discovered itself in that light to contain the most racially varied society in western Europe. The results were soon to be revolutionary: "Antagonism which had before been almost purely religious," writes the historian Henry Charles Lea, "became racial, while religious antagonism became heightened, and Spain, which through the earlier Middle Ages had been the most tolerant land in Christendom, became, as the fifteenth century advanced, the most fanatically intolerant." . . . They thus became the pioneers of our modern racial history in the West just as surely as they became the pioneers of European overseas colonization; indeed, after a brief prelude of racism in the Old World alone, the two roles often went hand in hand. (Sanders, 1978/2015)

PORTUGAL AND THE FIRST EXPEDITIONS IN THE ATLANTIC

In the 1300s, Prince Henry of Spain was given permission from the pope to separate from Spain and was granted lands along the Iberian coast which he named "Portugal." In late 1418, his descendent, Prince Henry "the Navigator," became anxious to find out what was beyond the coasts because at that time little was known about seas to the west and if there were any landforms. He began to follow this pursuit in earnest. Better shipbuilding techniques and technology, along with the ability to read the skies at night to determine direction, were decisive factors in making these undertakings possible.

While sailing along the coast of Africa, Henry's sailors encountered dark-skinned Africans. Africans had long been part of the Arabian slave trade and now were taken to be part of Henry's trade in slaves. Black slavery became associated with the legend of Ham, Noah's wayward son, who was said to carry a mark of his sins. At some point, the devil (who had no particular color) became Black, and was used to provide justification to enslave Africans as the term "black devils," was popularized to describe them (Sanders, 1978/2015).

At the end of the thirteenth century, a Genoese captain named Malocello found an island in the Atlantic that he named "Lanzarote." The island appeared to be uninhabited—of which many were—and he established a fortress there which did not survive. Later, the earliest record of encountering Native peoples in the western seas was made by Boccaccio who told of a meeting that took place in 1341 in the Canary Islands (Sanders, 1978/2015).

From the earliest encounters with Native island peoples by Italian and Portugal sailors, Native people were sensationalized. Boccaccio tells us that these people were largely unclothed and unable to communicate with the expedition leaders of the two ships (Sanders, 1978/2015). Natives were open and welcoming, and while swimming to greet the expedition, four of them were taken as "specimens" back to Portugal to be studied, beginning a long tradition of kidnapping Native peoples (Sanders, 1978/2015).

These proclaimed Christian navigators were overwhelmed with the fact that the people were unashamed of their nakedness, though it was noted that the married men and women wore woven aprons. This led to false premises about promiscuity in their culture. The expedition found a lack of war materials among these island peoples, indicating their lack of fear of strangers. The land was full of fresh fruit and other things to eat, as well as tropical birds unseen before by Europeans. They found animals that were unfamiliar to them, and the overall appearance of this land seemed like a beautiful garden to the sailors (Sanders, 1978/2015).

In describing the peoples, Boccaccio tells that they shared their food, had no knowledge of gold, danced and made merry along with others, did not drink wine, and spoke with signs to communicate their messages. His description becomes the first humanist report concerning these island people, though their ethnicity was never known (Sanders, 1978/2015).

The Europeans discovered the same conditions on other occupied islands they visited in the region. Many accompanying the expedition wondered if this was the Eden Paradise discussed in the scriptures. This was a question that continued throughout the period of conquest (Sanders, 1978/2011; Mann, 2005/2011).

Sixty years later, an expedition to the islands was led by a Norman (French) knight named Bethencourt, who had been promised lands for his heirs from his explorations. Two missionaries who accompanied him recorded what occurred with the Native peoples: some collaborated and some resisted; there were conspiracies between resisting Natives and rebel members of the conquering militia; Natives were either slaughtered or enslaved; and finally, conquered Natives were given the choice of death or conversion to Christianity (Sanders, 1978/2015). This established pattern of conquering Native peoples continued with future European voyages and colonizations.

Further excursions to the islands by European explorers from different countries led to encounters with some Native peoples who were not as docile as the people first encountered. Instead, these people were war-like and ready to attack the Europeans, which they did not hesitate to do. They were consumers of human flesh, a practice that had been widely denounced in Europe, especially in Christian Europe (Sanders, 1978/2011).

Cannibalism was not unknown in Europe; however, the punishment for this practice was enshrined in the unwritten Common Law for the European masses until the 1200s, when formal laws were recorded (Mueller, 1986). For this and the exercise of witchcraft, practitioners were burned alive or drowned, practices reflected in the folk tales collected by the Grimm Brothers. Examples are *The Wolf and the Seven Little Kids* and *Hansel and Gretel*, in which the perpetrator in each instance is drowned or burned alive as punishment for cannibalism (Mueller, 1986; Zipes, 1979).

We may never know what the reason was for the Native peoples who pursued this path of behavior, though some have conjectured that by doing so, warriors acquired the powers of the person who was devoured. Encountering these peoples did lend some caution to those involved in future expeditions as word of this behavior spread throughout Europe.

Meanwhile, Lagos, Portugal, became the center of the European slave trade in Africans. An estimated 5.8 million African slaves were carried eventually to Brazil, an area of South America colonized by Portugal. Lisbon, too, was an area where slave traders regularly sold Africans (Ames, 2018). Black slaves were introduced to Barbados and other islands for labor in the sugarcane fields.

Christopher Columbus Meets with the King and Queen of Spain

The Italian Christóbal Colón—later called Christopher Columbus (Mann, 2011)—approached the Spanish monarchy about his desires to launch an expedition to find a new western route to the Indies after being turned down by other European monarchs (Mann, 2005/2011; Sanders, 1978/2015). The monarchy had recently succeeded in their quest to oust the Islamists from Spain after the *Reconquista* and was not far from removing the Jewish populations there, whether converted or not (Sanders, 1978/2015).

The Spanish military was described as "brutal and efficient" after the long period of warfare and converting others to Christianity (Josephy, 1991). In need of funds to replenish the royal treasury, Ferdinand and Isabella agreed to finance the exploration proposed by Colón, particularly when he used the prospect of converting Native peoples found along the way to Christianity (Sanders, 1978/2015).

In addition to his crews, Colón brought along a recent Jewish convert named Luis de Torres who spoke Hebrew, Aramaic, and Arabic. As a side mission, Europeans and Israelites had been searching for the lost tribes of Israel since the release of the Jewish people from Babylonia under the Persian King Cyrus. There was a small hope that they would find these people along the way during their travels (Ghiuzeli, 1991; Mann, 2005/2011; Sanders, 1978/2015).

The Caribbean Island where Christóbal Colón landed and named Hispaniola on October 12, 1492, was full of treasures and animals unknown to Europe at the time. Estimates of the numbers of Taino Indians who lived on the island range to eight million (Native Circle, n.d.). The Taino excelled in their craftsmanship of ornamental goods, and the Spanish were taken with the immense amount of gold and silver they saw on the island (Barnes, 2010; Mann, 2011).

The Taino were élite members of the Arawak who inhabited the Greater Antilles, Puerto Rico, Jamaica, Cuba, and Hispaniola. The Caribs were more aggressive and lived in the Lesser Antilles, having forced others out. The Guanahatabeys originated in Florida and lived in the extreme western area of Cuba (Barnes, 2010).

The question concerning the Natives' lack of resistance to the Europeans who arrived in their lands is a puzzling one. As Mann (2005/2011) and others have postulated, the belief systems of Native peoples included that the Creator (by whatever name) had made man and then dispersed people throughout the earth. Some Native people thought the Conquistadors were holy beings with great power due to their metal armor and their weapons (Keillor, 1996). They were unafraid because, in Native belief systems, the Creator endows some individuals with powers to help their peoples, such as shamans who can look into the future and healers who can cure the sick.

It's possible that any of these explanations may be correct for any Indigenous people in the Americas (Mann, 2005/2011; Wilson, 1998). The writers at Native Circle state that Natives thought the intruders were gods, based on the way they looked and that it appeared they and their ships had come from the heavens ('Real' Columbus, n.d.). Part of Indigenous traditions throughout the Americas was the expectation that they would be hospitable to others, and may be the reason why Europeans might not have been repulsed initially.

Europeans were unknown quantities, not thought of as "enemies." With the Native beliefs that the Creator made men as equals, they would have found any kind of hierarchical system of the Europeans difficult to understand. Freedom of individuals to make their own choices (except in the cases of those who had been enslaved) was highly regarded and expected.

Colón and his two crews (one of his ships, the Santa Maria, had sunk) took samples of what they had found back to Spain, along with as many as ten Taino Indians, to present to Queen Isabella and King Ferdinand of Spain. Thirty-nine Spanish—all released convicts—were left behind on the island. While Colón was absent, the Spaniards committed atrocious acts against the Native peoples, starving and killing them, raping women and children. The Taino named Caonabo led the elimination of the Spanish who were torturing them ('Real' Columbus, n.d.).

When Colón came back on his second voyage, he found the fort, La Navidad, deserted. Colón determined to find out what had befallen the men left behind. Eventually the people were tricked into giving up Caonabo and he was sent off to Spain, never to be heard of again ('Real' Columbus, n.d.). This was the beginning of the horrendous treatment and enslavement of the Taino and future Native populations under the Spanish conquerors.

In 1493, Pope Alexander VI issued the Doctrine of Discovery (*Inter Caetera*), a papal bull that allowed Christian explorers under the patronage of a Christian monarch to plant a flag in the soil of the newly "discovered" pagan lands and waterways, and declare the territory now belonged to the monarch. The explorers had to return to their patron(s) and report their discoveries, then go back and occupy the lands that now belonged to Europeans. The doctrine gave conquerors the right to convert the Native peoples to Christianity if they deemed Native practices and belief systems were inferior to those of Christians (Doctrine of Discovery, n.d.). Pope Alexander VI proceeded to "give" most of the Americas to the Spanish (Keillor, 1996).

In 1495, Colón enraged Queen Isabella by sending 550 captured Taino to Spain to be sold as galley slaves (Mann, 2011). He justified this by using the argument that this was common practice in European wars, and it was his response to the attack on the Spaniards left on the island. The queen's anger did not dissipate, and in 1499, she ordered all Spanish who had acquired slaves to send them back to Hispaniola or face death for noncompliance (Mann, 2011).

Enslavement of the Indigenous peoples in the islands continued. The Spanish overseers were more brutish. Natives who refused to mine for gold had their limbs or parts of their bodies cut off and were left to die as examples to others who would dare to resist (Berkhofer, 1978).

The Spanish Dominican missionary, Father Bartolomé de las Casas saw the Natives as kind and humble when he came west. Nonetheless, Colón believed that only converting them to Christianity would change their reluctance to work as the

Spanish desired. The Spaniards used cavalry and dogs to crush rebellions. Colón introduced the Spanish practice of *encomienda* in the island, where individual Spaniards were given tracks of Native lands, along with everything on them, including the Indians who then became their slaves and were forced to work the lands and mine for precious metals (Barnes, 2010).

Many European disease outbreaks severely affected the Native populations on Hispaniola and the other Arawak islands. Food became a problem when there were famines. Some Aboriginals killed their own children or committed suicide to escape the cruelties of the Spanish (Barnes, 2010). European ships brought new invasive species to the islands by the way of plants, animals, and insects which had no natural enemies allowing their populations to multiply rapidly, forever affecting the ecology wherever the colonizers roamed (Mann, 2011).

In 1500, after listening to the reports of Father de las Casas, Queen Isabella and King Ferdinand denounced the enslavement of "Indians" by Colón and forbade its continuance. Nevertheless, with many exemptions to this decree, the practice persisted. Still opposing the Queen in 1513, the Spanish Roman Catholic Church theologians issued the *Requerimiento* giving religious and political justifications for conquest and taking of Native lands. At this point, the Church had benefitted in "converting" hundreds of Native peoples, and through the riches brought back and given to the church coffers (American Indian Histories and Cultures, n.d.).

Colón became known by the appellation of "the invader," which was used by Indigenous peoples when talking of him ('Real' Columbus, n.d.). Thirty-four years later, the Taino, with an estimated population of eight million people, had been reduced to a mere five hundred members, and at one point, were thought to be extinct (Mann, 2011).

Fifty years later, Charles V consulted a leading Spanish philosopher and theologian on what Spain could rightfully claim as theirs. In a surprising move, Vitoria proclaimed that the original inhabitants of the land rightfully owned the land (Doctrine of Discovery, n.d.). By this time, though, the damage had already been done.

The pattern of exploration was set and expanded to non-Christian lands around the globe. Christianity continued to be foisted upon Indigenous populations and gave legitimacy to white Europeans that they, their religion, and culture were superior to all others, a foundation for white supremacy that still exists to this day (Doctrine of Discovery, n.d.).

Later, in the early years of the United States, the Doctrine of Discovery was used to give legitimacy to the claim that Europeans owned the lands and Native Americans only had the "right of occupancy." This was the decision of the 1823

Supreme Court case *Johnson v M'Intosh*, which then made the Doctrine of Discovery part of U.S. federal law. It was used to justify the Monroe Doctrine and Manifest Destiny, as well as Western hegemony—or power—over the Americas and the egregious treatment of Native Americans throughout North America (Doctrine of Discovery, n.d.).

Invasion by the Spanish in the Andes and Mesoamerica

The postclassic period of the Andes and Mesoamerica from 900 CE–1519 CE ended with the coming of the Spanish in the sixteenth century (Editors, n.d.). Since the Inca and other Natives had no horses (then extinct from the Americas), they were completely surprised when Europeans on horseback in full armor attacked them on November 16, 1532.

The Inca had no conception of "wealth" in terms of precious metals and gems as did the Europeans. When the Inca ruler Atahualpa saw the Conquistador Pizarro's eyes alight at the sight of the city's wealth, he promised to empty the city of its gold, silver, and exquisite gems if they would leave him and the city alone. However, Pizarro decided to empty the city, kill Atahualpa, and take over the Empire. When Pizarro conquered the Inca, the city of Qosqo was in many ways the equivalent of any great European city (Mann, 2005/2011).

The Inca had a three-dimensional writing system that consisted of tying knots three different ways on strings that could be "read," called khipu. The strings were color-coded, dyed before they were tied. When the Spanish occupiers discovered that the Native version of their being conquered contained in the khipu was different from the Spanish version, they ordered all of the khipu burned. Recently, a cache of about six hundred of them was found (Mann, 2005/2011).

The Spanish invasion of the area brought with it many diseases, especially the feared smallpox, which killed entire villages. Native peoples did not have resistance to these diseases (Barnes, 2010; Mann, 2005/2011). While we think this was a period of devastation for Natives, evidence exists that the results of colonization were never complete or immediate.

Trade routes, maize production, hunting and fishing, and exploiting natural resources for food and clothing, ceremonies and festivals, all continued. The Native people of the Southern and Central Americas were accustomed to warring occupiers due to the Inca and Aztec conquerors, so they survived some of the worst brought by the colonizers (King, 2012).

Some researchers now note that these periods should be viewed as "transitions," taking place slowly over time and spreading toward North America. Traditional practices continued, accompanied by incorporation or blending (to an extent) of the new colonial ways and material culture with the old ways and material culture (King, 2012).

For example, after the Spanish conquest of Mexico in 1521 CE, Xaltocan was reduced even further in status to a *pueblo de indios* or Indian town. Notwithstanding these events, Xaltocan and its citizens continued to hold onto many of their religious ceremonies and practices, while incorporating the Christian ways forced onto them (Rodríguez-Algería, 2012).

The Spanish destroyed much in the way of cultural artifacts and tried to erase Indigenous histories by destroying their records. In this way, colonizers could continue to justify their inhumane treatments of Native peoples, insisting they were inferior to Europeans, and heathens in their ways and belief practices. This behavior continued with all European conquests (Stannard, 1992). As more city-states in the Andes and Mesoamerica are recovered from the dense jungle growths, we continue to learn about how wrong these perceptions were and how these untruths were deliberately perpetuated by the explorers.

Spanish Entrance into North America

In 1573, the Spanish decided to issue guidelines for setting up Indian missions and colonies (American Indian Histories and Cultures, n.d.). These missions were set up throughout the South and Central Americas and from Florida to California by missionaries who accompanied the Conquistadors. Meantime, the explorers prolonged their efforts of looking for cities of "gold" or the Fountain of Youth in the northern reaches, punishing and killing Native peoples for not telling them where to find these fantasies (Mann, 2005/2011; Wilson, 1998).

The southern part of the United States was under Spanish control at this time, complete with the same pattern of conquering Native peoples and then baptizing them. An alliance between the Utes and New Mexican authorities in the 1750s increased the demand for Native slaves in the New Mexico slave markets. The Utes used escaped Spanish horses to capture those neighboring Indigenous people without horses, who could not fend them off. Economically, this practice allowed the Utes to become more powerful than other Plains Natives (Blackhawk, 2006).

Some women and children captured by the Utes were incorporated into Ute families, becoming wives or servants of their lords. The Paiute in particular suffered much as slaves under the Utes, the Utes reacting as other colonial forces with harsh punishments and abuses of all kinds (Blackhawk, 2006). The Comanche were prepared for conflicts, especially with the Utes. They, too, captured women and children for use as slaves (warriors were usually killed on the battlefields).

When the European presence brought trade in Spanish goods, the Comanche, too, engaged in selling Natives from other tribes to the Spanish. As stated by Blackhawk (2006), "By the time of their earliest sustained appearance in Spanish sources . . . colonial violence had become woven into the fabric of Comanche society" (p. 46).

In New Mexico, especially, the demand was high for native women and girls to serve as slaves for the populace. Native women who were used for sexual pleasures by the colonizers delivered children with no patronyms, therefore these children suffered under even more prejudice and were considered at the bottom of the Spanish caste system (Blackhawk, 2006).

THE PROTESTANT REFORMATION AND OTHER EUROPEAN POWERS CLAIMING NORTH AMERICA

Eventually, all of the Church's power (exemplified by the Archbishops, Bishops, Popes, and common priests with uncommon powers) was questioned. Martin Luther, a German priest, was the first to do so, nailing his "Ninety-five Theses on the Power and Efficacy of Indulgences" to the church of Wittenberg's door in 1517. He then sent the document to the Archbishop of Mainz. Other reformers followed in what is known as the "Protestant Reformation," resulting in an examination of the Roman Catholic Church and claiming that salvation only came through the grace of God, not the Church, and that the Bible held the truths of God's intentions for man (Keillor, 1996; Biography.com Editors, 2014/2019).

The Renaissance began at the end of the Middle Ages and coincided with the Age of Discovery. It marked the beginning of a Europe where individuals lusted after their own power, and unity of Christian beliefs and practices was shattered. While different Protestant churches were founded and proclaimed to be more Christian than others, the élite made a semblance of following a Christian lifestyle, even while acquiring power and capital became justifiable goals for these Europeans (Keillor, 1996).

Freed from following the Roman Catholic principles of kindness towards others, equality for all, respect for others, and loving others as God loves us (some of which principals had only been marginally accepted by the élites in previous centuries), individualism and accumulating material wealth developed into a society of greed which grew to be limitless (Keillor, 1996).

As different groups broke away from the Catholic Church's teachings, they established their own churches, many of them still taking ideas from the church—such as the above—but with less emphasis on them.

Using the Doctrine of Discovery inspired travel to the Americas by these other groups. Owning American lands and slaves to work them became the goal of many Europeans of means. Therefore, the Dutch settled in New Amsterdam (now New York) and flourished in what they did best: becoming a worldwide trading post (Mann, 2011; Sanders, 1978/2015). The French, also looking for trade, went to Canada and upper New York, eventually adding the Louisiana Territory. The English went first to the East Coast to establish themselves.

Racism and Prejudice in North America after European Encroachment

The English who set sail for the Americas settled on the Eastern seaboard of what is now the United States. They met little resistance as smallpox had decimated the Native peoples a few years before their arrival. At first, there was concern and resentment from the Native peoples who did not show themselves because a sea trader had lately captured many local people to sell in the Mediterranean slave trade (Josephy, 1968/1991).

However, after it became apparent that the Pilgrims who arrived onshore in Plymouth in 1621 would need assistance to survive, Native peoples took mercy on them. A few months after landing, Samoset, who had picked up some English from traders, introduced to them the grand sachem of the Wampanoag, Massasoit (Josephy, 1991).

Trading between the two peoples ensued, and during Massasoit's lifetime, all lived in peace and harmony. One of the Indians, Squanto, learned English when he was captured and sold into slavery by a trader, bought by an Englishman and was later returned to his home. Squanto took particular care and showed the Pilgrims how to farm and survive in the wilderness. The new colony would not have survived without his assistance (Josephy, 1991; Wilson, 1998).

As always, some peaceful Native peoples befriended Europeans on the East Coast. The respect that both English and Indians felt towards each other in New England and later in Virginia, changed when more and more groups of immigrants came and pushed inland (Josephy, 1991). The Puritans came to shore in Pequot territory—now Connecticut. They found that many areas appeared to them to be empty. They used the Bible to support the idea that God had cleared the land for their settlement, clearly a sign of their superiority (Keillor, 1996; Mann, 2005/2011; Wilson, 1998).

The Puritans had gotten to know some of the members of the Mohegans and Narraganset tribes in Rhode Island from trading with them. When the Puritans alleged members of the Pequot tribe had attacked some white men, they called upon the two tribes to come to their aid. A war ensued with the encouragement of clergymen who regarded the Indians as Satan. The Puritans destroyed the main Pequot town of Mystic River by firing upon it. Six hundred Pequots were burned or shot to death (Josephy, 1991).

As more North American Indians were pushed out of their territories in the East by immigrants, they came into contact with other tribes. The results of these encounters began the newcomers' struggles for their own territories. Some of these groups became more prone to attacking others, including Europeans illegally infringing on Native lands. These events marked the end of peaceful relations with many of the Native peoples in New England (Wilson, 1998).

While they may have engaged in some trade with Europeans, Indigenous peoples would never feel completely comfortable with the white presence, specifically when clashes between the two cultures unfolded. To add insult to injury, immigrants unearthed the food stashes of Native peoples away from their villages on their annual rounds. Whites helped themselves to these and other Indian goods, such as grave goods, and built settlements on their lands (Wilson, 1998). By the second generation, the Pilgrims had forgotten about what the Wampanoag did to help their parents survive. They now saw themselves as the true Americans, and that they had the right to take as much land as they wanted (Josephy, 1991).

A war ensued in 1671 with Metacomet (also called King Philip), Massasoit's son and now sachem of the Wampanoag, leading other Indians who had allied with him to try to rid the area of the English. Much blood was shed, and the Natives ran out of food and ammunition. When the war was over, Metacomet, his family, and relatives were sent to be slaves in Bermuda (Togias, 2000). Afterward, things were never the same for Aboriginals in English North America.

The French Come to North America

Meanwhile, the French settled in Canada and the Northwest, encouraging people to become fur trappers, intermarrying, and engaging in negotiations with Native Americans throughout the land. A population of Métis of mixed French and American Indian parentage grew up in Acadia and elsewhere (Woodward, 2011).

The colonial élite looked down on the blended societies where the Métis were equally at home in Native and French societies, even though they had initially encouraged this mingling together. It vexed the colonials that this group of children grew up as independent thinkers and doers, not relying on or even obeying all of the government dictates, but as proud and self-reliant as their Native relatives (Woodward, 2011).

The French also settled in the area of the Louisiana Territory, again negotiating in peace and respect with the Native peoples who they believed to be equals (Woodward, 2011). The Jesuits who accompanied the French introduced Christianity, but it was not the fanatic Christianization engaged in by the Spanish. Many of the Indian nations they converted, such as the Hurons, included their religion in Christian ceremonies (Wilson, 1998).

Prejudice and Racism after the Beginning of the Republic

The history of racism in this country continued after the establishment of the United States as a republic with a constitution that made promises of freedom for its citizens and freedom from religious persecution. Yet, beginning with George Washington, the nation's first president and a landed member of the gentry, it is now known that he kept hundreds of African slaves working in his homes and on his land.

Washington was not the only elected official to do so, as we know now about Thomas Jefferson and others who kept African slaves to do the work required to run large households, carriage houses, and fulfill the needs required for the successful planting and harvesting of the day, including taking care of the animals needed for transportation as well as farming.

While some authors of history have excluded mentioning these behaviors in the past, considering them "normal" for the time, we can no longer afford to tolerate half-truths about our country's early leaders. This is especially true in the case of George Washington as he set the tone for the treatment of Indigenous and African peoples in this country, continuing the previous patterns of disrespect, racism, and prejudices against Indigenous and African peoples.

Galloway (2018) reveals how George Washington mastered Indian protocol while a commander in the Continental Army, yet he abandoned all he knew in subsequent years once he became president of the nation. Washington's goal was to acquire more land for the survival of the young nation, and the only way to get land was to take it, by offering payments or by force if necessary, from Indian nations.

Washington worked with leaders of the Shingas, Tanaghrisson, Guyasuta, Attakullakulla, and individuals such as Joseph Brant, Cornplanter, Red Jacket, and others who represented the Iroquois Confederacy. It didn't take long for Indian peoples to realize that despite all the promises made, the "Great Father" at the head of the new country did not have their best interests in mind as he set about building the new country.

A common colonial misunderstanding regarding Indigenous use of land was that they weren't occupying it or farming it, and therefore it should be up for grabs. Little did the colonists understand the importance of allowing land to lay fallow for a while before replanting it. In addition, Europeans and Euro-Americans did not understand that unlike religions in Europe where worship took place in a building, their land comprised American Indians' places of worship where sacred ceremonies were held in the open for thousands of years.

In the times that U.S. military forces met imperial armies, they were composed of very few colonists and large numbers of Indian supporters (Wilson, 1998). Instead of rewarding these people for their services to the country, the mistreatment continued. Regrettably, a precedent began of punishing Indian nations by taking their lands if they were supporters of the losing side in later wars and conflicts in which the young nation became involved. Such was the case with the imperial wars of Europe that extended into the Americas and the wars for freedom from the British (Galloway, 2018; Wilson, 1998).

In the Civil War, the Cherokee supported the Southern resistance to the Union. They lost large numbers of warriors in this conflict. Again, a great deal of land was taken by the United States, eventually leading to the Trail of Tears and loss of more lives when the Cherokee were forced to leave their homeland. The Cherokee, one of the Five Civilized Tribes, had done all they could to protect their people by emulating Europeans. Yet, with the pervasive anti-Indian views, even becoming "civilized" hadn't protected them (Mann, 2005/2011; Wilson, 1998).

President Andrew Jackson's zealous anti-Indian stance and shoddy treatment of Native tribes increased as he was determined to remove all Native peoples and open their lands for settlement by whites (Josephy, 1991; Wilson, 1998). This poor treatment of Native Americans by representatives of the U.S. government at the very pinnacle of governmental offices inculcated the idea within the populace that this treatment of Indians was "normal" and "warranted," similar to punishing children for doing wrong.

Indeed, in the minds of Western Europeans, the Indigenous peoples needed to be treated like children. Native American cultures, values, and morals, were considered antithetical to Protestantism with its focus on working hard, gathering individual wealth, and being concerned more with self than others (Stannard, 1992; Wilson, 1968).

Spanish Territories Become Part of the United States

The Navajos, Pueblo, and other Native tribes initially resisted the Spanish incursion into their lands. Nonetheless, because the Spanish were better armed and not afraid to inflict terrible harm on them, many of the Aboriginal peoples in El Norte succumbed to their rule. The Spanish gathered up thousands of Native peoples to be part of their economically fruitful slave trade, where Indigenous peoples were sent to Europe and beyond (Wilson, 1998).

The Spanish had been intolerant of the practices of Indians for hundreds of years, and that attitude persisted in the El Norte areas. Missionaries burned Natives' homes, food stocks, and everything that was related to Native religions. When the Spanish government determined that the missionaries should set up settlements for Natives to convert and educate them, this was done throughout their territories.

However, in El Norte, the missionaries were especially harsh, denigrating Indigenous peoples even though they had evidence, especially in California, of Native societies with nobles and hierarchies established, as well as laws to be obeyed. To justify their actions of making Indians virtual slaves, they had to completely ignore the complex civilizations of all these various Tribal groups, some of whom were related by language, others of which were not (Wilson, 1998).

Missionaries continued in their insistence that the heathens had nothing of worth in their own cultures, so they had to become baptized and practice European ways of living to be considered of consequence. When missionaries went out to round up Native families, they subsequently separated them in the barracks-like missions. Instead of education, Indigenous peoples were given onerous agricultural chores to perform using implements they had never seen before to do so. If mistakes were made, the consequences were severe lashings to teach them their lessons, some so harsh Natives were affected for life by their injuries (Wilson, 1998).

According to Wilson (1998),

> At the same time, the friars' assault on native culture, and particularly the merciless beatings they administered to offenders, left a legacy of bitterness and resentment. When the church accused settlers of corruption and of exploiting Indians economically and sexually, the colonists riposted that the missionaries' excessively harsh treatment of dissenters risked a full-scale rebellion against Spanish rule. (p. 201)

Indeed, this was a prophetic statement, and in 1680, pueblos in New Spain (New Mexico) revolted, killing four hundred soldiers and driving out two thousand Spanish settlers. A hundred years later, with some Indigenous peoples continuing to resist, Viceroy Galvez implemented a new approach in 1786 which was to enter into trade agreements with the Native peoples as a way to pacify their resistance (Wilson, 1998).

Eventually, though, the call for more land by white Americans continued and now involved the area of Texas. White immigrants surged into this territory, leading to war with Mexico (Wilson, 1998). Texas as its own state was proclaimed by the victors. Texas was annexed to the United States in 1844; when it entered the Union as a slave state in December 1845, it set off the Mexican-American War.

While U.S. forces trespassed on Mexican lands, resulting in skirmishes, President Polk decided this was "Mexican aggression," with the response of Congress voting to go to war with Mexico over the territories. These territories in El Norte—California, Arizona, New Mexico, Nevada, Utah, Colorado, and Wyoming, plus all claims to Texas—were turned over to the United States as a result of the victory over the Mexicans in the Treaty of Guadalupe Hildago (Woodward, 2011).

In addition, the United States received Cuba, Puerto Rico, Guam, and the Philippines. All of this was seen as God's favor of North America and its white leadership (Woodward, 2011). Still, white Americans looked down on Mexicans, or Mestizos, who were racially mixed and spoke Spanish. In colonial Mexico, there were 128 different racial categories, all on a hierarchy.

The United States decided that their duty to Mexicans was to eliminate any special racial categories previously reserved for Indians. Native peoples lost over half a million acres of land in El Norte through these political decisions, as well as the islands. Mestizos including islanders—many of whom now prefer the term "Latinx"—were subject to racism and racists attitudes by white Protestants, in particular if they were Catholic (Wilson, 1998). There was a determination to settle the land as quickly as possible with Europeans and Euro-Americans, which they did, making Native peoples outsiders in their own lands.

THE ULTIMATE RESULTS OF COLONIZATION

Colonization by all of the different European powers brought devastation to Native American peoples through disease, warfare, and slavery. Actions were justified as "God's will" by various clergy who attended the colonizers of each area. With the loss of so much land and lives, Native cultures were impacted with a cultural and a physical genocide (Stannard, 1992).

In the meantime, anti-Indian wars continued in the West during the three-fifths plus of the 1800s. Civilian militias meant for use in the Civil War were used against Indigenous tribes in the Northwest with the horrendous massacres of Bear River (Shoshone) in 1863 (in what is now Idaho) led by Col. Connors, and the Sand Creek (Cheyanne) massacre in 1864 (in what is now Colorado) led by Col. Chivington. Civilians showed their lust for killing Indians, attacking Indigenous peoples at dawn even though they had agreements with the federal government. Connors destroyed everything in sight, including foodstuffs, clothing, and lodges. He then left 160 Native women and children on the "battleground" to starve (Blackhawk, 2006).

The next action by the United States was to make treaties with different Native tribes and round up Indian people who were not yet on reservations. Again, harsh actions were meted out by the military including marching Natives in chains to their new homes (Klug & Whitfield, 2003). Reservation superintendents were often corrupt; the food mostly rancid; and the cloth given to make clothing substandard. Native peoples trying to leave reservations to hunt for additional food were shot by soldiers. Effectively, Indian peoples were held as prisoners in their lands and often placed with their traditional enemies as a way to (hopefully) kill one another (Klug & Whitfield, 2003).

In the following section, we will investigate how education was used to assimilate American Indians into Western European civilization, causing disaster for Native Americans. Western European hegemony established throughout the country resulted in racism and prejudicial actions towards Native students, continuing into the twentieth century and still alive today. The importance of student resiliency will be presented along with incorporating Native cultures and histories into schools, a viable solution for success of Indigenous students in our nation.

REFERENCES

American Indian Histories and Cultures. (n.d.). *History*. Adam Matthew Digital. Thousand Oaks, CA: Sage. Retrieved from https://www.aihc.amdigital.co.uk/.

Ames, P. (2018, February 6; February 12). Portugal confronts its slave trade past: Planned monument in Lisbon sparks debate over race and history. *Politico*, Europe Edition. Retrieved from https://www.politico.eu/article/portual-slave-trade-confronts-its-past/.

Barnes, I. (2010). *The historical atlas of Native Americans*. New York, NY: Chartwell Books.

Berkhofer, R. F., Jr. (1978). *The White man's Indian: Images of the American Indian from Columbus to the present*. New York, NY: Vintage Books.

Biography.com Editors. (2014, April 2, 2019; September 20, 2019). *Martin Luther Biography*. A & E Television Networks. Retrieved from https://www.biography.com/religious-figure/martin-luther.

Blackhawk, N. (2006). *Violence over the Land: Indians and Empires in the Early American West*. Cambridge, MA: Harvard University Press.

Doctrine of Discovery. (n.d.). *Upstander project*. Boston: Massachuset, Nipmuc, and Wampanoag Territory: Dawnlander.org. Retrieved from https://upstanderproject.org/firstlight/doctrine.

Galloway, C. G. (2018). *The Indian World of George Washington: The First President, the First Americans, and the Birth of the Nation*. New York, NY: Oxford University Press.

Ghiuzeli, H. F. (1991, August). *The myth of the Ten Lost Tribes*. The Museum of the Jewish People at Beit Hatfutsot, Tel Aviv: Museum Catalogue. Retrieved from https://www.bh.org.il/the-myth-of-the-ten-lost-tribes-article/.

Josephy, A. M., Jr. (1991). *The Indian heritage of America* (Rev. Ed.). Boston, MA: Houghton Mifflin. (Original work published in 1968.)

Keillor, S. J. (1996). *This rebellious house: American history & the truth of Christianity*. Downers Grove, IL: InterVarsity Press.

Kendi, I. X. (2016). *Stamped from the beginning: The definitive history of racist ideas in America*. New York, NY: Nation Books.

King, S. M. (2012). Hidden transcripts, contested landscapes, and long-term Indigenous history in Oaxaca, Mexico. In M. Oland, S. M. Hart, & L. Frink (Eds.), *Decolonizing Indigenous histories: Exploring prehistoric colonial transitions in Archaeology* (pp. 230–63). Tucson: University of Arizona Press.

Klug, B. J. & Whitfield, P. T. (2003). *Widening the Circle: Culturally relevant pedagogy for American Indian children*. New York, NY: RoutledgeFalmer.

Mann, C. C. (2005/2011). *1491: New revelations of the Americas before Columbus*. New York, NY: Random House, Inc.

Mann, C. C. (2011). *1493: Uncovering the New World Columbus created*. New York, NY: Albert A. Knopf.

Mueller, G. O. (1986). The criminological significance of Grimms' tales. In R. B. Bottigheimer (Ed.), *Folk tales and society: Illusion, allusion, and paradigm* (pp. 217–27). Philadelphia: University of Pennsylvania Press.

Native Circle. (n.d.). *American Indian Wisdom, Spirit, Culture and Tradition*. Retrieved from http://www.nativecircle.com/.

'Real' Columbus, The. (n.d.). *American Indian wisdom, spirit, culture and tradition*. Native Circle.com. Retrieved from http://www.nativecircle.com.

Rodríguez-Algería, E. (2012). Discovery and decolonization of Xaltocan. In M. Oland, S. M. Hart, and L. Frink (Eds.), *Decolonizing Indigenous histories: Exploring prehistoric colonial transitions in Archaeology* (pp. 45–65). Tucson: University of Arizona Press.

Sanders, R. (1978/2015). *Lost tribes and promised lands: The origins of American Racism*. Brattleboro, VT: Echo Point Books & Media.

Stannard, D. E. (1992). *American holocaust: The conquest of the New World*. New York, NY: Oxford University Press.

Togias, M. (2000). *King Philip's War in New England*. Retrieved from http://historyplace.com/specials/kingphilip.htm.

Wilson, J. E. (1998). *The earth shall weep: A history of Native America*. New York, NY: Grove Press.

Woodward, C. (2011). *American Nations: A history of the eleven rival regional cultures of North America*. New York, NY: Penguin Books.

Zipes, J. (1979). *Breaking the magic spell: Radical theories of folk and fairy tales*. New York, NY: Methuen.

Part II

Past and Present Education of Indigenous Students in This Country

The majority of Americans have images of Aboriginals as particular types of people living in particular areas, primarily in the western United States. The reality is quite different. The 2010 Census was probably the most sensitive of all of those that had taken place in prior history in terms of trying to categorize the populations of the United States by both number and racial or ethnic groups. Respondents were given the choice of five race categories from which to choose: white, Black or African American, American Indian or Alaska Native, Asian, and Native Hawaiian or Other Pacific Islander. An additional category, Other Race, was added for those who did not identify with any of the five categories. Further, respondents could indicate that they were a combination of different races, which reflected more accurately who makes up this country (Norris, Vines, & Hoeffel, 2012).

The results of the 2010 U.S. Census showed that the total U.S. population grew by 9.7 percent to 309.7 million. The population of American Indians and Alaska Natives—including those from Central American and South American Indian groups for the first time—grew substantially by 39 percent from 2000 to 5.2 million reported in 2010, almost twice as much as the general population. The figures for these Native Americans alone or in combination with other races increased in almost every area throughout the union, with a few states losing some of their Indigenous population numbers (Norris, Vines, & Hoeffel, 2012). This includes reservations, rural areas not part of reservation Trust lands, and urban areas.

Almost half of the American Indian/Alaska Native populations reported "in combination" with other races in the 2010 census. This led to the finding that California and Oklahoma had the largest in combination populations, followed by Texas and New York. The most often reported race in combination was white, followed by Black or African American, then Alaskan Native and other combinations (Norris, Vines, & Hoeffel, 2012).

The number of Native Hawaiians and Pacific Islanders—also considered Indigenous Native Americans—who reported to the 2010 Census was 1.2 million. Of this number, 56 percent reported in combination with other races, most often white. Of the respondents, 540,013 were Hawaiian or Pacific Islander alone, and 685,182 were in combination with other races, a 44 percent increase in size since the 2000 Census. Of this group, only 355,816 persons live in Hawaii or on other Pacific Islands (Hixson, Hepler, & Kim, 2012).

Many times, we are unaware of Native populations living in our areas. Part of this may be because not all Aboriginals are darker-skinned. There is also a myth in numerous areas of the United States that all American Indians perished; therefore people are not consciously aware of Indigenous peoples in their midst.

In Figure Part II.1, we can see that New York City, with a total population of 8,175,133, has a total population of Indigenous peoples of 111,749 for the 2010 Census, ranking it the highest in number of Native American citizens (see Figure Part II.1). The city of Los Angeles in California is ranked second with 54,236 Native Americans out of its total of 3,792,621, and so on. Some of this is a result of the Bureau of Indian Affairs' (BIA) efforts to relocate Native Americans after World War II into urban areas as another way to attempt to assimilate them (Wax, 1971).

In 1952, Relocation Centers were set up in Chicago, Illinois; Denver, Colorado; Los Angeles, California; San Francisco, California; San José, California; St. Louis, Missouri; Cincinnati, Ohio; Cleveland, Ohio; and Dallas, Texas. This became the largest mass movement of Indigenous peoples from across the country into urban areas in the hopes that their moving away from Native communities would cause Native Americans to assimilate completely (Urban Relocation Program, n.d.).

Some of those families stayed and were successful, denying their Indian heritages and looking down on their relatives back home as backward and primitive. Some consistently moved back and forth between the cities and reservations, trying to maintain family and identity ties while at the same time denying who they were due to prejudice at work in urban areas. Other families did not make the transition to urban life and remained impoverished, not a part of either world,

Place	Total population	Rank	American Indians and Alaska Natives Alone or in Combination
New York, NY	8,175,133	1	111,749
Los Angeles, CA	3,792,621	2	54,236
Phoenix, AZ	1,445,632	3	43,724
Oklahoma City, OK	579,999	4	36,572
Anchorage, AK	291,826	5	36,062
Tulsa, OK	391,906	6	35,990
Albuquerque, NM	545,852	7	32,571
Chicago, IL	2,695,598	8	26,933
Houston, TX	2,099,451	9	25,521
San Antonio, TX	1,327,407	10	20,137
Additional Places:			
Tucson, AZ	520,116	11	19,903
Philadelphia, PA	1,526,006	13	17,495
San Diego, CA	1,307,402	12	17,865

Figure Part II.1. Places with the Largest Number of American Indians and Alaska Natives, 2010. Only those places listed in Table 4 of the 2010 Census Brief Report are included here. Adapted from "Table 3: Ten Places with the Largest Number of American Indians and Alaska Natives: 2010" by T. Norris, P. L. Vines, & E. M. Hoeffel, January 2012, *The American Indian and Alaska Native Population: 2010, Census Brief (C2010BR-10)*. Copyright 2012 U.S. by the Census Bureau, U.S. Department of Commerce Economics and Statistics Administration.

especially after BIA supportive services were withdrawn later when the program closed (Wax, 1971). Since then, many Native Americans have moved to cities as opportunities for education and employment have arisen.

In Figure Part II.2, we can see that there are places within the United States that have the highest percentages of American Indians and Alaska Natives living in this country whether or not they have the highest numbers of Native American students (see Figure Part II.2). Again, these percentages may change with the 2020 Census, the results of which will probably not be available until 2022. For educators, this is important information since it confirms that of our student populations, there are a greater number of American Indians, Alaska Natives, and Hawaiian/ Pacific Islanders than may have been perceived before this information being released.

Hence a place like Green Bay, Wisconsin, with a total of 104,057 citizens has the seventh-highest percentage of Indigenous people. Or Tacoma, Washington, with a total population of 198,397 citizens has the eighth-highest percentage of Native Americans. The consequences of this information for public schools is very important, as we know that not only does this mean that there may be needs for

Place Name	Total No. for Entire Population	Percentage Ranking for AI & AN
Anchorage, AK	291,826	1
Tulsa, OK	391,906	2
Norman, OK	110,925	3
Oklahoma City, OK	579,999	4
Billings, MT	104,170	5
Albuquerque, NM	545,852	6
Green Bay, WI	104,057	7
Tacoma, WA	198,397	8
Tempe, AZ	161,719	9
Tucson, AZ	520,116	10
Additional Places:		
Sioux Falls, SD	153,888	13
Spokane, WA	208,916	11
Eugene, OR	156,185	24
Topeka, KS	127,473	17
Sacramento, CA	466,488	23
Santa Rosa, CA	167,815	15

Figure Part II.2. Places with the Highest Percentages of American Indians and Alaska Natives Living in the United States. Only those places listed in Table 4 of the 2010 Census Brief Report are included here. Adapted from "Table 4: Ten Places with the Highest Percentage of American Indians and Alaska Natives: 2010" by T. Norris, P. L. Vines, & E. M. Hoeffel, January 2012, *The American Indian and Alaska Native Population: 2010, Census Brief* **(C2010BR-10). Copyright 2012 U.S. by the Census Bureau, U.S. Department of Commerce Economics and Statistics Administration.**

more funding from the federal government for low-income students, but that there will also be large numbers of Indigenous students attending schools from all different socioeconomic levels throughout their districts.

In this section, we will address Indian education initiatives in terms of the earliest efforts to present endeavors to enhance educational achievements for Indigenous students both on and off reservations; areas of Native American identity; and the importance of resiliency development for Indigenous students. All of these areas impact our Aboriginal students in our schools.

REFERENCES

Hixson, L., Hepler, B. B., & Kim, M. O. (2012, May). *The Native Hawaiian and Other Pacific Islander Population: 2010, C2010BR-12. 2010 Census Briefs*. Washington, DC: U.S. Census Bureau, U.S. Department of Commerce Economics and Statistics Administration. Retrieved from https://www.census.gov/prod/cen2010/briefs/c2010br-12.pdf.

Norris, T., Vines, P. L., & Hoeffel, E. M. (2012, January). *The American Indian and Alaska Native Population: 2010, C2010BR-10. 2010 Census Briefs*. Washington, DC: U.S. Census Bureau, U.S. Department of Commerce Economics and Statistics Administration. Retrieved from https://www.census.gov/history/pdf/c2010br-10.pdf.

Urban Relocation Program. (n.d.). *Articles*. WERNATIVE. Retrieved from https://www.wernative.org/articles/the-urban-relocation-program?sa=X&ved=2ahUKEwiM84-MvbjnAhVKITQIHVUtD-IQ1i8wEnoECA4QJA.

Wax, M. (1971). *Indian Americans: Unity and diversity*. Englewood Cliffs, NJ: Prentice-Hall.

Chapter Five

Racism, Stereotypes, and Education for Assimilation

Racism is the promotion of hatred towards one group or another based on the particular ethnic group they belong to, in the case of American Indians and Alaska Natives, the color of skin plus group affiliation. Racism and racist thinking block the realities of what people are really like as individuals believe the worst they have been told about others, leading to prejudices against those who are unlike themselves.

Europeans who traveled to North America had nothing but good things to say about American Indians. They especially noted their love of liberty, and this thinking influenced the European Enlightenment. Thomas Paine, who came to America in 1774, became very involved with the Iroquois, learned their customs and language, and . . .

> throughout the remainder of his political and writing career he used the Indians as models of how society might be organized. . . . Paine castigated Britain for her abusive treatment of the Indians, and he became the first American to call for the abolition of slavery. . . . After the victory [over the British], he returned to Europe in 1787 to carry the Indian spark of liberty. (Weatherford, 1988, p. 125)

Nevertheless, Native peoples were disparaged on a regular basis in the Americas.

THE ROLE OF WRITERS AND MEDIA IN ON-GOING RACISM AND PREJUDICE

The power to persuade people—positively or negatively—concerning their values, viewpoints, ideas of the world, racist attitudes, prejudices and actions belongs to the media. It also has the power to confirm our perceptions and sometimes, our greatest fears. We can witness this regularly when we watch television advertisements with children: their view of the world becomes shaped immediately by what they see on television, and now also social media. If not discussed, children can grow up with distortions of their worlds as presented through the media.

The media of some of the early groups of colonizers on the east coast of the country from Europe, in particular the Puritans and the Pilgrims, was that of the Bible; writings of church doctrine and literature, including sermons by famous pastors; and oral stories that circulated through their communities. They brought with them a faith that was contemptuous of the human body, which they believed represented sin and evil. Carnal desires were to be fought, people to be ashamed of themselves; strict rules of behavior were to be obeyed in order to avoid contamination by the evil one (Mann, 2005/2011; Stannard, 1992). Religious leaders, supposed to tell the truth, would equate Native peoples with the devil, and rail against them.

The Massachusetts Bay Colony had explicitly demanded that settlers were not to harm the Indians in their region (Wilson, 1998). However, one of the first large-scale massacres of Indians occurred in Mystic, Connecticut in 1637, discussed previously. The Pequots had joined other Indian nations in a pact of resistance to the white intrusions onto their lands. Upon learning of this, the Puritans then decided that the only way they could reverse this action was to annihilate the Pequots at their two encampments; the first attack was to be at Mystic (Wilson, 1998).

The Pequots were attacked at night by a militia and some Narragansets while they were meeting together. Not only were they fired upon by guns, but the torch was put to their fort and homes burning all who were there. The Narragansets did not know the full extent of the Puritans' intentions when they were called upon to provide assistance to them. They were appalled by the carnage, crying "Too much! Too much!" Cotton Mather, a renowned Puritan Minister, delighted in the bloodbath and incineration of the Pequots. He viewed this atrocious event as "the just Judgment of God," calling it "a barbeque" (cited in Stannard, 1992).

Continued Prejudicial Literature, Stories, and Racist Attitudes

In spite of observations to the contrary, Indigenous peoples were viewed heathens, as a dirty, slovenly, people. They supposedly had no ethics or morals; the men were perceived to be extremely lazy. Indigenous peoples in North America were viewed as primitive savages who must be saved through Christianity. They were held to be extremely violent, ready to attack anyone—Native or Non-Native—

instantaneously (Josephy, 1991; Mann, 2005/2011; Stannard, 1992; Wilson, 1998).

In none of these stories are provocations against Native Americans part of the narratives. Europeans and Euro-Americans were always shown to be innocent and on the receiving end of Indian aggressions. These stories would continue to be spread as a way to justify actions of the government, settlers, and miners as they took more and more Indian lands for themselves. The prejudice and racism that resulted from this literature ensured that Natives would continue to be on the losing end of colonial bargaining agreements (Davidson, 2012).

The fact that Indians contracted European diseases and drank alcohol (provided by traders) was proof that they were inferior to Europeans from birth. Territories where Indigenous peoples had perished due to European epidemics were viewed as fulfillment of "God's promise" to Puritans and other religious that the earth would be cleared of Indigenous people—so that a superior civilization could take over the land (Davidson, 2012; Wilson, 1998). Passages from the Bible were used to support God's promise to these "religious" Europeans. Promises made in exchange for Indian lands were rarely kept, subject to amendments and the whims of the government (Wilson, 1998).

Visitors from overseas noted at the end of the 1700s that there was palpable hatred of American Indians, even though they had been the principal volunteers in the war for independence from England. The greed that was so much a part of the character of the colonizing forces at this time was hidden under racist ideas that the Aboriginals of this land could not possibly be civilized. Indigenous peoples were not only heathens, but savages, wolves, bears, vermin, and needed to be exterminated. All of this propaganda was spread to fulfill God's will and promises to his faithful people (Stannard, 1992).

Davidson (2012) explains this phenomenon below:

> Thought collectives [of societies] often transform stereotypes and unanalyzed assertions into firmly implanted assumptions of truth. This applies to the white American perceptions of the Indian in the seventeenth through nineteenth centuries. That in this process there was a war of extermination going on was, as a consequence, easily explained away. (p. 33)

In the late 1700s through the late 1800s, many people only relied on a few media resources to tell them the truth about Native Americans. Education was not universal in this country; the ability to read and compute was mainly the purview of the upper classes, therefore those without the means relied on the current oral discourse of the day.

People depended on oral storytelling as well as portrayals in paintings; those who could read shared information in newspaper accounts, government reports, newspaper articles, eye-witness accounts (some falsified), and books which sensationalized Native peoples either as Nobel Savages or as the embodiment of evil. James Fennimore Cooper's books about the vanishing Indians were taken as a sure sign of destiny being fulfilled for both Indians and non-Indians (Wilson, 1998). Consequently, readers and non-readers alike were influenced by this campaign of propaganda against Indigenous peoples.

After 1812, the federal government—under the auspices of the War Department—was determined to put all Indians on reservations, removing them from their homelands and segregating them from others. Art became a medium through which preservation of these doomed peoples could be recorded for posterity. George Catlin produced 478 paintings of people from 47 different tribes as a tribute to them. The War Department collected paintings of American Indians so they could look back at the people they had vanquished to justify their actions (Davidson, 2012).

The 1800s and Manifest Destiny

The population in the United States grew from 5 million in 1800 to 23 million by 1850, and continued to grow during the last half of the 1800s with more immigration coming from different parts of Europe as a result of famines and other disasters. These migrations grew from the U.S. acquisitions of new lands in the middle, Northwest, and Far West of the territory. Americans entered former French territories after President Thomas Jefferson acquired these territories through the Louisiana Purchase in 1803.

Between 1804 and 1806, President Jefferson sent Lewis and Clark on an expedition to find out what these territories were like and to find a route to the Pacific Ocean to advance American commerce. The expedition encountered numerous American Indians who had never seen Europeans before, many of whom were friendly to them and assisted them in their journey. This was due primarily to the presence of Sacajawea. As a young Shoshoni girl she had been captured in a Hidatsa (a tribe related to the Sioux) raid against the Shoshoni. She was enslaved and later bought by her fur-trader husband, Charbonneau, to be one of his three wives (Duncan & Burns, 1997).

As Sacajawea accompanied the expedition and gave birth to her son, her presence in the expedition signaled to other Natives that the expedition had a peaceful mission. Her knowledge of the territory and Native customs, her quick-thinking in disasters, and abilities to find food and medicinals from nature were skills sorely needed for the campaign to survive. When the travelers required additional horses, they met a group of Shoshoni Indians in the Lemhi Mountains on August 13, 1805. Sacajawea originated from this band and recognized her relatives, resulting in a tribal celebration of her return. It was this meeting with her brother, Cameahwait, chief of the Lemhis, which saved the expedition from failure (Duncan & Burns, 1997).

The Oregon Trail, which later brought European/American settlers to the far west, was used first by American Indians and then by Mountain men through the 1830s in their search for beaver for the European fur trade. Eventually, the American Fur Company, which had bought out others, and the British Hudson Bay Fur Company, competed in the area of Oregon Territory, which was under joint governance as a result of the War of 1812. The Treaty of Oregon signed on June 15, 1846, established the boundary between the United States and Canada. This area of expansion brought invasions into Indian Territory, though because of the difficult terrain, the process took longer than in other areas of the country (Wilson, 1998).

All the while, treaties were enacted with Native peoples in these areas. Nonetheless, settlers constantly violated the treaties and made incursions into Indian lands (Nabovkov, 1978; Wilson, 1998). Education, which had been promised in treaties for Indian tribes, rarely was provided unless by missionaries. Altogether, the U.S. enacted 370 treaties with Native tribes, only to be broken by citizens time and again (Wilson, 1998).

Manifest Destiny and the West

The philosophy of Manifest Destiny, that God had ordained the expansion of the U.S. across the continent, was first espoused in 1845, reinforcing the notion that what was occurring in this country with Indigenous peoples was natural and right. The Mormons under Brigham Young emigrated from Nauvoo, Illinois in the U.S. to Utah territory. They settled in the area now known as Salt Lake City on July 24, 1847, and Young became the territorial governor there (Blackhawk, 2006). The Mexican-American War ended shortly after, on February 2, 1848, with awarding the former territories of Mexico in El Norte to the U.S.

The many thousands of Aboriginals from Florida to California, having already suffered under the Spaniards, now suffered under the Anglo-Europeans. In California, Native Americans were estimated at 350,000 at first encounter with the Spanish, many of whom perished through disease and treatment under them. There were approximately 100,000 Native Americans when the U.S. took possession there. These tribes still had some of their rituals, mythologies, musical instruments, dances, and customs at this time; the exception were the Mission Tribes, which had been forced to become Christian and accept Spanish ways (Josephy, 1991).

The finding of gold in California in 1848 resulted in hordes of Americans coming into California with the goal of making it rich. They massacred whole tribes, destroying their food supplies and gathering places. It is estimated that by 1859, 70,000 Indians were killed. By the end of the nineteen century, Indians were reduced to approximately 15,000 of those Indigenous peoples who had survived by hiding in caves and other places away from American eyes (Josephy, 1991).

Congress ceased treaty-making between the United States and Native American tribes in 1871 (Wilson, 1998). The Oregon Trail was used as the U.S. population exploded, bringing in new emigrants as the U.S. economy had experienced two recessions. People moved west for the promise of "free land." Missionaries and traders, families and communities were established; they made no considerations nor concessions to Indians who were losing their lands to them.

A new dilemma faced the U.S.: What to do with the Native Americans who had survived efforts to eliminate them? Government officials made the decision to remove American Indians from their homelands and place them on reservations where they would be civilized and Christianized. However, even this approach of a "peace policy" was opposed by many.

Massacres of Aboriginals in the West

The Sand Creek massacre, led by Colonel John Chivington, a Methodist minister, is an example of the treachery that occurred throughout the West during this period. In 1864, Major Edward Wynkoop succeeded in bringing the Cheyanne "peace chiefs" Black Kettle and White Antelope and their people closer to Fort Lyon (now in Colorado) for their protection and so they would not join other hostile groups.

When Chivington came, he had Wynkoop removed because he was too sympathetic to the Indians. Chivington stated he had come to kill Indians, justifying his actions by stating "nits make lice" and then ordering his men to kill all the Indians they found. On the morning of November 29, 1864, Black Kettle raised the American and white flags as told to do and went out to meet the soldiers to talk to them. But the soldiers would not stop firing, shooting men, women, children of all ages. All the while people begged for mercy as the soldiers approached each teepee. Afterwards, the soldiers proceeded to scalp everyone.

Next on the agenda was to eliminate additional Native peoples, employing Colonel George Armstrong Custer among others to do so. The Lakota chief Red Cloud fought back. According to one survivor, Indians felt that they were going to be wiped out completely, and there were no alternatives to fighting back if they were going to survive. There would be no peace with the whites as long as they continued to believe the propaganda against Indian people.

The Massacre of Wounded Knee, December 29, 1890, proved to be one of the determining factors for ending these wars. Big Foot and his group of about 400 Sioux were on their way to meet with other groups of Lakota where they had settled in the South. When they arrived at Pine Ridge, South Dakota, Custer's 7th Calvary ordered them to camp at Wounded Knee Creek (Wilson, 1998).

In the early morning hours of the next day, the soldiers disarmed the Sioux, searched their teepees for additional weapons, and then set about killing approximately 300 Indians outright; many later died as a result of their wounds (Wilson, 1998). Several of the militia received medals for what they did. In the East, news of this latest massacre finally made Euro-Americans take notice of what was occurring to Native peoples in the West (Wilson, 1998).

The Works of Writers in the Late 1800s Contributing to White Prejudices

Blackhawk (2006), cites the work of Mark Twain, a.k.a. Samuel Clemmons, as an example of how one author was able to influence generations of thought about Native peoples. Clemmons had visited the Shoshones in the Great Plains, an arid landscape that Native peoples had lived in for thousands of years. Clemmons declared the Shoshone to be the most primitive and debased human beings he ever met, and used them to illustrate the character of all Native peoples.

Again, Clemmons did not choose to write about the deprivations that led to the Shoshones' conditions in 1872. There was no discussion of the Spanish slave trade in Aboriginal peoples; no discussion of the fact that those "pioneers" going to settle California and their animals destroyed a great deal of arable land, and dug up plants that had previously supplied nutritious diets. There was no discussion that the white people helped themselves to the bison—on which the Shoshone and other tribes depended—which had numbered more than 30 million in the first half of the century and were reduced to just 1,000 by the end of the 1800s (Are bison an endangered species? 2001; Wilson, 1998).

General Sheridan concluded that the way to rid the plains of Indians was to destroy their stock, forcing them onto reservations. Cody (later called "Buffalo Bill Cody") led wealthy men from the East on trips to kill the buffalo; runners each killed up to 50 buffalo a day. The military accompanied by citizens killed bison with glee, skinning them and leaving the meat to rot in the fields. With the slaughter of the bison, Indigenous economies were destroyed. A deep wound was driven into the central part of American Indians' material and spiritual worlds, driving Indians to starvation (Madsen, 1986; Smits, 1994; Wilson, 1998).

Still feeding the prejudice and racist attitudes against Native Americans, dime novels sensationalized the violence of Indians against white settlers, depicting scalping of "innocent" pioneers. Revenge by citizens against natives in these novels fed the fires in the imaginations of Euro-Americans who justified their rights to the "open" lands in the West (Wilson, 1998).

Stories of white captives, untrue and sensationalized, depicted cruel trials white women and girls supposedly underwent when taken as captives of the Indians. Yet, in truth, those taken captive were usually adopted into tribes and treated much better than in their Euro-American settlements. White women were reluctant to leave their Native families when "rescued" by the military and forced to leave their children and spouses behind. Cynthia Ann Parker, the mother of the Comanche Chief Quanah Parker, is probably the best known of these (Berkhofer, 1978).

Fantasies concerning Aboriginal peoples ignored the truths of their conditions, the results of colonization and in many cases, the great poverty that had been produced by the influx of non-Native peoples into the country. For a proud people confronted with a seemingly endless demand for more land—ongoing even today—the last five hundred years plus have been grievous to endure.

> Through it all . . . the Christian Europeans continued to display a seemingly antithetical set of tendencies: . . . [the antiracial tendencies along with] the same inner prompting that drove missionaries to the ends of the earth to Christianize people of color, but to insist that their new converts worship in segregated churches. Beginning in the late eighteen century in this conflict of racial abhorrence and mission—and along with it a redefined concept of holy war—became secularized in the form of an internally contradictory political ideology. In the same way that the Protestant Ethic was transformed into the Spirit of Capitalism, while the Christian right to private property became justifiable in wholly secular terms, America as Redeemer Nation became Imperial America, fulfilling its irresistible manifest destiny. (Stannard, 1992, p. 242–43)

EDUCATION OF AMERICAN INDIANS IN THE 1800s

Early Spanish and French monasteries and convents were established in the Americas in the 1600s and 1700s with the goals of teaching Spanish and French to Native students, along with Christian values. Few schools had been established by the British, with most of their children from upper classes sent to boarding schools in Europe.

The Puritans established schools for children in New England, following their religious beliefs in the inherent evil of human nature. These values of neatness, punctuality, hard work, competition, honesty, patriotism, respect for authority and the rights of others, and especially of individualism, formed the basis for all schools in this country to follow (Pulliam, 1987). Corporal punishment was a given in this environment.

In the early part of the 1800s, missionaries were sent to Indian peoples in the East, determined that they could teach American Indians agriculture and industrial arts as a way for them to become civilized, and therefore saved from impending doom (Nabovkov, 1978). In 1819, the Indian Civilization Act was signed by President Monroe distributing subsidies to missionary societies if they were involved in civilizing Indians (Davidson, 2012).

The Choctaw and the Cherokee looked at these offers to educate children as a way to preserve their cultures and for their survival (Spring, 1994). Cyrus Kingsbury was a Presbyterian minister who brought European education to these people. He selected tribal members who were bilingual in both Cherokee/Choctaw and English and prepared them to teach.

Meanwhile, Sequoyah, a member of the Cherokee nation, invented a written form of the Cherokee language called the *syllabary*, which included all of the syllables that made up the Cherokee language. As a consequence, the Bible, Cherokee Constitution, and other important documents were now translated into Cherokee. With using the Cherokee language in their schools, students were able to read both Cherokee and English with almost 100% literacy rates. The literacy rates in Choctaw schools were also the same, mainly due to bilingual teachers and their abilities to translate information in a way that made sense to students (Spring, 1994).

Many of the Cherokee and Choctaw youth went on to college, and they were able to succeed there and become doctors and members of other professions in their own right. Charles Eastman, called Ohiyesa in Lakota, became one of the best known Indians in his time, having been raised partly on the Pine Ridge Reservation and in Canada with his Grandmother and Uncle until he was fifteen.

Ohiyesa graduated from Dartmouth in 1887, and wrote nine books throughout his lifetime to educate non-Natives about Native belief systems and knowledge while helping his contemporaries adapt to white ways (Eastman, 1911).

The Long Walks

One unstated goal of educating Native Americans was to convince them to agree to move onto reservations. "That they usually did not do this, but rather opposed removal, caused repeated protests by those who wished to steal Indian land officially" (Davidson, 2012, p. 39). There were fifty-two schools throughout the country by 1836 teaching 1,381 Indian students. The mixing of Christianization with curriculum continued since missionaries were the primary teachers in these schools (Davidson, 2012).

Congress passed the Indian Removal Act of 1830 (Cave, 2003; Pruca, 2000) under pressure from citizens who felt Indians had to leave so settlers could have more land. Initially, many whites and Chief Justice John Marshall were resistant to the removal of the Cherokee, Choctaw, Chickasaw, Seminole and Muskogee Creek from their lands. In a move now called "ethnic cleansing," Chief Justice Marshall, under pressure from the Indian-hating President Jackson, reversed his opinion. Natives were herded into makeshift forts, and then began the horror of being forced to walk in chains over 1,000 miles in the dead of winter to Oklahoma ("home of the red man"), where the land was promised to be theirs forever (Adams, 1995).

As we know today, thousands of Native Americans died or were killed on this walk. Soldiers were indifferent, and if someone became ill or died, they were unchained and left in the open where the animals could scavenge their bodies. It is estimated that over 4,000 Cherokee alone died during this "Trail of Tears." Other Tribal nations suffered similarly, and later, when additional territories were claimed by the U.S., Tribal nations in those areas were also put on forced walks to reservations again, most of the time in chains (Madsen, 1986; Walker, 1985; Zinn, 1999).

Schooling under Indian Agents and Later Superintendents

The accomplishments by countless Native American students were ignored when the government decided that in order to educate Native children they had to be separated from the influences of their families and communities. Schools were taken out of the hands of tribes and missionaries in the late 1800s as several commissioners of Indian affairs imposed sanctions against Indian languages, values, cultures, and customs (Spring, 1994).

There were still difficulties with Congress appropriating monies for promised education guaranteed in the treaties with Native tribes. Education for Shoshoni, Ute, and Paiute at this time provides a case in point. In addition, finding teachers who were of upright character and had the ability to teach was another challenge, as was acquiring a building to house students and materials to teach them (Madsen, 1980). In a December 18, 1873, report produced by Commissioners J. W. Powell and G. W. Ingalls concerning the Shoshoni, Ute, and Paiute tribes, the Commissioners made the following statement:

> It is unnecessary to mention the power which schools would have over the rising generation of Indians. Next to teaching them to work, the most important thing is to teach them the English language. Into their own language there is woven so much mythology and sorcery that a new one is needed in order to aid them in advancing beyond their baneful superstitions; and the ideas and thoughts of civilized life cannot be communicated to them in their own tongues. (Cited in Madsen, 1980, p. 181)

There was no action to build a school for Native students at Fort Hall, Idaho between 1869–1873 due to lack of interest by the government and assigned Indian agents. Agent Henry Reed started a school that first had to be built in 1874 and hired an educated Indian, Peter O. Mathews, to be the teacher. With a small number of students, the school was declared a success (Madsen, 1980). However, with the lack of funding, Reed tried to find ways to raise the money for school repairs and supplies. In addition, some of the boys were boarding at the school in a loft above the schoolroom. There were not enough funds to take care of these students or allow others to attend school (Madsen, 1980).

For a couple of years the school could not operate due to lack of a teacher. In 1879, the Office of Indian Affairs wanted to have a day school established, which was built, but the children were still surrounded by their families and cultures at home. In September 1879, it was decided by the commissioner of Indian Affairs that a boarding school should be built to separate the students from "what was held to be the debilitating and retrograding influence of 'blanket Indians' and camp life" (Madsen, 1980, p. 182).

Still the government did not provide the funding necessary to take care of building repairs, teachers, and care of the children at a second school established to replace the first inadequate one. In addition, there was reluctance on the part of families to send their children to school. Finally, after one of the Medicine Men was convinced to send his children to school, other families agreed to do so. The school was in operation with forty-seven pupils, a laundress, and a cook, and operated for nine and a half months before closing yet again (Madsen, 1980).

A new office of Indian School Superintendent was created by Congress in 1882. Attempting to improve conditions at the school, in 1887 an investigation revealed "buildings in disrepair; dead cattle in the springs which supplied drinking water; two broken plows and one shovel to . . . work the school farm; and [students] . . . locked in their rooms at night . . . which presented a hazard in case of fire" (Madsen. 1980, p. 184).

Again, additional parents had been convinced that sending their children to the school would be good, and enrollment went from thirty-eight to seventy-five students. Because of lack of funding, problems ensued. A special investigation by an agent found that the conditions under Superintendent Everest were untenable (Madsen, 1980).

In his defense, Everest described the following conditions: 250 panes of glass were missing from windows, children were filthy (with little access to water to bathe), there was no discipline in the school, only two old buggy horses were available to get supplies from the nearest town, and there was not enough bedding to keep the children warm. These circumstances foretold the state of education for many years on one reservation, with similar conditions on others. Scarlet Fever and other illnesses that spread through the schools resulted in death for some; child suicides took place due to the shock some suffered from being separated from their families (Madsen, 1980).

In 1895, the first graduation class was held for the school at Fort Hall, Idaho. All told, there were 250 people in attendance: families, whites, and other Fort Hall community members (Madsen, 1980). This event was a cause for celebration, in which everyone participated. At this time, Shoshones and Bannocks recognized that education could be used to hold onto their Native cultures and ceremonies, and protecting their lands from more depredations by non-Indians and the government. There was still a long way to go toward actually providing education as we think of it today.

Pratt and the Boarding School Movement

Richard Henry Pratt, an officer in the army, was assigned to oversee Native prisoners at Fort Marion in Augustine, Florida. He decided that to Americanize them, he needed to cut Indians' hair and dress them in uniforms, make them learn English, and work for others (called the "Outing Program"). He first led Indian prisoners in 1878 to the Hampton Normal and Agricultural Institute in Hampton, Virginia. Later, he moved them to an old army barracks in Carlisle, Pennsylvania. Chiricahua Apache child prisoners were taken to Carlisle in 1886, beginning the Carlisle Indian Industrial School (Heard Museum, 2019).

At Carlisle, children had their hair cut—only done to Indians who were cowardly or grieving the loss of family members—leaving children to wonder about what they had done wrong and/or who had died in their families. Their Native clothing and beads—associated with spiritual practices—were replaced with uniforms and never returned. Native children were given Christian names, taught to rise early at 5 a.m., put on their uniforms, and march outdoors.

Children spent part of their days in the classroom, where boys would learn about agriculture and animal husbandry, and girls would learn about industrial arts. Harsh punishments were meted out for offenses such as speaking in Indian languages. Students completed heavy chores in school and outdoors (Reyhner & Eder, 2004; Spring, 1994).

Indigenous students were put on display at Carlisle, to show that this was the way to Americanize them. Towards the late 1800s, photography and the development of the film industry became additional sources utilized in creating campaigns about the benefits of forcing Native children into boarding schools to civilize them (Heard Museum, 2019). Pratt lobbied Congress to make his model the one used for educating American Indian children.

In his defense, Pratt's intentions were to develop a system where children would learn the white culture because he perceived that they could be taught, a perception not shared by everyone at the time (Child, 2018). Pratt also fought with the government to increase the amount of monies for providing food for the children, and got them involved with sports, intending to show the rest of the country how capable Indian people were. He made life-long friendships with many students and their families (Child, 2018).

When the government decided to establish boarding schools around the country, opportunities presented themselves for behaviors that would not be tolerated today, including rounding up Indigenous students to be taken by rail to boarding schools established around the country. The idea was to take children far away from their homes, leaving them in the company of other children not of their own tribes, therefore preventing them from speaking in their Native tongues or practicing any cultural rituals (Meriam, 1977).

In some cases, whites received bounties for Indian children they brought into train stations for transport to the schools in what has been dubbed "Kid Catching" (Merriam, 1977). Some children did not have a chance to say goodbye to their families, nor did their families know where they were. Christian names were given, and many records of children's original names and Tribal nations were lost, leaving graduates with no knowledge of where they belonged (Meriam, 1977).

For some Indigenous students, opportunities were provided through the schools that would not have happened otherwise. The Chilocco Boarding School established in Oklahoma in 1884 is one such example (Lomawaima, 1994). While run in much the same way as others, there was communication with Native families. Students ended up making friends for life, and a few students found ways far from prying eyes to practice some of their cultural rituals. In the one-hundred years the school operated, we can see the beginnings of a pan-Indian movement that forged relationships with others of different Tribal nations and reinforced older relationships. This was done in spite of the agenda of the school administration (Lomawaima, 1994).

For others, the boarding school experiences were nightmares of starvation, degradation and despair, where Native children often contracted sicknesses and died, or committed suicide. They were buried in on-site graveyards, commonly without notifying their families. All kinds of abuses took place at multitudes of these schools, including authorities taking money for themselves that should have gone for students' welfare (Johansen, 2000; Meriam, 1977).

It is clear that there are mixed feelings regarding the boarding schools, and that there were mixed results. Some communities felt that the boarding schools benefited their children, while others abhorred the forced attendance at these schools. Child (2018) makes the case that the "boarding school" is really a metaphor for all of the efforts to assimilate Aboriginals, and of all the evil acts that were perpetrated against them:

> It makes sense to implicate boarding schools. Boarding school has become the most tangible symbol of widespread turmoil that sprang from the allotment and assimilation era; for some indigenous people boarding school may be the "mnemonic benchmark," or even an "aboriginal Auschwitz." . . . Boarding school history, like all of American Indian history, is also about agency, resistance, survival, and the sometimes heroic actions of people young and adult who had lost significant freedoms. Without that, as Basil Johnston suggests, there is no story. (Child, 2018, p. 53)

The Dawes Act

During the same period, the Dawes Act was passed February 8, 1887, in order to break up Tribal Indian land holdings and sell the "surplus" lands to white farmers and ranchers. Again, this was another example of breaking the treaties with Indigenous peoples who had been promised their land in perpetuity by government representatives. Each Native American adult was to receive 160 acres of land, with 80 acres given to each child on the reservations. Aboriginals who had not gotten the word of when to come to the Indian Agencies for land distribution lost their claims to any of the land that was being divided, creating more havoc on some reservations.

Needless to say, the unremitting attacks on Native lives, cultures, and languages contributed to the historical trauma that Indigenous people endured. When it became obvious that Aboriginal peoples were not going to disappear as foretold, the federal government realized their programs were not working to eliminate all Native peoples and cultures. Settlers continued to demand Indian land. In 1885, newspapers in Kansas still advertised bounties for "Redskin scalps," supposedly to discourage Apache warriors and to get them to agree to relocate on reservations (Moya-Smith, 2015).

The Meriam Report of 1928

In reality, there was very little academic learning going on at the majority of boarding schools. Children were being used only as labor to keep the schools going. The food offered was gruel and gravy, and provided little nutrition to growing bodies. The Outing Programs with non-Native families could last for several years and were more like free labor programs than learning programs. The poverty levels of graduates of these schools were extremely high (Meriam, 1977).

American Indian youth, some who had been forced to leave their families at age five and had not seen them until they were released from the schools at eighteen, could no longer communicate with their relatives as they did not speak their languages. They did not understand their Native cultures, which made them outsiders in their communities (Meriam, 1977).

Feelings of despair, loneliness, and desperation were common for graduates. They were neither Indian nor American in terms of their cultural affiliations. Some graduates where students were used primarily for labor still did not know English when they left the boarding schools, leaving them with communication problems in both worlds.

Countless boarding school graduates and others married out to non-Indians, though these marriages had begun early in the history of the country and been hidden from others (McGrath, 2015). Anti-miscegenation laws against interracial marriages were passed by states, and were either ignored or couples entered into common law marriages.

Enough instances of boarding school graduates living in abject poverty occurred that finally the government took notice in the late 1920s. An inquiry was commissioned and led by Lewis Meriam to investigate the effects of the boarding schools on Native American children. The report was scathing in its indictment of what had happened to children in Native communities, and how it contributed to the breakdown in Aboriginal families. There were reports of all types of physical abuse, emotional abuse, and other abuses of students while attending these boarding schools (Meriam, 1977; Johansen, 2000).

With Congressional hearings and publication of the Meriam Report (Meriam, 1977), it was determined that Day Schools be built on Indian reservations as an alternative to the boarding schools. The worst boarding schools were closed down; others remained open when there were few alternatives in terms of a public education system nearby that could take on the education of Native American students. Since segregation was still a part of American society at this time, the day schools for Indigenous students were segregated from local public schools.

The memory of this time in history is deeply etched on the American Indian collective consciousness. Even after the time when the Indian boarding schools were reformed, and some of the worst had been shut down, the idea of these schools was fearsome to Aboriginals.

Indian boarding schools from the 1930s on had to reflect more of what was happening in the rest of the country for education. There is still resentment toward "White man's education" on many reservations throughout the country today. Even in the day schools, though, Native American languages and practices were forbidden. Constant reminders of the boarding school days were embedded in Aboriginal students' psyche because of outlawing Native American religious practices, including naming ceremonies, and children themselves had been given European surnames which did not relate to their tribal ancestors.

The Influence of the Field of Anthropology on Indian Life and Education

At the same time this was going on with the boarding schools, Franz Boas from Germany began fieldwork among Canadian natives in 1883, and formulated a very different notion of Indigenous peoples than what was being touted in the Americas. At the beginning, his intention was to document the demise of all of these various cultures who shared some similarities but also many differences. Through his observations of Native Inuit people and meetings with other Canadian First Peoples, he diverged from the theory that Western Civilization was at the pinnacle of all civilizations. He developed a great respect for the Indigenous peoples (Biography.com Editors, 2014/2019).

Boas decided to move to the U.S. after one of his many trips to Canada, securing a position as a science editor, and continuing his interest in Aboriginal peoples. In 1896, he secured a position to lecture in the field of Anthropology at Columbia University, and three years later became the first professor of Anthropology there. Later, Columbia established the first department of Anthropology in the U.S. (Biography.com Editors, 2014/2019).

One of the challenges for ethnographers—anthropologists relying primarily on observations and interviews with those being studied—was to separate truth from fiction about Native peoples. Even so, some of the interpretations made by anthropologists were not neutral observations but were based on the particular Western-European middle- and upper-class biases of those doing the research. Boas created the idea of "Cultural Relativism": that anthropologists should not let contemporary ideas and cultures influence their interpretations of other groups, as happened frequently (Carr, 1996; Jacobs, 2012).

In other words, what humans did in one group to survive and which became part of their cultures must have had some purpose, perhaps one that has been forgotten or obscured. One area Boas and his followers overlooked in their studies, though, was that of racist ideologies held by others that negated the importance of Indigenous populations, that those of darker skin colors could not really have contributed information of value to humanity (Blackhawk, 2006).

That Boas's notions differed from those of other anthropologists is quite apparent when compared to the ideas formulated by Steward who followed him at Columbia. Julian Steward used the plight of the plains Shoshoni to expand his racist notions. These Shoshoni had little left and were starving from the land and game depletion by those who were emigrating to California. Steward used their plight to declare that all Indians were like the Shoshoni at the very earliest stage of civilization: that of the poorest hunter-gatherers (Blackhawk, 2006).

Steward took this opportunity to criticize Indigenous lifestyles and political structures to conclude that theirs was the most basic existence, and from this, created a hierarchy of cultural achievement based on the idea that ecology determined the cultures of Native American peoples. This provincial view was widely adopted by other ethnographers of the period. The Bureau of Indian Affairs (BIA) adopted Steward's position of different hierarchical levels of civilization and used it in dealings with American Indians (Blackhawk, 2006; Carr, 1996).

Realigning the Position of the BIA

Luckily, the ideas promoted by Boas, who was called "The Father of Modern Anthropology," and followers like Alice Fletcher, Mable Dodge Luhan, A. L. Kroeber, Ruth Benedict, and others, were becoming popularized by the turn of the 1800s. Even then, these scientists hoped to understand American Indians on their own terms, positioning them as co-creators of knowledge, though there were still Western influences in their interpretations (Carr, 1996).

The Meriam Report (Meriam, 1977) was very troubling to members of the BIA such as John Collier, the future Commissioner of Bureau of Indian Affairs in 1933. He was an acquaintance of Luhan's and spent some time at her ranch in New Mexico where she and others had relocated to "save the Indians." There were also those whose intentions were good in adopting American Indian children who were very poor or were orphaned; however, they raised these children in Western ways without any contact with their Natal groups, alienating them from their heritages (Adam & De Luzio, 2012).

Collier was influenced greatly by what he experienced in New Mexico, witnessing American Indians who were still struggling to survive amidst the pressure to assimilate (Carr, 1996; Smith, 2000). He became an advocate for Native American rights, and his influence changed much of the negative thought about the degradation and decline of Native populations as he adopted some of the ideas proposed by these intellectuals.

Mabel Dodge Luhan produced a series of articles and books, as well as unpublished manuscripts, on the Pueblo Indians. She held "salons" where she and other intellectuals could discuss what they learned about Native Americans, contrasting their lives with European Americans (Smith, 2000). A turning point concerning the view of non-Native Americans towards Aboriginals was coming; Indigenous peoples began to be viewed as true and good by the common man (Kuper, 1997).

In 1924, Native Americans were granted citizenship in the United States based on their sacrifices made in wars fought for the country, especially in World War I (Indian Citizenship Act, 1924). Yet, in some states Aboriginals were still not allowed to vote because states' make the determination of who is allowed to vote. Recognition of Indigenous contributions to the country were still far away, but this was the beginning of attitude change regarding overall perceptions of Native Americans. There were still problems in some areas of the country, but there was agreement that Indigenous Americans and those of other ethnicities, particularly Euro-Americans, could live together in peace in this country.

FORCES CHALLENGING NATIVE SOVEREIGNTY AND MOVEMENT FORWARD

We see from this chapter that there were tremendous forces aligned against Native Americans and their plight to remain connected to their homelands. These were the lands upon which their cultures, spirituality, and hearts were engraved. In the following chapter, we will address changes in attitudes toward Indigenous peoples; the Civil Rights Movement; the efforts of the federal government to eliminate poverty in this country; beginning efforts to incorporate culturally relevant/responsive teaching in educating Native American students; and the direction of Indigenous education during the latter part of the twentieth century.

REFERENCES

Adams, D. W. (1995). *Education for extinction: American Indians and the boarding school experience, 1875–1928*. Lawrence: University Press of Kansas.

Adams, D. W., & De Luzio, C. (2012). *On the borders of love and power: Family and kinship in the intercultural American Southwest*. Berkeley: University of California Press.

Are Bison an Endangered species? (2001, November 17). Fermilab Flora and Fauna Virtual Exhibit. Batavia, IL: Leon M. Lederman Science Education Center.Retrieved from https://ed.fnal.gov/entryexhibits/bison/endangered.html.

Berkhofer, R. F., Jr. (1978). *The White man's Indian: Images of the American Indian from Columbus to the present*. New York, NY: Vintage Books.

Biography.com Editors. (2014, April 2; 2019, July 26). Biography of Franz Boas. *The Biography.com website*. A & E Television Networks. Retrieved from https://www.biography.com/scientist/franz-boas.

Blackhawk, N. (2006). *Violence over the land: Indians and empires in the early American West*. Cambridge, MA: Harvard University Press.

Carr, H. (1996). *Inventing the American primitive: Politics, gender, and the representation of Native American literary traditions, 1789–1936*. New York, NY: New York University Press.

Cave, A. A. (2003). Abuse of power: Andrew Jackson and the Indian Removal Act of 1830. *Historian, 65* (6), 1130–53.

Child, B. J. (2018). The boarding school as metaphor. *Journal of American Indian Education, 57*(1), 37–57.

Davidson, L. (2012). *Cultural genocide*. New Brunswick, NJ: Rutgers University Press.

Duncan, D., & Burns, K. (1997). *Lewis & Clark: The Journey of the Corps of Discovery*. New York, NY: Alfred A. Knopf.

Eastman, C. A. (Ohiyesa). (1911). *The soul of the Indian: An interpretation*. Lincoln: University of Nebraska Press.

Heard Museum. (2019). *Remembering our Indian school days: The boarding school experience*. Exhibit. Phoenix, AZ: Author.

Indian Removal Act of 1830. U.S.C., Title 25, §174.

Indian Citizenship Act of 1924, Pub. L 68–175. U.S.C., Title 8, §1401b.

Jacobs, M. (2012). Breaking and remaking families: The fostering and adoption of Native American children in non-Native families in the American West, 1880–1940. In D. W. Adams &

C. De Luzio (Eds.), *On the borders of love and power: Family and kinship in the intercultural American Southwest* (pp. 19–46). Berkeley: University of California Press.

Johansen, B. E. (2000). Education: The nightmare and the dream. *Native Peoples Magazine, 13* (1), 10–20.

Josephy, A. M., Jr. (1991). *The Indian heritage of America* (Rev. Ed.). Boston, MA: Houghton Mifflin. (Original work published in 1968).

Kuper, A. (1997). *Invention of primitive society: Transformation of an illusion*. New York, NY: Routledge. (Original work published in 1988).

Lomawaima, K. T. (1994). *The called it Prairie Light: The story of the Chilocco Indian Boarding School*. Lincoln: University of Nebraska Press.

Madsen, B. D. (1980). *The Northern Shoshoni*. Caldwell, ID: Caxton Printers.

Madsen, B. D. (1986). *Chief Pocatello*. Caldwell, ID: Caxton Press.

Mann, C. C. (2005/2011). *1491: New revelations of the Americas before Columbus*. New York, NY: Random House, Inc.

McGrath, A. (2015). *Illicit love: Interracial sex and marriage in the United States and Australia*. Lincoln: University of Nebraska Press.

Meriam, L. (1977). The effects of the boarding schools on Indian family life: 1928. In S. Unger (Ed.), *Destruction of American Indian families*. New York, NY: Association on American Indian Affairs. (Original work published 1928.)

Moya-Smith, S. (2015, January 26). Seeking $250 reward, settlers hunted for "Redskin Scalps" during extermination effort. *Indian Country Today Media Network.com*. Retrieved from http://indiancountrytodaymedianetwork.com.

Nabovkov, P. (1978). Introduction to "The Treaty Trail." In P. Nabovkov (Ed.), *Native American testimony: An anthology of Indian and White relations, first encounter to dispossession* (pp. 147–52). New York, NY: Thomas Y. Crowell.

Pruca, F. P. (Ed.). (2000). *Documents of United States Indian Policy* (3rd ed.). Lincoln: University of Nebraska Press.

Pulliam, J. D. (1987). *History of education in America* (4th ed.). Columbus, OH: Merrill.

Rehyner, J. A., & Oyawin Eder, J. M. (2004). *American Indian education: A history*. Norman: University of Oklahoma Press.

Smith, S. L. (2000). *Reimagining Indians: Native Americans through Anglo eyes 1880–1940*. New York, NY: Oxford University Press.

Smits, D. D. (1994). The frontier army and the destruction of the buffalo: 1865–1883. *Western Historical Quarterly, 25* (3), 312–38.

Spring, J. (1994). *Deculturalization and the struggle for equality: A brief history of the education of dominated cultures in the United States*. New York, NY: McGraw-Hill.

Stannard, D. E. (1992). *American holocaust: The conquest of the New World*. New York, NY: Oxford University Press.

Walker, D. E., Jr. (1985). *Conflict and schism in Nez Perce acculturation: A study of religion and politics*. Moscow: University of Idaho Press.

Weatherford, J. (1988). *Indian givers: How the Indians of the Americas transformed the world*. New York, NY: Fawcett Columbine.

Wilson, J. (1998). *The earth shall weep: A history of Native America*. New York, NY: Grove Press.

Zinn, H. (1999). *A people's history of the United States*. New York, NY: HarperCollins.

Chapter Six

Twentieth-Century Change and Rising Native American Voices

In the four centuries since contact was made with Indigenous peoples in the Americas, various theories were proposed concerning their origins. For many at the time, the Bible held all of the answers to questions, and the idea was quickly disseminated that Indians must be part of the Lost Tribes of Israel, though a different and more inferior version (Sanders, 2015).

Some thought of Native Americans in terms of being Noble Savages, while others proclaimed them to be just plain savages. Contrary to these perceptions, Jefferson and many other members of the thinking public from the 1780s to 1830s believed that American Indians were the equivalent of Europeans (Berkhofer, 1978).

Propositions put forward in Europe after Darwin's 1859 publication of *On the Origin of Species by Means of Natural Selection, or the Preservation of Favoured Races in the Struggle for Life*, included that Native peoples must be of an inferior species of human beings. Indigenous peoples surely were not the equivalent of the strongest Europeans, who were set to inherit the earth as predicted by Darwin's theory of the "survival of the fittest" (Berkhofer, 1978).

In other words, many Euro-Americans could not decide who, indeed, Native Americans were or where they had come from; nevertheless, conjectures were made throughout the 1800s that the present conditions of Indigenous peoples represented the earliest conditions of primitive people, reflecting Steward's theory discussed previously. To support this theory, writers just had to fill in the gaps and put forth inferior Native practices to support their stories (Berkhofer, 1978).

In terms of the general public, the idea of "the Indian" was held up in contrast to the idea of the "white American" to assuage white guilt over the treatment of

Native peoples, and to allow atrocities to continue to be committed. The latter part of the 1800s was a period where the media constantly focused on Native peoples as backward, resistant to government influences to tame their wild characters. Supposed "battles"—euphemisms for outright efforts to exterminate Native nations—took place resulting in the massacres of hundreds of Native Americans at a time. California itself had five major massacres of Native nations, activity that had increased with the discovery of gold at Sutter's Mill in 1848.

Treaties with California Indians were locked in a drawer before they could be ratified by Congress because of the pressures put on the U.S. Senate by the Senators and governor of California at that time. Instead, the California legislature made it legal to hire Aboriginals as farm and ranch hands, housemaids and servants, and enabled the kidnapping of Native American children for sale as labor without any repercussions. Meanwhile, the killing of American Indians went on without trials or punishments against the white killers. This went on unheeded well into the twentieth century (Chavers, 2012).

The media was focused on giving vivid descriptions of American Indians either as courageous defenders of their people or as the enemies—mostly the latter—attacking white settlers only to be defeated by the "good guys," the white armies and settlers. Over 90 percent of the thirty thousand books published about Indians have been authored by non-Natives, the majority since the latter part of the 1800s and through the twentieth century (Fixico, 1997).

Films made about Indians were usually about the reoccurring battles between American Indians and settlers (Fixico, 1997). When television became a reality in the homes of most Americans during the 1940s and 1950s, cowboy and Indian programs became a standard, with of course everyone, including Indigenous children, wanting to be the cowboys who were always the "winners."

Realizing the diminishing numbers of American Indians toward the end of the 1800s, and with the thought that Native peoples were dying out, some expressed a type of nostalgia at this thought. They felt that there needed to be records made of these people who once occupied the entire hemisphere. The Bureau of American Ethnology was founded in 1879 by the government to preserve some of the literature and histories of Native peoples. This included pieces of "oral texts that were transcribed, recontextualized, edited and used as evidence for particular anthropological theories and for Western ends" (Carr, 1996).

"American primitivism" was invented as a result of these efforts. The people who interviewed Native Americans interpreted what they were hearing through their Western lens of understanding, concluding that these Indigenous peoples must be naturalists, relying on physical reality rather than having any higher philosophical thinking powers. They did not take into consideration that these cultures had been virtually destroyed by pestilence and through governmental actions taken to segregate their nations. The result was a narrative molded for Western minds. These perceptions about Indigenous peoples cloud Euro-American thinking even to this day and must be investigated as to the degree of truth they contain (Kuper, 1997).

BEGINNING OF THE TWENTIETH CENTURY AND CHANGING THE NARRATIVE

> The white man does not understand the Indian for the reason that he does not understand America. He is too far removed from its formative processes. The roots of the tree of his life have not yet grasped the rock and soil. The white man is still troubled with primitive fears; he still has in his consciousness the perils of this frontier continent, some of its fastnesses not yet having yielded to his questing footsteps and inquiring eyes. He shudders still with the memory of the loss of his forefathers upon its scorching deserts and forbidding mountain-tops. The man from Europe is still a foreigner and an alien. And he still hates the man who questioned his path across the continent. (Luther Standing Bear, 1973, p. 307)

One of the results of the boarding school movement was the introduction of American Indians to those from other Native nations as mentioned previously. This led to cross-fertilization of ideas for some students, forging bonds that would endure even after leaving the schools (Child, 2018). Several students went on to be recognized by the general public, one of them being the great athlete Jim Thorpe—Wa Tha Huch, or Bright Path—the ingenious football hero from Carlisle who would go on to win Olympic medals in Sweden in 1912. He played professional baseball with both the New York Giants and the Boston Braves, as well as professional football. Thorpe was of Sauk and Fox, Potawatomi, Kickapoo, Menominee, Irish, and French ancestry (Barnes, 2010).

Luther Standing Bear was another success. He was Brulé Sioux and returned to his reservation to help with the school there. Standing Bear wrote articles, essays, and four autobiographical books, hoping to confront the prejudices toward Native Americans in his day. He advocated for Indigenous rights as members of American society (Barnes, 2010).

Will Rogers (1879–1935), of Cherokee descent and from Oklahoma, was one of the American Indians who had survived the attempts to deculturalize him in schools, becoming adept at navigating both the dominant culture and his Native community. Rogers was the son of a prominent Cherokee politician, was raised in the Cherokee nation, and drew on his Native heritage as part of his way to educate Americans about "modern" Indians (Ware, 2015).

Rogers was able to do this while unapologetically insisting that people knew who he was—the Cherokee kid who became famous as a comedian, actor, political pundit, and journalist. He traditionally introduced himself in terms of his tribal ties with the Cherokee Nation and underscored the Native American influence on U.S. popular culture. In the 1920s and 1930s, Rogers starred in nearly seventy movies, hosted a regular radio show, and penned more than four thousand syndicated columns for newspapers (Ware, 2015).

"Rogers was, to put it lightly, a Cherokee who carried substantial cultural capital in the United States during the first half of the twentieth century" (Ware, 2015, p. 2). Rogers considered himself a dual citizen of both the Cherokee Nation and the United States and used the technology of the dominant culture to demonstrate cultural survival and endurance for the American public.

Native American Intellectuals Making a Difference

In 1911, the Society of American Indians was formed by a group of American Indian scholars who came together to combat prejudice and racism by educating the public about the achievements of American Indians. Among this group were Charles A. Eastman (Santee), Arthur Parker (Seneca), Carlos Montezuma (Yavapai), Charles E. Daganett (Peoria), Gertrude Simmons Bonin (Yankton), and Minnie Kellogg (Oneida). All these individuals were strong writers who published widely. Some were for complete assimilation while others were not, but together they made their voices representing Indian country thunderous (Barnes, 2010).

Membership in the society was by individuals; they also allowed non-Native associate membership. Many tribes were represented in the society, and at one point in 1913, there were 619 memberships with 400 associate nontribal memberships. Conferences were held in which the current issues of the day were considered, one of which was the importance of U.S. citizenship for Native Americans. They worked closely with the BIA, as well with Boas and ethnographers mentioned in the previous chapter, to secure universal U.S. citizenship for Native peoples (Barnes, 2010).

Other inter-tribal organizations came into being as a result of these first activists: The All Pueblo Council (1922); The Grand Council Fire of Native Americans (1923); the Indian Association of America (1932); and the Indian Confederation of America (1933). Later, the National Congress of American Indians (1944) and the Red Power Movement of the 1950s, as well as others all came together to advocate for the rights of American Indians and ensuring their success economically as well as in life. They vehemently disclosed their concerns about education, health, and living conditions for Aboriginals in the United States (Barnes, 2010).

Education for Native American Students in the Post-Meriam Era

Traditionally, Native American children were taught by using the whole environment as a "classroom" (Pewewardy, 1994). Tribal members would teach children skills or information, and then the children would be expected to practice what they learned until they had perfected the skill or could relay information accurately. There were no tests, and children waited until they had mastered the material before giving demonstrations to adults (Pewewardy, 1994). Demonstrations included actual experiences such as accompanying an adult to gather roots and being able to identify what they were and what medicinal purpose they were used for (R. Walema, 2009, personal communication).

Education for Native Americans did improve during the 1930s and 1940s. Henry Roe Cloud—a Winnebago who had received a master's degree in Anthropology from Yale University—and W. Carson Ryan Jr. wrote the section that dealt with Indian education in the Meriam Report (1928). Their conclusions included that education provided for Indigenous students must match their interests, especially in the area of reading materials (Rehyner, 2012).

Additionally, Roe Cloud and Ryan advocated for progressive education as conceptualized by John Dewey. This education would be rooted in experiential activities planned to develop Native American students' cognitive abilities, similar to traditional Indigenous learning activities. Planned learning outcomes guided activities based on the knowledge needed for children at different developmental stages (Rehyner, 2012).

This was a first step toward what we now call culturally relevant/responsive teaching, or pedagogy, for American Indian students. Workshops and institutes were held during the summers by the Indian Service's education department to assist teachers in developing materials that would be effective for their students (Rehyner, 2012).

Ideally, Indian education was supposed to be a combination of academics and vocational training. Again, that was not always the case, though Aboriginal children fared better in some schools than others. The Johnson-O'Malley Act was passed in 1934 to provide monies to school districts for Indigenous children attending local schools. However, these funds were not monitored well and became incorporated into general school district revenue funds (Stahl, 1979).

Day Schools for Aboriginals were segregated from schools serving white students. The conditions in these schools were not as good as in neighboring schools. While teachers were mandated to attend to Native American student learning styles to assist them in being successful in their studies, cultural and language factors were ignored. Students still had their mouths washed out with lye soap when they spoke any "Indian."

Boarding schools were still operating during this time, as well as BIA schools, which basically constituted a fifty-first state in terms of regulations for K–12 education (St. Germain, 2000). The Bilingual Education Act was passed in 1934—and continues to be amended—which ended repression of Native languages, though the goal was to teach English more intensely to Indigenous children. Because this was the era of recovery following the Great Depression, the School Lunch Indemnity Plan was passed in 1943 and the National School Lunch Act in 1946 to ensure that all students had the nourishment they needed during the day to learn (Stahl, 1979).

The majority of teachers outside of the Indian Service were not trained to teach Native American students. Consequently, education was presented from a dominant-culture viewpoint. Many times, the teachers who were hired to teach Indigenous students were not of the highest quality, because it was considered a job only for the most unsatisfactory or youngest teachers.

The same struggles faced by African Americans in the South were faced by Native Americans in the West where signs proclaiming "No dogs or Indians allowed" were posted in store windows; Indians had to drink from different water fountains than whites; and they had to swim in different public swimming areas (D. McArthur, personal communication, 1995). These social factors could not help but influence Native Americans' views of themselves as "less than" those of the dominant culture.

Native American Rights to Sovereignty

With the passage of the Indian Reorganization Act (IRA) in 1934, not only could Tribal nations have their own sovereign governments, but they were accorded other rights that formerly had been handled only by the BIA (Barnes, 2010). After World War II, the United Nations proclaimed that Indigenous peoples around the world had basic human rights, including the right to self-determination. Though nothing changed immediately, gradually the federal government did begin to make some changes in relationships with Native American peoples.

This act included the right to determine who would qualify to be members of particular Tribal nations, based on a person's "blood quantum," a practice begun by the government during the 1700s and that continues to this day. It was believed that the determination of one's ethnicity was carried in the blood. Consequently, the amount of degree of American Indian "blood quantum" determines whether an individual can be enrolled in a particular Tribal nation (Sheffield, 1997).

For most Tribal nations, enrollees must have at least one-quarter Indian ancestry (or blood). In some cases, as with some of the Pueblos, the requirement is one-half Indian ancestry.

American Indians carry a Certificate of Degree of Indian Blood, usually referred to as their CDIB (Snipp, 2000). However, this enrollment by blood quantum is causing more difficulties today as American Indian populations are growing.

BACKWARD JOURNEYS—TERMINATION, RELOCATION, AND SPECIAL EDUCATION

Just when it appeared that the government was ready to accept sovereign Tribal nations and work as coequals with them, Congress began a program of terminating them in 1945 (Sheffield, 1997). The Termination Act of 1953 severed relationships with 109 Tribal nations (Termination Policy 1953–1968) and ended the trust protection of their lands (American Indian Urban Relocation, n.d.). In addition, funding for education of Native children that was now supposed to become the duty of state governments did not come to fruition, leaving many Native American children without schools to attend.

Many more Tribal nations were set for termination when there were protests by American Indians against these actions beginning in the 1950s with the Red Power movement (American Indian Movement, 1998). There are still Tribal nations that are trying to regain their sovereign nation status, though the process is very costly. That is why the number of federally recognized Tribal nations is continually being adjusted.

Simultaneously, after World War II numerous American Indians and Alaska Natives who had served in the military wanted to live in other areas of the country rather than being confined on their reservations. An experiment of "relocating" Native Americans to urban settings took place as discussed previously. Not only did the government want to do this as a way to continue the assimilation process, but with the intent of eventually completing the process of severing all Tribal nation relationships, therefore abrogating treaties with Native nations (Wax, 1971). This was not a goal stated aloud for the program but became obvious as the program continued throughout the years of its operation along with termination procedures.

The Indian Relocation Act was passed in 1956. While the government set up so-called support centers for Indians who were relocating, these centers were seriously underfunded and closed without being able to entirely fulfill their promises to provide assistance to Native Americans coming into the cities. There were Native Americans who became homeless and then had no way to return to their reservations as a result. Some Indigenous people remained in the cities and tried to find work while others became drifters.

Native people experienced prejudices at their places of work or were attacked physically on the streets. To hide their identities, nothing was discussed at home except work and school. Numerous children did not learn about their Indian heritage and little, if any, time was spent traveling back to reservations (Gonzales, 2001; Jackson, 2001).

With both of these efforts, relocation and termination, suddenly Indigenous students were becoming part of public schools in greater numbers. In the case of urban areas, they were placed in school systems that hadn't had American Indians or Alaska Natives in the past. Some urban Indians did grow up knowing about their heritages, and while they could show outward signs of Indianness, they did not necessarily know or understand their cultures, languages, mythologies, or traditions.

Travel was difficult and costly at this juncture, and long-distance telephone conversations were rare. As a result, a type of common "pan-Indianness" developed in some urban areas, a sort of extension of the movement which had begun during the boarding school days (Strauss & Valentino, 2001).

PREPARING EDUCATORS FOR TEACHING ALL STUDENTS

Preparation of potential teachers in the United States from 1839 to 1940 took place in Normal Schools around the country. The emphasis of these programs was on practical education training which took place over two years. Administrators were typically teachers who were thought to be able to handle older students and budgets but did not necessarily have advanced training. The majority of these facilities closed in the early 1940s, though some closed later when teacher preparation programs moved into universities granting four-year degrees (Levine, 2011).

Teachers who received their education from Normal Schools were still teaching through the 1980s, depending on the state from which they received their licensure. With little training in pedagogy provided, teachers persisted in teaching the way they had been taught with an emphasis on memorization and recitation.

There was not an emphasis on experiential learning or on connecting learning to students' cultural capital, or what they had learned from their families and communities. Most of the education in mathematics and other areas was abstract, not connected to students' real worlds. There was not an emphasis on teaching ethnically diverse populations or exceptional student populations. This situation only enhanced the dropout problem for Native Americans and other students.

During the Depression in the 1930s, compulsory education laws—enacted to keep students in school during the 1800s and 1900s mainly as a way to keep children from entering the workforce—raised the age of school leaving to 16 instead of 14. For the first time, children who previously would have dropped out of school earlier due to lack of academic achievement or lack of reading skills were forced to stay in the school systems. Teachers were unprepared to teach all of these children in their classrooms.

AMERICAN CIVIL RIGHTS ERA AND NEW LEGISLATION IMPACTING AMERICAN INDIAN EDUCATION

I grew up in upstate New York, Greenfield Center. I was raised by my Indian side of my family, my maternal grandparents. My great-grandfather had earned money to purchase land by joining the Irish Brigade during the Civil War. After the battle of Gettysburg, American Indians were recruited to fill the ranks since so many soldiers had died. Lots of Abenakis were recruited and joined the military.

My Grandparents lived/worked in the area of Saratoga Springs. The springs were well known by Natives. My grandparents were involved in traditional basket making and sold the baskets to tourists as did other Natives. . . . Many Abenaki refer to themselves as French Canadian, as did Jesse Bowman (my grandfather) because of the prejudice against Indians in this area. During the Census, it was common for many Indians around Indian Lake to say they were white and other family members to say they were Indian or Abenaki. In fact, many Abenaki became models or worked in the movie industry before the industry moved to California.

There is still so much going on in New York as in other places around [the country]. Indians are loved in absentia. [For instance, I attended schools in the 1950s], and the superintendent stated that, "Everybody knows those people aren't Indians and I'm not letting those savages into my schools!"

> There were challenges [in school] in terms of having people assume that they know who you are before you can prove yourself. For example, for me, the way one teacher taught math was boring. His wife taught social studies, and I naturally gravitated to the social studies. I did well in this area. One day, the math teacher said to me in the hallway, "My wife tells me you're not an idiot after all!"
>
> Students live up or down to the expectations of their teachers. An assumption was made by the math teacher that since I wasn't performing well in math, that I couldn't learn anything at all. —Joseph Bruchac, Nulhegan Abenaki (Interviewed by B. J. Klug, September 2010)

Segregation was still alive and well when Mr. Bruchac attended school. His is only one case of how Native American students were treated in schools at the time. Then in middle 1950s and 1960s a period of activism for American Indians began with the Red Power movement. The National Indian Youth Council aligned itself with African Americans and the Black Power movement. This was the first time that American consciousness was substantially raised about the conditions of Native America around the country (American Indian Movement, 1998).

The year 1954 marks the beginnings of radical changes regarding the education of ethnically diverse populations in this country. In that year, *Brown v. the Board of Education* overturned *Plessy v Ferguson*, the 1896 ruling that separate schools for teaching ethnically diverse populations were permitted as long as students received equal educations.

With *Brown*, the wealth of testimony concerning the poor conditions and materials used in separate schools for children of color demonstrated quite clearly that separate was not equal.

Schools were ordered to desegregate their students, a situation for which the majority of white teachers had not been adequately prepared. Some school districts (and even some districts today) completely ignored the order to desegregate their schools, especially in the southern states. As the era of civil rights drew nearer, and access to televised programming became more of a reality in everyday households, for the first time many white households witnessed what was really going on in the treatment of ethnically diverse groups of people around the country.

Education for All

In previous eras, those who were mentally or physically impaired were kept at home instead of going to school. Since 1910, parents had drawn attention to the need for schooling for their mildly mentally retarded children. In 1958, the Education of Mentally Retarded Children Act was finally passed, with funding for teachers to learn how to educate those with special needs (Education of All Handicapped Children Act of 1975; History of Special Education Law, 2003). Those severely mentally impaired were still excluded from local schools. Innumerable children of color, including Native Americans, were consigned to these classes.

This was due more to cultural and English dialect mismatches with students' new schools and teachers rather than a lack of mental abilities. White teachers were not accustomed to educating children who had obvious physical or mental disabilities, nor were they prepared to teach children of different cultural backgrounds. The assumption that anyone could learn the standard curriculum if they were intelligent enough led to false conclusions that those who had difficulties must be mentally impaired.

> [I was in] a public rural school with only a few Indians, and this is a funny story. So one day in fifth grade the principal of our school came, there was myself and another Indian from [the reservation] named Kevin, one of my best friends. [The principal] goes, "you two come with me" and I thought uh, oh, we are in trouble again. And so he took us to a room and said, "You two are now in special education." And I said, "Well what does that mean?" [He said], "Well you are going to be pulled from the school and work with this new teacher, and she [is] a wonderful lady." And I said "Okay," but I didn't know what special education meant, but I said okay....
>
> So two years go by and I am having a talk with my mom and I said yeah I am doing this and that [as well as teaching other students]. And she said, "Where is that at?" and I said, "It's in this class called Special Education" and she goes, "What does that mean?" and I go, "I don't know; it's where they put me." So she said, "Well I better go down to that school and see what that means."
>
> And so she has an appointment with the principal and says, "What does this mean, Special Education?" "Well they have been pulled here," [says the principal]. She asks, "But why?" They couldn't give [her] a good reason. But the reasoning was this, because you fit a profile and you were round and brown, now you are going to be a Special Education person. That's what it was. Just to fill some numbers for the school and my mom didn't take kindly to that. And so, [the principal] said, "Okay, okay we goofed up there. We will test people as we are supposed to do, okay?" —Ed Galindo, Yaqui (Interviewed by B. J. Klug, September, 2010)

Civil Rights and Education

Red Power and Black Power movements began coalescing in the 1950s, and by the middle of the decade were generating a great deal of attention. Martin Luther King led the first nonviolent demonstration for civil rights in 1955. It was apparent that political action must be taken in order to change the conditions in this country to fully realize equality for all of the citizens of this nation.

This was a time of great upheaval in the country with powerful élitists trying to maintain the status quo even in the face of the dire conditions for ethnically diverse populations. During the Kennedy administration (1961–1963), close attention began to be paid to the plight of the poor in the United States, and the connections between low-income levels and academic achievement.

Robert F. Kennedy, as the U.S. Attorney General, toured Indian reservations throughout the country, and made a speech to Native American leaders calling their treatment a "national disgrace." He made public in the media the treatment of Indigenous peoples, and the deplorable conditions found on the reservations, which were supposed to be under the trust provisions of the government. Robert Kennedy then created a Senate Subcommittee on Indian Education and served as its chair (Widmere, 2018).

President Kennedy supported making changes in laws to create more equality in wealth and power around the country, engaging Native Americans and African Americans. Sadly, he did not live to see these young efforts make a difference.

Lyndon Johnson took over the reins from the Kennedy administration after Kennedy's assassination. Johnson's War on Poverty was introduced in his State of the Union Address on January 8, 1964. This legislation finally addressed the U.S. poverty rate of approximately 19 percent of the population. The Civil Rights Act was passed on July 2, 1964, outlawing discrimination based on race, color, religion, sex, or national origin.

Voter suppression—as well as segregated schools, places of business, and public accommodations—were all prohibited. School districts which had refused integration were threatened with the loss of federal funding if they did not commence to do so. This act, then, became responsible in large measure for the desegregation of a great number of school districts, especially in the South.

As a senator, Robert Kennedy continued to visit American Indian reservations and schools, again noting the inequities apparent in housing, education, and the failure of a high percentage of Native Americans to graduate from high school (Widmere, 2018). Congress began to pass a spate of legislation to address the inequalities in schools and the needs of Indigenous students. This was due to the federal government's efforts to positively affect education changes since state governments and local governments had been unable—and many times unwilling—to approve of the extra funding needed to bring education up to par in areas of high poverty (Glover, 1999). This legislation included passage of the Bilingual Education Act of 1965, though its intent was not on preserving students' languages but on teaching English to those who did not have any English, spoke limited English, or spoke dialects of English.

Congress has continued to pass or renew additional legislation for low-income education since the Civil Rights era. (A list of important legislation affecting Native American education can be found in Appendix A.) All these acts helped to address American Indian education by providing federal funding for school districts to teach underserved populations. Additional acts have passed specifically targeting American Indian/Alaska Native populations in this country.

The American Indian Movement (AIM; 1988) under Dennis Banks, Clyde Bellecourt, Edie Benton Benai, George Mitchell, Russell Means, and others used radical means to draw attention to the plight of urban Indians and of the conditions on reservations. The hated Termination Act of Tribal nation status ultimately ended in 1968 (Termination Policy 1953–1968, 1980).

A New Explanation for School Failure Arises

The Cultural Deficit Theory arose in the 1960s as psychologists and others determined that it was because of inferior ethnically diverse cultures that children were unable to master the standard school curriculum (Ausubel, 1966; Brophy, 1983). At that time, there were few who understood the impact of language and cultural differences—in addition to racism, classism, sexism, and socioeconomic status (SES)—and how those areas impacted children's understandings and success within the formal education system.

Instead of taking the time to assist students with their understandings of Standard English—now sometimes referred to as "school English"—educators assumed that ethnically diverse children must be of low intelligence. Thus, instead of challenging Native American students to see how much they could learn, they treated them as if they couldn't learn at all. In addition, the cultural reprimand of not making oneself look better than others was not understood by white teachers. When teachers called on Indigenous students' individually, many invariably gave the wrong answer so they would not look smarter than their peers.

This idea of Cultural Deficit was confirmed through administrations of IQ tests by white teachers and psychologists. The tests were written in Standard English (Rosenblatt, 1983). Many of these tests were given in schools where children were expected to read the entire test and answer the questions to determine what their IQ was compared to those of white student peers upon which the tests had been standardized. This complicated the situation for ethnically diverse students even more as they usually had not been taught the same way as white peers, spoke dialects in their homes and were not familiar with "school talk," and were not expected to be intelligent due to stereotypes and prejudices about low SES populations.

By the 1980s, this theory had largely run its course. Variations on this theme still reemerge and today are used to "explain" the differences in achievement test scores between high and low SES level students under the heading of the "Culture of Poverty" (Gorski, 2018). Unfortunately, low teacher expectations usually result in low achievement for all students.

This deficit model rests on the belief that there are differences in wants and goals between the rich and the poor of society. In effect, this mythology is a remnant of imperialism and is built on the very real class system that we choose not to acknowledge in this country. Here, we are supposed to have an equal chance of achieving dreams by overcoming obstacles (Gladwell, 2005; Gorski, 2010). However, systemic racism is still present in our society and rules the day for many ethnically diverse populations.

The Multicultural Education Movement

The curriculum used in schools throughout the country was finally examined and found to contain many of the country's biases and stereotypes about people of color (Banks, 1991; Gollnick & Chinn, 1990). While white European culture was praised, that of children of color was treated as not worthy of study. For American Indians, the typical description of them as savages, heathens, violent, cruel, unworthy occupants of this country was clearly displayed in textbooks, along with the also damaging stereotype of the Nobel Savage who gives way to "civilization" (Berkhofer, 1978).

With the country still experiencing many of the upheavals of the Civil Rights Movement, communities of color began demanding changes for the education of their children. Committees were formed to examine textbooks for biases and stereotypes, and this became one of the criteria for state adoption of textbooks for school districts. American Indians made known their goals for their children through the "Trail of Broken Treaties 20-Point Position Paper" published by the AIM in 1972. The American Indian Education Act of 1972 resulted from Robert Kennedy's detailing of conditions in schools and Indian Nation reservations throughout the country (Widmere, 2018).

In 1974–1975, the National Advisory Council on Indian Education was established (National Advisory on Indian Education, 1987). This group of distinguished American Indians called for more local and tribal control for education of Native students. Their goal was to focus on the unique cultural strengths and traditions found in Aboriginal students' communities. By incorporating these strengths in Native students' education, it was perceived that there would be more success for them in schools. The Indian Self-Determination and Education Assistance Act of 1975 resulted from the desires of the National Advisory Council (Deloria, 1974; St. Germaine, 2000).

Multicultural Education added to a dimension of awareness of accomplishments of people of color (primarily men) in the curriculum that had been missing previously. For Euro-Americans whose families had immigrated to the country in the 1800s, this information assisted in changing the perceptions of many. However, since the emphasis was more on heroes and a few sheroes, it did not change very much in the way of how schools approached teaching Native Americans and other students of color. The Multicultural Education Movement was also opposed by many conservatives in and out of government and in teacher education programs.

One outcome of Multicultural Education should be real change in our schools (Grant & Sleeter, 1999). Change will not come until there are opportunities for ethnically diverse populations to be able to work through the social reconstruction of their worlds. As Tozer, Violas, and Senese (1993) state, schools, by nature of their hierarchical organization, do not promote student introspection. One of the goals of education, then, should be to assist students with examining their own circumstances and setting goals for their own lives.

Looking beyond Hegemony in Schools

Critical Theory challenges the hegemony—or power—of the white, middle-class, Anglo-Saxon, Protestant culture to serve as the framework for schools, teaching, and curriculum. This theory acknowledges that children from ethnically diverse and lower socioeconomic communities may not be engaged in school or education because they are not represented in the materials they are reading or the information they are expected to learn. This leads to students questioning of what use school is to them, instead of engaging students with the learning process (Tozer, Violas, & Senese, 1993).

Critical theory allows an interrogation of the relationships between schools and students, which reflects differences between children's cultures and schools. It marks changes in blaming the students or their cultures for difficulties experienced in schools, and asks for solutions when there are mismatches between schools and cultures (Tozer, Violas, & Senese, 1993).

Cultural Difference Theory marks a first social change from the Cultural Deficit theories. It is premised on the legitimacy of incorporating the multiple perspectives of the diverse cultures in our nation into our educational systems. It allows information from the social sciences of anthropology, psychology, and linguistics to play a role in the education of all students in a way that respects cultural practices and outlooks. With Cultural Difference Theory, there is no one right way of thinking or analyzing curriculua or content.

Cultural Difference Theory recognizes that the learning styles, practices, and expressive manners of different cultures are just that: different (Henry & Pepper, 1990). Cultural Difference Theory allows teachers to be flexible in their approaches to teaching and learning in the classroom dependent upon student population (Tozer, Violas, & Senese, 1993).

The Native American Indian Languages Act of 1991 finally gave full recognition to the importance of teaching Native languages to students within public or BIA schools, providing a way to reconnect with Native cultures which were becoming threatened in the midst of the modern world. One of the fears of some American Indians, though, was that their languages, too, would become used as a tool against them by Euro-Americans.

THE SEESAW OF PROGRESSIVE AND CONSERVATIVE EDUCATION

Ethnically diverse groups of people gained more power in our society after the civil rights movement and have joined together in efforts to demand that schooling be offered to their children in respectful and dignified modes. By admitting that there is built-in bias in curriculum and the way schools operate, changes can be made for teaching children who are from involuntary, underrepresented populations. This movement has led the way toward the creation of teaching which incorporated cultural knowledge and ways of knowing for American Indian students (Klug & Whitfield, 2003). Culturally relevant teaching applies to both the context of teaching and the content to be learned in schools.

The 1980s and 1990s saw a return to conservativism promoted by the ideas that our schools were failing to hold a high place in education internationally as reported in the 1983 document *A Nation at Risk* (National Commission, 1983). This report claimed the United States was falling behind other countries in terms of the achievement and high school graduation rates especially in terms of ethnically diverse students. While we know now that this was a "manufactured crisis," as Berliner and Biddle (1995) had insisted all along, recently one of the most ardent supporters of the conservative movement to fix our so-called failing schools, Diane Ravitch (2020), has recanted her previous position.

What Ravitch (2020) uncovered in her recent educational research was a staged attack—accomplished by manipulating tests scores reported in the Commission's 1983 report—by corporate America and supporters of privatization, neo-liberalism (actually a return to the "good old days" before Civil Rights), and those who determined to do away with social justice actions in this country. Members of this club include the Koch brothers, the Dick and Betsy DeVos Foundation (Amway), the Walton family (Walmart), the Bill and Melinda Gates Foundation, the Chan-Zuckerberg Initiative, Michael Bloomberg, and a long list of other millionaires, billionaires, and trillionaires. Their interests include privatizing all education, having all charter schools, keeping teacher pay low, and destroying teacher unions (see Ravitch, 2020, pp. 27–51).

Movements such as "Back to Basics" and the "Standards" implementations were efforts purportedly to reorganize education along recommended lines of:

a. increasing the demands of schools and school hours;
b. having high expectations and more rigorous content;
c. increasing graduation rates;
d. making elementary school content more rigorous;
e. making teaching a more desirable career option and increasing the quality of teachers through standardized testing; and
f. rewarding good teachers (those whose students had higher test scores) by providing higher salaries to them.

The School Dropout Prevention and Basic Skills Improvement Act of 1990 was also passed with the idea that this legislation would ensure all graduates had basic reading and writing skills, but the focus on comprehension and application of those skills was not necessarily a given in the teaching of these "basic" skills.

Those teachers in schools where students had lower test scores, mainly children of color and low SES, would be eliminated from the pool of available teachers. The public was told that these were failing teachers. However, the goals listed were only shields for covert conservative and neo-liberal efforts to do away with public education.

Ravitch and Cody have co-founded the Network for Public Education (NPE) in an effort to join educators, other advocates for social justice and separation of church and state in public schools, and "resistors" in this movement to de-skill teachers, end the professionalism in teacher certification and careers, and end public education in this country. They are joined by other groups who oppose what is going on in the fight to keep our public schools in this country (Ravitch, 2020).

Concurrently there have been real, ongoing efforts to increase the success of American Indians and Alaska Natives in our schools since the release of the *Indian Nations at Risk* report in 1991. This real report identified difficulties still faced by Indigenous youth in our schools (Cahape & Howley, 1992). The authors set out goals to be reached by the year 2000 for parents, students, teachers, and communities in terms of the curricula used in education for Aboriginal youth, in addition to increasing graduation rates for Indigenous students by involving Native American communities in the schools.

Efforts to increase American Indian languages and cultures in schools, along with incorporating culturally relevant teaching, and research on positive contributors to Native American educational achievement will be topics presented in the next chapter. Educators have come a long way in understanding how important collaboration with diverse families and communities is in educating their children. Teachers' abilities "to create culturally responsive learning experiences, including choices of content, representations, and forms of discourse that connect to student experiences, will help [them] create bridges for students into academic material" (Horowitz, Darling-Hammond, & Bransford, 2005, p. 115).

REFERENCES

American Indian Movement (AIM). (1998). *A brief history of the American Indian Movement.* Retrieved from http://www.aimovement.org.

American Indian Urban Relocation. (n.d.). *Educator Resources.* Washington, DC: National Archives. Retrieved from https://www.archives.gov/education/lessons/indian-relocation.html.

Ausubel, D. P. (1966). Effects of cultural deprivation on learning patterns. In S. W. Webster (Ed.), *The disadvantaged learner: Knowing, understanding, educating* (pp. 251–57). San Francisco, CA: Chandler.

Banks, J. A. (1991). Multicultural literacy and curriculum reform. *Educational Horizons, 69* (3), 135–40.

Barnes, I. (2010). *The historical atlas of Native Americans.* New York, NY: Chartwell Books.

Berliner, D., & Biddle, B. J. (1995). *The manufactured crisis: Myths, fraud, and the attack on America's public schools.* New York, NY: Basic Books.

Berkhofer, R. F., Jr. (1978). *The White man's Indian: Images of the American Indian from Columbus to the present.* New York, NY: Random House.

Bilingual Education Act of 1965, 20 U.S.C. § 7401 *et seq.* (U.S.C. 2000).

Brophy, J. (1983). Research on the self-fulfilling prophecy and teacher expectations. *Journal of Educational Psychology, 75* (5), 631–61.

Carr, H. (1996). *Inventing the American primitive: Politics, gender, and the representation of Native American literary traditions, 1789–1936.* New York, NY: New York University Press.

Cahape, P., & Howley, C. B. (Eds.). (1992). *Indian Nations at risk: Listening to the people— Summaries of papers commissioned by the Indian Nations at Risk task Force of the U.S. Depart-*

ment of Education. Appalachia Educational Laboratory, Charleston, WV: ERIC Clearinghouse on Rural Education and Small Schools.

Chavers, D. (2012). Leadership in Indian education. In B. J. Klug (Ed.), *Standing together: American Indian education as Culturally Responsive Pedagogy* (pp. 171–82). Lanham, MD: Rowman & Littlefield.

Child, B. (2018). The boarding school as metaphor. *Journal of American Indian Education, 57* (1), 37–57.

Civil Rights Act of 1964, 42 U.S.C. § 1901 et seq (U.S.C. 2000).

Deloria, V., Jr. (Ed.). (1974). *Indian education confronts the seventies. Volume No. 4: Technical Problems in Indian Education.* (ERIC Reproduction Service No. ED 113084).

Education of All Handicapped Children Act of 1975, 20 U.S.C. § 1400 et seq. (U.S.C. 2000; Public Law 94–142).).

Education of Mentally Retarded Children Act of 1958 (Public Law 85–926).

Fixico, D. L. (1997). *Rethinking American Indian history.* Albuquerque, NM: University of New Mexico Press.

Gladwell, M. (2005). *Blink: The power of thinking without thinking.* New York, NY: Little, Brown, and Company.

Gollnick, D., & Chinn, P. C. (1990). *Multicultural education in a pluralistic society* (3rd ed.). Columbus, OH: Merrill.

Glover, K. D. (1999). *Congress back then: The lost War on Poverty.* Retrieved from http://www.intellectual capital.co/issue316/item7104.asp.

Gonzales, A. A. (2001). Urban (trans)formations: Changes in the meaning and use of American Indian identity. In S. Lobo & K. Peters (Eds.), *American Indians and the urban experience* (pp. 169–85). New York, NY: Altamira Press.

Gorski, P. C. (2010). *Unlearning the deficit theory and the scornful gaze: thoughts on authenticating the class discourse in education.* EdChange.Org. Washington, DC: George Mason University. Retrieved from http://www.EdChange.org.

Gorski, P. (2018). The myth of the Culture of Poverty. *Educational leadership, 65* (7), 32–36.

Grant, C. A., & Sleeter, C. E. (1999). *Making choices for multicultural education: Five approaches to race, class, and gender* (3rd ed.). New York, NY: John Wiley & Sons.

Henry, S. T., & Pepper, F. C. (1990). Cognitive, social, and cultural effects of Indian learning style: Classroom implications. *Journal of Educational Issues of Language Minority Students, 7.* (Special Issue).

History of Special Education Law. (2003, June). Handout. Department of Education, University of Kentucky. Retrieved from http://www.uky.edu/~kmkram1/eds413/eds515.

Horowitz, F. D., Darling-Hammond, L., & Bransford, J. (with Comer, J., Rosebrock, K., & Rust, F.). (2005). Educating teachers for developmentally appropriate practice. In L. Darling-Hammond & J. Bransford (Eds.), *Preparing teachers for a changing world: What teachers should learn and be able to do* (pp. 88–185). San Francisco, CA: Jossey-Bass.

Indian Education Act of 1972, 20 U.S.C. § 3385 *et seq.* (U.S.C. 2000).

Indian Nations at Risk Task Force. (1991, October). *Indian Nations at risk: An educational strategy for action* (Final Report of the Indian Nations at Risk Task Force). Washington, DC: U.S. Department of Education. Retrieved from https://narf.org/nill/resources/education/reports/nationsatrisk.pdf.

Indian Reorganization Act of 1934, 25 U. S. C. § 461 *et seq.* (U.S.C. 2000).

Jackson, D. D. (2001). "This hole in our heart": The urban-raised generation and the legacy of silence. In S. Lobo & K. Peters (Eds.), *American Indians and the urban experience* (pp. 189–206). New York, NY: Altamira Press.

Klug, B. J., & Whitfield, P. T. (2003). *Widening the Circle: Culturally relevant pedagogy for American Indian children.* New York, NY: RoutledgeFalmer.

Kuper, A. (1997). *Invention of primitive society: Transformation of an illusion.* New York, NY: Routledge. (Original work published in 1988).

Levine, A. (2011). The new normal of teacher education. *The Chronicle of Higher Education.* Retrieved from https://www.chronicle.com/article/The-New-Normal-of-Teacher/127430.

National Commission on Excellence in Education. (1983). *A Nation at Risk: The Imperative for Educational Reform. A Report to the Nation and the Secretary of Education United States Department of Education.* Retrieved from https://edreform.com/wp-content/uploads/2013/02/A_Nation_At_Risk_1983.pdf.

Pewewardy, C. D. (1994). Culturally responsible pedagogy in action: An American Indian magnet school. In E. R. Hollins, J. E. King, & W. C. Hayman (Eds.), *Teaching diverse populations: Formulating a knowledge base* (pp. 77–92). New York, NY: State University of New York Press.

Ravitch, D. (2020). *Slaying Goliath: The passionate resistance to privatization and the fight to save America's public schools.* New York, NY: Alfred A. Knopf.

Rehyner, J. (2012). A history of American Indian culturally sensitive education. In B. J. Klug (Eds), *Standing together: American Indian education as Culturally responsive pedagogy* (pp. 25–36). Lanham, MD: Rowman & Littlefield.

Rosenblatt, L. M. (1983). *Literature as Exploration.* New York, NY: Modern Language Association of America.

Sanders, R. (2015). *Lost tribes and promised lands: The origins of American racism.* Brattleboro, VT: Echo Pointe Books. (Originally published in 1978).

School Dropout Prevention and Basic Skills Improvement Act of 1990, Public Law 101–600; H.R. 5140.).

Sheffield, G. K. (1997). *The arbitrary Indian: The Indian Arts and Crafts Act of 1990.* Norman, OK: University of Oklahoma Press.

Snipp, C. M. (2000). *Some alternate approaches to the classification of American Indian and Alaska Natives.* Paper prepared for Executive Order 13096 National American and Alaska Native Education Research Agenda Conference, Albuquerque, New Mexico.

St. Germaine, R. D. (2000). *A chance to go full circle: Building on reforms to create effective learning.* Paper prepared for the National American Indian and Alaska Native Education Research Agenda Conference, Albuquerque, NM.

Stahl, W. K. (1979). The U.S. and Native American Education: A survey of federal legislation. *Journal of American Indian Education, 18* (3), pp. 28–32.

Standing Bear, L. (1973). What the Indian means to America (1933). In W. Moquin & C. Van Doren, *Great documents in American Indian history* (pp. 306–308). New York, NY: Praeger.

Strauss, T., & Valentino, D. (2001). Retribalization in urban Indian communities. In S. Lobo & K. Peters (Eds.), *American Indians and the Urban experience* (pp. 85–94). New York, NY: Altamira Press.

Termination Policy 1953–1968. (1980). Partnership with Native Americans. Retrieved from http://www.nativepartnership.org.

Tozer, S. E., Violas, P. C., & Senese, G. (1993). *School & society: Educational practice as social expression.* New York, NY: McGraw-Hill.

Wax, M. (1971). *Indian Americans: Unity and diversity.* Englewood Cliffs, NJ: Prentice-Hall.

Ware, A. M. (2015). *The Cherokee Kid: Will Rogers, Tribal identity, and the making of an American icon.* Lawrence: University Press of Kansas.

Widmere, T. (2018, April 16). Why Robert Kennedy went to Pine Ridge. Opinion. *New York Times.* Retrieved from https://www.nytimes.com/2018/04/16/opinion/robert-kennedy-pine-ridge.html.

Chapter Seven

Indigenous Families, Communities, and Ways of Learning

The Heart of Resiliency for Native Students

In the period of the late twentieth century and early twenty-first century, several developments occurred partly as a backlash to Civil Rights and Multicultural Education (McLean, 2017). A conservative movement within the federal government was underway, promoting the idea that our students in the United States were falling behind, not keeping up with the rest of the world, due to a lowering of standards in our nation's schools.

We know that this was a fabricated crisis, an attempt to keep the official cannon of public school education unchanged. Corporations became involved in the discussion of what they wanted to see in future workers, noting that many of their current employees were not reading or had poor skills in mathematics, delivering the idea that the schools must move "back to basics" (Ravitch, 2020).

In switching the emphasis to what industry required for their workers, or only educating students for employment and training, part of the dominion over education was given over to large corporations. These corporations, now seen as taxpayers contributing to the funding of education, desired that the focus change to outcomes in education, not inquiry. They did not want schools to operate in ways that encouraged students to question what they were learning nor the official history of the country (the hegemonic narrative) presented in the approved textbooks for public school use (Tozer, Violas, & Senese, 1993).

Fear of not keeping up with other industrialized nations in the world took hold of the public and in schools, even though information regarding who was tested in other countries (primarily the top students) was being withheld from the U.S. media and public. In the United States, all students are tested from the highest to the lowest achievers. A false perception of what was occurring in our American schools was created by reporting and averaging all of the test scores to "prove" that our test scores were lower and that schools were "failing" (Testing, 2020).

Statistically speaking, the "average" for achievement test results is different depending on when the tests are taken and who is taking them. The statistical bell curve is utilized to determine the average or the middle range where the majority of student populations taking the standardized assessments score at any given point in time. Then some score both above the average and below the average on the assessments. When you are talking about human beings and testing, there are many influences on students' test scores. Educational testing is different than assessing the quality of a line of products in an industry.

Standardized tests in this country reflect the white, Anglo-Saxon middle- and upper-middle classes, the standardized English language, and the knowledge supposedly acquired by these students at different grade levels. Indigenous students who are middle and upper-middle class tend to score similarly to those for whom the assessments were standardized. For those Aboriginal students living in isolated areas of the country, poverty, health, living conditions, social status, understanding of the use of Standard English, and lack of experiential knowledge many middle and upper-middle class students have acquired, all have influences on test results. For example, a question regarding instruments typically played in a symphony could be answered by many lower-middle- and upper-middle-class dominant culture students, but may not be answered by Native students. However, a question easily answered by the majority of Indigenous students living on reservations about the composition of an Indian flute would be failed by many non-Indigenous students. Questions about tracking animals during hunting season, an activity that many Indigenous children are engaged in, are not usually part of achievement tests although these are life skills just as important as learning about finances to other populations.

UNCOVERING THE HIDDEN POCKETS OF POVERTY IN THE NATION

Up until the War on Poverty in the 1960s and the Civil Rights Act of 1964, schools had always been under "local" control. That changed with the pieces of legislation such as the Elementary and Secondary Education Act of 1965 and its several later iterations, which increased federal funding for schools, mainly in the area of compensatory or remedial programs for students who were having difficulty in reading and mathematics.

Because people are usually concerned with what is occurring in their local communities, the poverty in this country came as a surprise to many. The concept of poverty previously for many in the middle class related primarily to growing up during the Great Depression. The idea that there were large areas of poverty everywhere—and educational opportunities for children were not the same as for middle-class populations—was shocking and inconceivable.

In addition, the idea that those who were in poverty brought this condition on themselves due to their laziness or stupidity was widely believed, an idea that heralds back to the Puritan values incorporated in our schools. The efforts to create more equity in education did shine a light on the disparities in low-income schools due to lack of funding, a dearth of textbooks and other instructional materials available, as well as low educational achievement and high school graduation rates. Schools for Native Americans in impoverished communities were at the bottom of all areas.

Focusing on New Psychological Theories of Learning

Many individuals in psychology, special education, linguistics, and literacy became involved in exploring how children learn, moving away from the psychological behaviorist theories of Watson (1925) and Skinner (1974) that had dominated education beginning in the late 1930s, and which continue in some circles to this day. Now researchers began to examine the processes themselves involved, including the area of cognition, or thinking, reexamining the works of Piaget in the 1950s (Wadsworth, 1996) and Vygotsky in the 1970s (Vygotsky, 1978).

In the area of literacy education, particularly reading, the pendulum from the 1950s onward has always swung between teaching children how to decode words through teaching either phonics or linguistic approaches emphasizing how word patterns are made. The two main approaches were classified as phonetic (sound it out) or visual (look-say). However, there was little emphasis on comprehension or how students "make meaning" or sense of what they read.

During the late 1970s through 2000, new research emphasized student psychological processes as they read: which cognitive or thinking processes were children using as they learned? What modalities or learning styles—visual, phonetic, tactile, or kinesthetic (whole body) were children using as they read? What were children's funds of knowledge or cultural capital that they could utilize as they tried to understand information from their textbooks or what teachers taught them? Were their English dialect differences preventing students from learning?

New methods of teaching reading and writing, such as the Whole Language Approach espoused by Ken Goodman (1986), Frank Smith (1985), and others, emerged. In 1973, the first children's multicultural book emerged with the publication of Arnold Adoff's *Black Is Brown Is Tan*, an autobiographical book about his own blended race family. Recognition of the nonexistence multicultural texts for reading material in this country began a movement in the publishing industry toward more inclusive literature as well as inclusion of diverse ethnicities in subject area textbooks.

With the development of a broader range of inclusive materials for placement in textbooks, the industry began to satisfy those involved in multiculturalism, whereas the conservatives in the country promoted the idea that schools were providing an inferior or watered-down curriculum to students (Edelsky, 2006). One of the results of this was the increased call for testing to "prove" that teachers were teaching and students were learning. With federal strings attached to programs for equitable education, the demand from corporate America for standardized testing that would "prove" that students were learning was increased and became part of the requirements for receiving federal dollars beginning at the end of the twentieth century (Tozer, Violas, & Senese, 1993).

American Indian/Native Alaska Education

There were still needs for changes in education for Native Americans that testing could not solve. Indigenous peoples expressed that:

> The mainstream orientation of school curricula disorients many Indian students rooted in traditional culture. Because most teachers are non-Indian, school districts do not provide Indian students with positive role models, nor have they developed effective teaching strategies based upon the learning styles of Indian children. . . . [Native Americans] wanted curricula to include Indian languages, world views, cultures, concepts, values, and perspectives. They articulated the need for schools to offer course work designed to reinforce parental and community teachings. [Indigenous people] asserted that children instilled with traditional tribal values could live successfully in the modern world. (Saravia-Shore & Arvizu, 1992, p. 61)

That message is still strong today and led to the development of culturally relevant teaching or pedagogy for American Indian children. This type of instruction incorporates knowledge about Native worldviews; practices; belief systems; and learning styles; it acknowledges the need to incorporate students' cultural capital which they bring with them to school each day (Castagno & Brayboy,

2008; Klug & Whitfield, 2003; Pewewardy, 1994). In other words, culturally relevant teaching applies to both the context of teaching and the content to be learned in schools.

For too long, educators have assumed that schools were places where all children could learn. We did not realize that because most teachers belonged to the dominant culture, that incorporating these values, mores, and ways of teaching, plus the dominant culture capital, would be problematic for children of different ethnicities. Walking into a school like this for Indigenous students would be like going into a foreign place across the globe and feeling strange and alienated. Students need to feel comfortable in their physical surroundings and with their teachers to be able to learn optimally. This means being able to see themselves reflected in their curricula as well as having teachers who are schooled in the appropriate ways to teach Indigenous students.

Tribal nations have responded to this message by developing some of their own curricula materials related to their nations. In 1972, Montana decided to draft a new constitution that included recognition of Montana's twelve Tribal nations. Rick Champoux, a delegate involved with this action, stated the following:

> Are we to tell the Indian people that their history has no place in our schools? . . . That their ways, their governments were wrong and that they must accept ours, because ours are better? Or, will we help them to retain their ethnic identity and make their adaptations as Americans? If there is ever to be a solution to the Indian problem in this country, it will come about when our educational system provides the knowledge which is needed to understand and respect the cultural differences between us and the state helps to preserve and protect their cultural integrity. (Indian Education for All, 2010)

While a mandate to include Indian education in all school curricula was passed, there was no money attached to the order to make that happen. Finally, the Montana Indian Education for All Act (IEFA) was passed by the legislature in 1999 with the intention that not only their large American Indian student population in Montana schools needed Native knowledge, but that all students would benefit through this knowledge (Indian Education for All, 2010; Thompson & Lugthart, 2009). The curriculum was developed with the assistance of Native peoples and integrated throughout instructional teaching materials.

The developers of the IEFA identified seven Essential Understandings that were deemed necessary for all students to understand about American Indian Tribal nations in Montana (Indian Education for All, 2010; Thompson & Lugthart, 2009). In essence, they call for recognition of the sovereignty and legitimacy of

Tribal nations and their rights to a continuance of their traditional beliefs, spiritual practices, languages, and ways of life, which predate colonialism.

In addition, the Essential Understandings call for the recognition that Montana Indians—like all U.S. Indian Nations—gave up portions of their lands through treaties with the U.S. government; they were not given reservation lands by the government. Through education, citizens and future citizens can learn about and understand the histories and cultures of American Indians, thereby engendering respect for Montana Indians and their Tribal Nations (Indian Education for All, 2010; Thompson & Lugthart, 2009).

The Alaska Knowledge Network (ANKN; 2011) has publications and resources for Indigenous education that are free to the public and accessible online. These materials are developed for different subject areas across the curricula and provide teachers with more understanding of Native American cultures and how to approach particular subject areas for teaching. (See Appendix B for a list of resources for educators.)

Students who have had access to these materials have done well in their classes. This knowledge has made a tremendous difference for all of Montana's students, especially Aboriginal students attending schools. The same is true for those students who have had access to the materials provided through the ANKN and other Tribal resources.

It is important to keep in mind that the central concepts needing to be addressed in students' educations have not been compromised. They have been positioned in a new fashion matching Native students' epistemologies, culturally developed knowledge, and ideas about the world (Klug, 2014). Non-Native students have a chance to better understand their Indigenous classmates and neighbors and respect them and their cultural practices through these efforts.

THE ESSENTIAL ROLE OF FAMILY IN ABORIGINAL COMMUNITIES

An area that has not been fully presented in other discussions of Native education is that of the role of Indigenous families in the education of their children. For too long, carrying a mindset in schools that Native American families are exactly like white middle-class families, or should be, has done a disservice to our Indigenous students. This may be true for families of Aboriginal students who are considered completely assimilated into the dominant society. On the contrary, Aboriginal families may be anywhere on the spectrum from very traditional, to bicultural, to acculturated, to fully assimilated to Western society.

Traditional Native Americans retain the languages, practices, mores, and belief systems of their ancestors. In today's world, with the infusion of technology in our everyday lives, it is more difficult to have a completely traditional lifestyle. However, numerous families have preserved their Aboriginal lifestyles.

Many students may be bicultural to a more or less degree. Biculturalism is the ability to be comfortable operating in both the Native American and dominant societies equally. For those who are acculturated, they may lessen their Indigenous cultures in terms of language, practices, and belief systems while adopting more of the practices of the dominant culture and speak or understand only English.

Due to educational efforts to suppress Native American and Alaska Native languages in schools, many of these languages are now in danger of completely being lost or being moribund (Fishman, 2001; Hinton & Hale, 2001/2013).

Every time a language is lost, we also lose aspects of culture as ideas expressed in one language do not always translate well into another language. People can see this with the different translations of "holy books" used around the world, and how they become "retranslated" to more accurately reflect the original meanings in their different translations.

Through research on the brain and cognition—thinking and learning—we now know that being able to speak more than one language grows the brain and children become smarter. Most recently, the Commission on Language Learning was formed by the American Academy of Arts and Sciences in 2015 in response to a bipartisan request from Congress. It not only investigated the state of affairs concerning learning foreign languages but of learning Native American heritage languages as well (American Academy, 2020).

The report, *America's Languages: Investing in Language Education for the 21st Century*, was released in 2017. It focused on the positive effects of language programs for the social, cultural, and economic life of the country, and second language use in business, science, technology, international affairs, and civic life. The report included information about the positive effects of dual immersion programs for students. Among the Commission's recommendations was the need to debunk the myths that only English will be needed for the twenty-first century, and that Americans were not very good at learning second languages (American Academy, 2020).

The report also contains the following statement: "Heritage language initiatives at schools and colleges are important, in part, because they recognize forms of self and cultural expression that have been devalued by our educational policies and practices, sometimes to devastating effect" (American Academy, 2020). The report was influential in the reauthorization of the Esther Martinez Native American

Languages Programs Reauthorization Act in 2019, followed by additional acts for teaching languages in the United States. The report also has influenced the passage of the 2020 National Defense Authorization Act (NDAA). The World Language Advancement and Readiness Act became the first piece of federal legislation focusing on language needs in this period (American Academy, 2020).

Study of High School Completion and Resilience for American Indian Students

Resilience is related to being able to succeed in accomplishing goals, and in the case of education, to completing high school (Hupfield, 2010; Loukas, Ripperger-Suhler, & Horton, 2009; Martin & Halperin, 2006). A criterion for resilience is the ability to adapt to unfamiliar situations or situations that may pose risk for individuals; in other words, providing an effective response to stress while maintaining one's sense of psychological well-being (Wu et al., 2013).

Forty-six (n = 46) Native Americans participated in a recent ethnographic study focusing on high school completion and resiliency. Participants were aged eighteen to fifty-six and older and represented Tribal nations across the United States (Klug, 2011; 2013; 2015). Twenty-one (n = 21) of these participants were interviewed through a semistructured interview protocol about their school experiences. Of these, ten had completed or were in the process of completing bachelor's degrees; two had completed master's degrees, and nine had completed doctoral degrees. An additional twenty-five (n = 25) Native Americans, several with advanced degrees, participated in the survey portion of the study (Klug, 2011a; 2011b; 2013; 2015).

The two most salient themes that emerged from the study were: (a) the importance of family support—in particular that of grandparents—in Native students' lives and decisions to complete high school; and (b) the importance of having at least one K–12 teacher/coach who supported them and made a difference in their lives (Klug, 2011a; 2011b; 2013).

Command of English was not found to be the premier determinant of school success as it has been presented in the past. Eleven (n = 11) of the survey participants grew up in households where all Indian or a combination of Indian and English languages were used. Only eight participants (n = 8) grew up in all-English speaking homes (Klug, 2015). All of the survey participants succeeded in obtaining their high school diplomas, with the majority going on to attaining advanced degrees (Klug, 2015).

Self-identity and self-efficacy go hand in hand. When interviewees did not have a sense of "belonging" in the United States as a whole, they had difficulty with developing "can-do" attitudes, willingness to try new things, and risk-taking. The question of "Who am I as an Indian" was very important to their overall development in all realms (Klug, 2011a; 2011b; 2013).

Interviewees indicated that because of the support they received from family and at least one teacher or coach, they were able to persist in achieving their goals even in the face of their struggles. We must note here that in the case of three individuals, support equivalent to that of family was given by mentors when there were no family members to provide this during teen years and young adulthood. These mentors recognized the talents of the interviewees and encouraged them to continue their educations beyond their high school or GED completions.

One of the comments that was frequently made by interviewees was that they didn't know they were smart: No one had ever told them this while they attended K–12 schools. Almost all of them had experienced some degree of prejudice as they attended schools, whether in boarding schools, BIE schools, contract schools, private or mission schools, or public schools (Klug, 2011a; 2011b; 2013).

It needs to be noted that Native American interviewees with poor facility in English may have had a more difficult time in terms of learning the content of the curriculum, but that did not hinder them from reaching their goals. None of the interviewees had experienced much in the way of access to materials related to Indigenous cultures in their schools. A few of the younger participants who took part in the study had belonged to clubs at school. Almost all of the participants in the study had participated in sports at some point in their educational careers, and a few had dropped out of school and reentered later or completed their GED (General Education Diploma) certificates (Klug, 2011a; 2011b; 2013).

Information about Indigenous Families and Communities for Educators

Most of the information in teacher preparation programs is presented from a dominant culture point of view. When students do not fit this "profile," new teachers and teachers new to working with diverse populations, are left to figure things out on their own. They know that there are differences within Native American families, but we do not provide information about what some of these differences may be. We need to understand that family constellation differences arise due to historical circumstances for different ethnicities.

These differences are not good or bad: all differences have arisen as a way to help humans survive in many different circumstances. For this reason, we are going to explore some of the differences that may exist within Native communities, many of which are matrilineal societies (Sillars, 1995). In this way teachers have a clearer understanding of why practices may be different in Aboriginal communities than in the dominant culture. In presenting this information, it is important not to rely on stereotypes. We will present generalized information that may or may not apply to particular Indigenous communities who are traditional or bicultural.

Family Constellations

Urie Bronfenbrenner (1979) is known for his pioneering work in the area of child psychology and development, specifically in the area of the human socioecological development of children. From his perspective, the growth of children from babyhood on is a reflection of their interactions with different substrata systems of communities and societies. These are the following, presented from his Western-European dominant culture framework:

- The **microsystem**, or the smallest system, which is the home in which the child grows up and the people in the children's lives: mothers, fathers, sisters, brothers, and the interactions with each other in their environments. Interactions may be influenced by SES due to the kinds or quality of experiences children have in their early years which determine their cognitive growth. Other areas such as number of children, divorce, stepfamilies, or blended families can also impact children's development.

    In addition, if children are enrolled in preschool, this institution is included in their microsystem as many of the relationships are similar to home with dyads (one-to-one) interacting, such as child and adult or child and child. This is the case with children enrolled in Head Start or other early childhood programs.
- The **mesosystem**, or middle system, is that of K–12 institutions where children are participating with many more individuals at a time. It is also represented by sport activities, participation in band, clubs, or other types of different school environments. Children interact with individuals who are not connected to their immediate home environments. The extended family, cousins, aunts, and uncles in the dominant culture may be part of the child's mesosystem. People can have multiple links if they are part of both microsystems and mesosystems, such as when fathers and coaches are friends.

Successful mesosystems provide links with microsystems through communications, whether face-to-face or by telephone; email, text messaging, Facebook, FaceTime, or other social media used today which were not yet invented when Bronfenbrenner began his work in the 1960s and 1970s but are included here. If communication is only one-sided, coming from the power source to the home, parents may feel disenfranchised by the institutions. This is experienced often in the lives of ethnically diverse members of our society, especially if they are in lower SES levels.

- The **exosystem** is comprised of institutions outside of the home, but which impinge on the people in the home in some ways. For example, mom is working and has to get permission from her superior to attend parent-teacher conferences.

School boards and their decisions impact families in terms of when children go to school, how long, and how many days a week. Even trips to the dentist or going to a summer camp require the interplay between the child's microsystems and exosystems, whether planned or not.

When children take school field trips to the symphony, or to a museum, they are encountering additional types of exosystems that have an impact on their perceptions of the world and cognitive development. It would be hoped and expected that children's self-confidence in new settings would be enhanced through interactions across systems, allowing them to expand their knowledge of other systems in their worlds.

- Finally, we have the **macrosystem**. This system is the furthest away from children's microsystems though it may impact the children's growth and development in several ways. Bronfenbrenner explains the macrosystem as "the consistency within a given culture or subculture in the form and content of its constituent micro-, meso-, and exosystems, as well as any belief systems or ideology underlying such consistencies" (1979, p. 258).

This concept is referring to the macroculture of a country that impacts the particular ways people think, interact, practice their faiths, and recreate. The macrosystem is at work when we discuss universal family leave for the birth of children in the United States, and whether different companies grant this or not. It is at work in the amount of vacation time expected in this country. For example, in Germany and other European countries there is an expectation of a three-week vacation during the summer for family and renewal of working individuals. If a person moved from Germany to the states, they may be very surprised by the little amount of vacation time allowed, causing some disillusionment in the workplace.

We see the macrosystem in our government, laws, and in the U.S. Office of Education which dictates the operation of public schools in this country, and the Bureau of Indian Education (BIE) which is concerned with Indigenous education. This office was formerly the Office of Indian Education with the BIA, and was renamed and established in August 2006. The BIE operates from two polar views that do not pair well: (1) from the dominant culture as laws are formulated by Congress for American Indians, and (2) from Indigenous perspectives of taking care of the whole person: their spiritual, mental, physical, and cultural aspects (Bureau of Indian Education [BIE]; n.d.).

Unlearning Stereotypes about Diverse Families and Cultures

Bronfenbrenner's conceptualization (1979) works well when it applies to homogenous dominant-culture societies. It does not work well when we are educating diverse populations of students. Ogbu (1991) discovered through his ethnographic research that "voluntary minorities" to another country are quick to acculturate because they have made a conscious decision, even under duress, to leave their countries of origin. "Involuntary minorities," such as Indigenous peoples, however, are reluctant to make changes forced on them by a conquering nation.

This is where confusion lies between Native American families who are not assimilated and schools as institutions, especially for families who are living on reservations as well as for those who migrate between reservations and other urban or suburban settings. As teachers, we tend to assume that all of our students and their families will think just like white, middle-class families, in other words, be like the dominant culture.

Instead of blaming SES or determining that some cultures just "don't put much stock into learning," we need to unlearn these stereotypes with regard to American Indian and Alaska Natives. The important differences are within the children's microsystems and mesosystems which differ from those of the dominant culture. In fact, all of the systems are somewhat different except in the case of assimilated students.

The first commandment in teaching is to know your audience. While teacher preparation programs ensure those enrolled have had classes in child psychology, what is not usually stated is that most of what is written and taught holds true for students from the dominant Western-European culture or those who have assimilated fully into this culture. As a result, what the teacher does or the way content matter is delivered is in synchrony with what Euro-American students bring with them as their cultural capital to school (see Figure 7.1a).

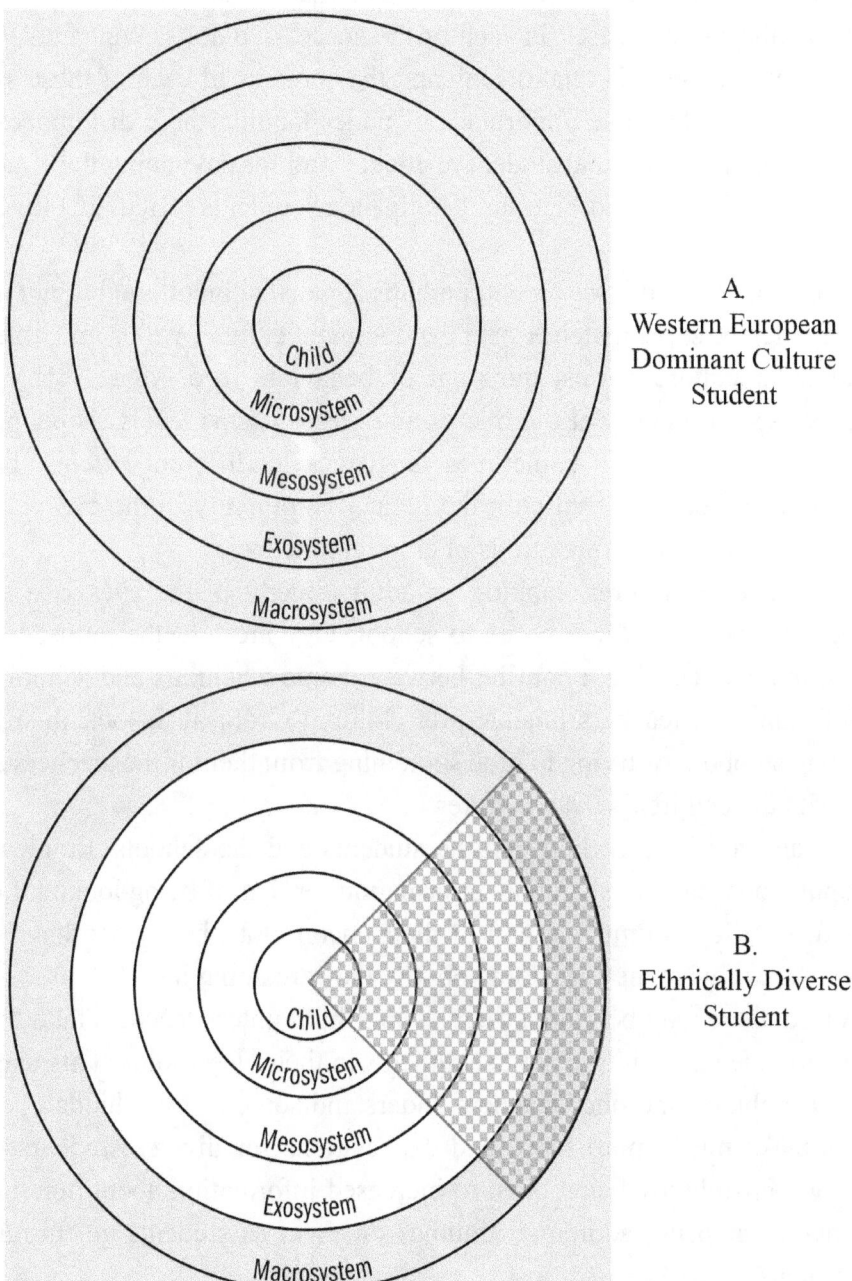

Figure 7.1. Bronfenbrenner's Socioecological Systems for the Dominant Culture. Visual representation of the Human Socioecological Systems model (Bronfenbrenner, 1979) from an educational standpoint, examining relationships among teachers, students, curriculum, and teaching practices: (A) represents the cultural match among teachers, school, and students who are of the dominant Western-European culture in the U.S.; (B) represents children who are not assimilated causing a cultural mismatch. Adapted from *The ecology of human development: Experiments in nature and design*, by U. Bronfenbrenner, Cambridge, MA: Harvard University Press, 1979. Visual models developed by the author.

We can think of the micro-, meso-, exo-, and macrosystems as a set of Russian dolls, the smallest one encased in each of the successive dolls. We can also use a Venn diagram to show this relationship and the contents of each of these systems for Indigenous peoples. The importance of understanding these differences is related to developing Aboriginal student resiliency and for navigating the educational system for traditional and bicultural Indigenous students (Klug, 2011a; 2011b; 2012).

With an ethnically diverse student, perhaps somewhat bicultural but not assimilated, there may be some matches with the dominant culture, with some diversions from dominant culture norms, thinking, or behaviors (see Figure 7.1b). These conflicts are seen primarily at the micro- and mesosystems levels, as people tend to retain their cultures and sometimes languages to different extents, but this information may not be shared with the greater community in the exo-or macrosystems, leading to misinterpretations of cultural practices.

In many diverse cultures, looking an adult directly in the eyes is a sign of disrespect. Yet when children come to school, they are told they must look the teacher in the eye, causing a conflict between home teachings and school teachings. Unfortunately, teachers misinterpret children's refusal to look them in the eye as being stubborn or trying to hide something from them if the teachers are not familiar with the children's natal cultures.

This creates a mismatch between the students and the schools. Ethnically diverse populations may not share this information for fear of being looked down on by educators, or it is so much a part of their unconscious behaviors that they are not even aware of what they are doing or why they are doing it.

Therefore, there may be more struggles in school unless teachers take the time to understand the natal cultures of the students in their classrooms. This usually is not a great problem, and once teachers understand some of this "hidden" culture, behaviors make much more sense and expectations for diverse students can be adjusted. Meanwhile, by being open to increased information about our students, we can avoid imposing additional traumas on them as students go through our school systems.

When we examine Figure 7.2, an adaptation of Bronfenbrenner's (1979) systems for Indigenous peoples, we find there are many disconnects between the dominant culture and Native American cultures (see Figure 7.2). This is important in light of the dominant culture's continual pressure on American Indians and Alaska Natives to fully adopt the Western-European culture and English language, using educational institutions to accomplish this mission.

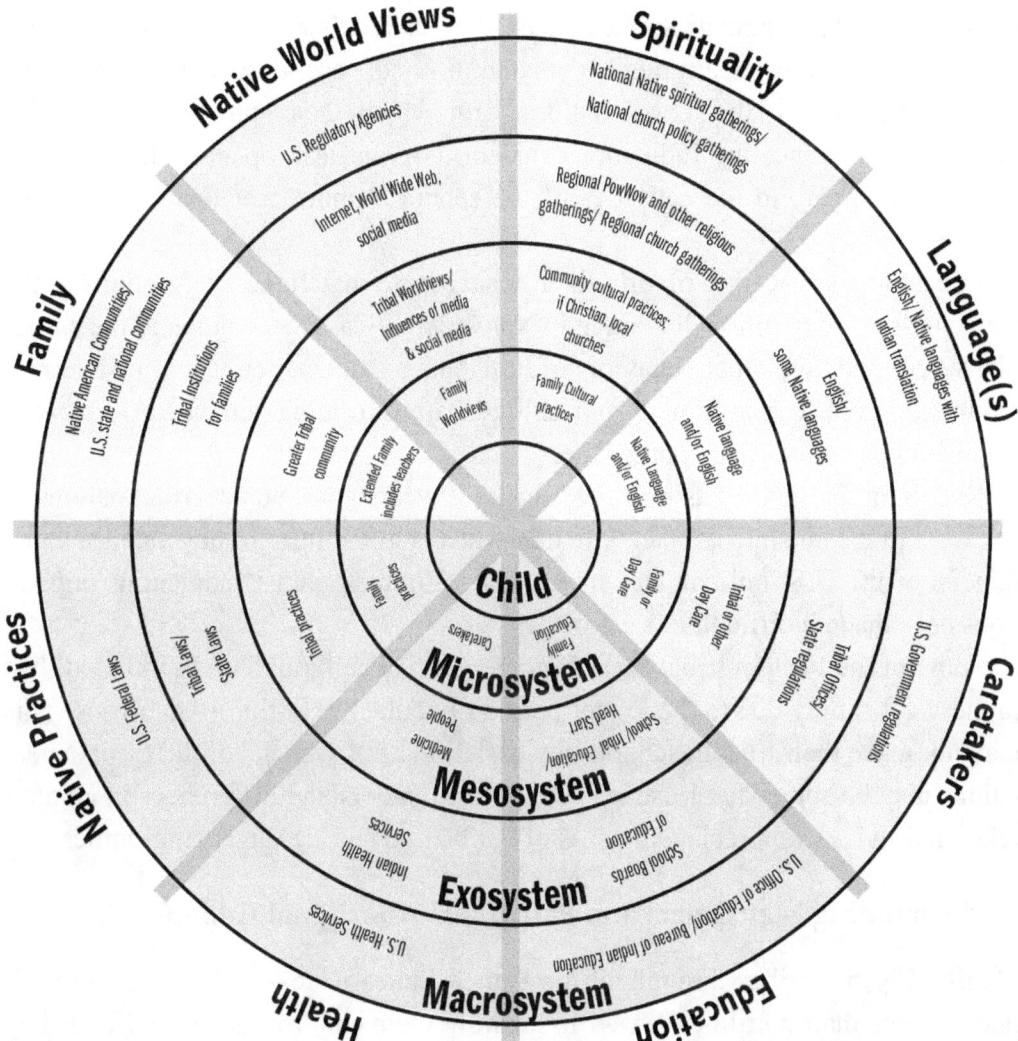

Figure 7.2. Traditional and Bicultural Native American Human Socioecological Systems. Adapted from Bronfenbrenner's Human Socioecological Systems.

In Figure 7.2, Native Americans' dual citizenship in both their Tribal nations and in the United States is recognized. Schools they attend may be either public school districts, charter schools, contract schools, or BIE schools, including the four remaining off-reservation boarding schools in the United States. We can see in this depiction that the traditional extended family is represented, whether it is a matrilineal or patrilineal Tribal nation (see Figure 7.2). Traditional spiritual and cultural practices are represented, as well as Native languages.

While Standard English may be the official language of the school, Native American students may speak a dialect of English called American Indian English

(AIE or "Red English"), which is based on the grammar of the particular ancestral or heritage Tribal language spoken (Leap, 1993). Teachers need to become bicultural in terms of the learning, understanding, and accepting of the verbal and nonverbal norms of the Tribal nations with which their students identify. By accepting and respecting Indigenous students, we are also opening their willingness to participate in the activities of the school without fear that they may be rejected.

Educators may need to modify their behaviors to match the expectations of the way children are traditionally taught in Native America. By recognizing the particular verbal and nonverbal behaviors of Indigenous students' cultures, misinterpretations are kept to a minimum and children are not being forced to do what is deemed to be culturally inappropriate.

Keep in mind that it has been less than 170 years since some Tribal nations in the West first came into contact with non-Natives in the form of unwanted settlers, miners, or the U.S. militia. The atrocities committed against Indigenous populations have made it difficult to trust whites.

Some of the Eastern tribes have become more acculturated or assimilated than in the West simply due to the longer period of contact with Euro-Americans. This may not make their trust in schools any easier, but the "shock" of different expectations may be somewhat lessened. We need to understand differences in cultural relational styles to appreciate the gifts of our Native families and communities.

Understanding Matrilineal and Patrilineal Aboriginal Communities

Manifold Native tribes throughout the United States were—and still are—matrilineal rather than patrilineal in terms of how their children are raised and they operate as communities. The dominant culture is patrilineal in this country and fathers are considered the head of households unless there has been a death or divorce. This pattern comes from Europe where wives and children up until the late 1800s were considered the property of the male head of house, with the father administering discipline and taking care of the needs of the family.

Euro-American children almost always carry their fathers' names or their mothers' and fathers' names combined. While before Industrialization, the extended family played a part in the lives of family members living closely together, this changed with immigration to America and the lack of extended family generations when the majority of Europeans came to the country in the mid- to late 1800s. Here, the extended family does not usually play a large role in the raising of children except in cases of illness or other necessities.

In Native American matrilineal societies—as can be seen by examining the child's microsystem in Figure 7.2—children belong to everyone in the community (D. Gould, 2010, personal communication). The children and their nuclear families are not considered to be separate entities. Grandparents play an important role in the lives of their grandchildren, and part of their role is to teach the cultural histories, values, ethics, and practices of their Tribal nations to their grandchildren.

However—and this is the part that many non-Native educators do not understand—grandmothers are the matriarchs in this system, and all of the grandmother's sisters and brothers are grandparents to the children. Therefore it is not uncommon for children to be living with grandparents throughout the year, even though they may not be direct descendants of that particular grandparent.

In the same way, sisters and brothers of the child's mother are considered the same as their mothers and fathers, and children may refer to aunties as "mom" and so forth. Cousins are referred to traditionally as "brothers and sisters." One can see in the microsystem of the Native American children who are being brought up traditionally or biculturally, that the community has a responsibility for all of the children.

In this manner, children are always welcomed into the homes of their extended family and made to feel they belong there, because they do. In some cases and communities, grandparents perform the majority of the caretaking and raising of the children, actually the first daycare system in this country, as their parents traditionally were responsible for providing food and protection to the community and taking care of elders.

In schools, it is not uncommon for grandparents to be the ones to enroll the children and accompany them to school their first day. In terms of discipline, grandmothers are usually involved with the discipline of children. Grandmothers will report to an uncle—usually the mother's brother—that a child needs attention for something that is going on. This is to preserve the sacred bond between parents and their children. While these are generalizations, some form of this structure is usually in place in Native communities. Variations can be found when grandparents have an interethnic marriage and the Native American partner is the grandfather.

Before the boarding school era, children were not beaten in terms of discipline. Children were talked to apart from others until they understood what they did wrong and were able to change their ways. This is reinforced through celebrations and ceremonies held during different times of the year.

These practices are in contrast to the non-Native community, so that teachers who are unfamiliar with these patterns may misinterpret the absence of parents at different events as the parents being irresponsible or negligent of the child's academic career, or that the parents "don't care," when just the opposite is true. When relatives attend special events with or without parents, powwows held during the year, and sometimes parent-teacher conferences, that sends a message to the children that they are cared for by everyone.

In terms of schools, we must be open to these variations of family and community micro- and mesosystems. Instead of limiting invitations to children's events, we need to open them up to extended family and members of the community. If we can keep in mind that in this way, the students are given even more support than what we might see in the dominant culture, we can see the benefits of this system.

> I think one of the biggest things that really helped me was family life in general. We had a pretty stable family. I had my mother and grandmother and my dad and grandpa. And they always told us you can do anything you put your mind to. Instead of saying, "Oh, you can't do that!" or "You shouldn't do that!" They always said, "Well figure it out for yourself and if you can do it, do it. If you can't, don't."
>
> And the other thing was they always said, "If you do something you are going to take whatever consequences come with it." And that really shaped the way I looked at school, and even later in life. Because, honestly, [school] didn't interest me in any way, shape, or form. But knowing that if I accomplished it, then I could move on, I think was one of the reasons I pushed so hard to get through it.
> —Jason Pretty Boy, Lakota (Interviewed by B. J. Klug, November 2010)

In the same way, non-Native teachers may have difficulty with understanding the practice of children staying overnight at their auntie's home during the school week. The belief seems to be that children will do better in school if they stay only in their parents' residence during the week. There is no proof that this is true: rather, this is more a belief based on the dominant culture's nuclear family than knowledge of Indigenous traditions. Today, we find a wide variation of practices taking place on reservations, depending on the degree of assimilation or acculturation of Native families.

In patrilineal Native American societies, lineage is linked through the father's side of the family, and children are given their father's last names. However, even if mothers and children use the father's last name, the family in reality can still act as if they are matrilineal. If one member of the family is non-Indian, the family may act more like a patrilineal family with the father in charge of the nuclear family.

Again, this causes confusion when students have last names that are English, but if we revisit Native American history, students who attended the boarding schools and did not have English names or their names translated into English were often given the patronyms of the supporters of the schools, especially those that were missionary schools. Sometimes the soldiers who were in command of the different reservations gave families the patronyms of the soldiers since many Native American Tribes did not employ last names.

Other times, last names were given as a description of what the particular clan elder was especially good at, or where the clan lived on the reservation. In other words, last names can be misleading in terms of whether a family is patrilineal or matrilineal, non-Indian, or of mixed heritage.

It was common for female graduates of boarding schools to take their husbands' last names since this was the custom of those who worked for the schools and it was part of the assimilation process into the dominant culture. Another variation that can be seen today is that mothers may retain their maiden names, but give their children their fathers' last names.

Consequently, we need to remember not to judge our Native students' level of being traditional to assimilated based on Western concepts of patrilineal families. What we need to remember is that the extended family is very important both on and off reservations and in urban areas, especially today with the easy linkage to social media. Even if family members are not living physically closeby, most are keeping daily or weekly ties to their loved ones through Skype, FaceTime, Facebook, Messenger, and other social media programs.

Teachers and Their Place in Native Students' Human Socioecological Models

Teachers need to realize that because of traditional practices, members of the community who possessed special knowledge or skills were selected to teach children. Children were taught to watch intently, not interrupt what was being taught, and then to practice what they were taught on their own. Children demonstrated their knowledge when they were ready and not before (Skinner, 1974). Traditionally, teachers were viewed as part of the children's families and treated as such. Therefore, we see teachers even today are placed within the Indigenous students' microsystems.

TAKING THE NEXT STEPS

In the following section of this book, we will detail the importance of developing resiliency for Native youth and the importance of families as protective determinants in healthy child development. The role of teachers in the education of American Indian students in buttressing our students during their educational experiences will be explored more fully as well.

In doing so, we are changing the narrative of Indigenous lives, capitalizing on student strengths and abilities as hallmarks of forward trajectories in Native education. We are also changing the greater narrative of the dominant culture from one of exclusion of Native peoples from the national consciousness to embracing all of our Native peoples and recognizing their gifts and talents.

REFERENCES

Adoff, A. (1973). *Black Is Brown Is Tan*. New York, NY: Harper & Row.

Alaska Knowledge Network. (2011). *Curriculum Resources*. Retrieved from http://www.ankn.uaf.edu/.

American Academy of Languages of Arts & Sciences. (2020, January 9). New Federal program among far-ranging achievements of Commission on Language and Learning. Retrieved from https://www.amacad.org/news/federal-bill-among-achievements-commission-language-learning.

Bureau of Indian Education (BIE). (n.d.). *Indian Affairs*. Washington, DC: U.S. Department of the Interior. Retrieved from https:///www.bia.gov.

Bronfenbrenner, U. (1979). *The ecology of human development: Experiments by nature and design*. Cambridge, MA: Harvard University Press.

Castagno, A. E., & Brayboy, B. M. K. J. (2008). Culturally responsive schooling for indigenous youth: A review of the literature. *Review of Education Research, 78* (4), 941–93. Retrieved from: https://doi.org/10.3102/0034654308323036.

Edelsky, C. (2006). *With literacy and justice for all: Rethinking the social in language and education* (3rd ed.). Mahwah, NJ: Lawrence Erlbaum Associates.

Elementary and Secondary Education Act of 1965—Amendment of 1995 Addressing American Indian Education specifically.

Elementary and Secondary Education Act of 1965—Title I of Improving America's Schools Act of 1994.

Elementary and Secondary Education Act of 1965, 20 U.S.C. § 6301 (U.S.C. 2000).

Esther Martinez Native American Languages Programs Reauthorization Act of 2019–2020, Public Law No: 116-101.

Fishman, J. A., Ed. (2001). *Can Threatened Languages Be Saved?* Clevedon, UK: Multilingual Matters.

Goodman, K. (1986). *What's whole in whole language?* Richmond Hill, Ontario: Scholastic TAB.

Hinton, L., & Hal, K. (2001/2013). *The Green Book of Language Revitalization in Practice*. San Diego, CA: Academic Press.

Hupfield, K. (2010). *A review of the literature: Resiliency skills and dropout prevention*. Denver, CO: Scholar Centric. Retrieved from http://www.scholarcentric.com/wp-content/uploads/2014/03/SC_Resiliency_Dropout-Prevention_WP_FNL.pdf.

Indian Education for All. (2010, August 4). Montana Education for All. Native American Netroots. Retrieved from http://nativeamericannetroots.net/diary/614.

Klug, B. J. (with Pewewardy, C. D.). (2011a, October). "A Study of Factors Influencing High School Completion and Resiliency for American Indian Youth. Preliminary results as of October, 2011." National Indian Education Association Annual Convention. Albuquerque, NM.

Klug, B. J. (with Pewewardy, C. D.). (2011b, October). "My Coach Really Wanted Me: A Study of Factors Influencing High School Completion and Resiliency for American Indian Youth. Preliminary results as of October, 2011." Idaho Association for Physical Education & Sport Science. Pocatello, ID.

Klug, B. J. (Ed.). (2012). *Standing together: American Indian education as Culturally Responsive Pedagogy*. Lanham, MD: Rowman & Littlefield.

Klug, B. J. (2013, February). "Children at the Center: A Constellation of Socioecological Factors Influencing Resiliency and High School Completion for American Indian Youth." Association of Teacher Educators Annual Meeting. Atlanta, GA.

Klug, B. J. (2014). Pedagogy for Aboriginal Students in the U.S.: Shattering walls of distorted glass. In C. Craig & L. Orland-Barak (Eds.), International Teacher Education: Promising Pedagogies (Vol. 2; pp. 179–208), Emerald Group Publishing Limited, Howard House, Wagon Lane, Bingley, BD16 1WA, United Kingdom.

Klug, B. J., (with Pewewardy, C. D.). (2015). *Part B: Survey results of American Indian youth resilience and high school completion*. Unpublished results.

Klug, B. J., & Whitfield, P. T. (2003). *Widening the circle: Culturally Relevant Pedagogy for American Indian children*. New York, NY: RoutledgeFalmer.

Leap, W. L. (1993). *American Indian English*. Salt Lake City: University of Utah Press.

Loukas, A., Ripperger-Suhler, K. G., & Horton, K. D. (2009). Examining temporal associations between school connectedness and early adolescent adjustment. *Journal of Youth and Adolescence, 38* (6), 804–12. https://doi.org/10.1007/s10964-008-9312-9.

Martin, N., & Halperin, S. (2006). Whatever it takes: How twelve communities are reconnecting out-of-school youth. Washington, DC: American Youth Policy Forum. Retrieved from www.aypf.org/publications/WateverItTakes/WIT_nineseconds.pdf.

National Defense Authorization Act (NDAA) of 2020, S. 1790—116th Congress (2019–2020).

Ogbu, J. U. (1991). Immigrant and involuntary minorities in comparative perspective. In M. A. Gibson & J. U. Ogbu (Eds.), *Minority status and schooling: A comparative study of immigrant and involuntary minorities* (pp. 3–33). New York, NY: Garland.

Pewewardy, C. (1994). Culturally responsive pedagogy in action: An American Indian Magnet School. In E. R. Hollins, J. E. King, & W. C. Hayman (Eds.), *Teaching diverse populations: Formulating a knowledge base* (pp. 72–92). New York, NY: State University of New York Press.

Ravitch, D. (2020). *Slaying Goliath: The passionate resistance to privatization and the fight to save America's public schools*. New York, NY: Alfred A. Knopf.

Saravia-Shore, M. & Arvizu, F. (1992). *Cross-cultural literacy*. London: Taylor & Francis.

Skinner, B. F. (1974). *About behaviorism*. New York, NY: Random House.

Smith, F. (1985). *Reading without nonsense* (2nd ed.). New York, NY: Teachers College Press.

Sillars, A. L. (1995). Communication and family culture. In M. A. Fitzpatrick & A. L. Vangelisti (Eds.), *Explaining family interactions* (pp. 375–99). Thousand Oaks, CA: Sage.

Testing. (2020). National achievement tests, international. *Education Encyclopedia—StateUniversity.com*. Retrieved from https://education.stateuniversity.com/pages/2503/Testing-NATIONAL-ACHIEVEMENT-TESTS-INTERNATIONAL.html.

Thompson, S. & Lugthart, K. (2009). IEFA: The big picture. University of Montana & Montana Office of Public Instruction. Retrieved from https://montanatribes.org/.

Tozer, S. E., Violas, P. C., & Senese, G. (1993). *School & society: Educational practice as social expression* (7th ed.). New York, NY: McGraw-Hill.

Vygotsky, L. S. (1978). *Mind in society: The development of higher psychological processes.* Cambridge, MA: Harvard University Press.

Wadsworth, B. J. (1996). *Piaget's Constructivism theory of cognitive and affective development: Foundations of Constuctivism.* White Plains, NY: Longman.

Watson, J. B. (1925). *Behaviorism.* New York, NY: W. W. Norton.

World Language Advancement and Readiness Act of 2019, H.R. 1094.

Wu, G., Feder, A., Cohen, H., Kim, J. J., Calderon, S., Charney, D. S., & Mathé, A. A. (2013). Understanding resilience, *Frontiers in behavioral neuroscience.* Retrieved from https://www.frontiersin.org/articles/10.3389/fnbeh.2013.00010/full.

Part III

Designing Schools in Partnership: Educators, Schools, Native American and Non-Native Communities

There were families, white families, who helped me get through school. There were my best friend's parents and his whole family, his uncle, [and] his grandpa [who] supported me and helped me along. My neighbors that lived up the street, they were very supportive. When I couldn't stay at home certain nights, I would always have a place there to lay on their couch. And so I can't stress enough how [that made a difference to me].

There was a coach who lived down the street: He was always there to listen to me. So I can't stress that enough. There were a lot of non-Indian families in the community who also played a big part in my growing up and graduating. Definitely have to point that out, too. It wasn't just my Indian family, it was my white family, too, that helped me, [because] it really did. I couldn't have done it without them. —Harlan McKosato, Sac & Fox (Interviewed by B. J. Klug, October, 2010)

Harlan grew up in a small rural community where his family was the only Native family in the town. He attended school with the same group of students who started kindergarten together and was an honor roll student and football player. Both his parents and grandparents were "intelligent people," and all of his four siblings and he graduated from high school.

There were difficulties at home, as with many Indigenous families suffering through the resulting effects of colonialism and poverty. The care of people around these children is what makes communities, whether Native or non-Native, effective in ameliorating some of the difficulties faced by a great number of Indigenous students.

Other interviewees in the *Study of American Indian Youth High School Completion and Resilience* (Klug, 2011a; 2011b; 2013) who grew up outside of their family's reservation area (or region where they had settled when their tribe was terminated) made similar comments. People who were caring to them, whether Native or non-Native, made a difference in their lives for the best.

Harlan goes on to say in his interview:

> I never had any doubt that [I would finish high school] and I also saw it as a way to improve my living conditions. And so I always saw school as something that [was good], and my teachers were very encouraging. I think they saw I had some talent, that they were very [supportive].
>
> I remember even in 4th grade or 5th grade I was acting up in class one day. And my teacher held me after class and she sat down with me. And she had a heart to heart with me and she said, "Harlan, you are talented and you can be anything you want." I remember this specifically. She said, "I know things are bad at home, but when you come here to my class if you ever need anything, you let me know." And it just touched my heart. —Harlan McKosato, Sac & Fox (Interviewed by B. J. Klug, October, 2010)

Very clearly, we can see the importance of this teacher in the microsystem of Harlan as a child. We can see how important the "ethic of caring" is for all of our students, particularly our Native American students, and that this ethic needs to be part of what is cultivated in the professional lives of teachers (Klug & Whitfield, 2003; Noddings, 1994).

From our previous discussion in the last chapter, we know that teachers are part of Native American students' microsystems, and as such, are also part of the Native community at large.

Not that teachers should be Indian "wannabes"—we've seen many people from the hippies in the 1960s and 1970s to the New Agers in the late 1970s and through the 1980s who fit this description, especially with the New Age movement.

The New Age religious beliefs are centered on four areas: belief in psychics; reincarnation; that spiritual energy can be found in objects; and in astrology (Gecewicz, 2018). Approximately six in ten Americans believe in at least one of these four concepts. What non-Native Americans need to understand is that one cannot just appropriate a culture's belief systems and "become" like them; for example, the number of reincarnated Cherokee princesses rose dramatically during this period. What you can do is appreciate and respect others' belief systems while not "owning" them for yourself.

There is a distinction between being spiritual and trying to convert others to one's religious faith. Educators can be very strong spiritually, practicing meditation, praying to a Supreme Being, and incorporating positive morality and ethics throughout their lives. This is important as too often people confuse religion with spirituality, not understanding that we can all be of different faiths (or no faith) and still be spiritual in our ways of being.

Indigenous peoples are known for their deep spirituality and connections to Mother Earth and Father Sky. The way we treat our Indigenous students, respecting their belief systems, providing caring atmospheres for them in which to learn, and holding high expectations for all of our Native American students constitutes a formula for their success.

INVOLVING THE MESO- AND MACROSYSTEMS IN THE EDUCATION OF OUR ABORIGINAL STUDENTS

> Throughout history, whoever is the wealthiest and the most technically advanced thinks that their way of life is the best, the most natural, the God-given, the surest means to salvation, or at least the fast lane to well-being in this world. . . . Dazzled by our contemporary inventions and toys (e.g., CNN, IBN, Big Mac, blue jeans, the birth control pill, the credit card) and at home in our own way of life, we are prone to similar illusions and the same type of conceits. (Shweder, 2000, p. 167)

Public school boards are not immune to believing that they are making the right decisions for all of their students, including their Native American communities. Unless members are well-versed in the needs of Indigenous students and have made an effort to learn about the cultures of Native communities in their area, they may make decisions that negatively affect Aboriginal students without understanding why their decisions are not producing positive results.

This is the reason we need to have strong ties between Indigenous communities and those controlling local and state school boards. Native Americans need to have a place at the table to give voice to what they perceive are the needs of Indigenous students in our schools. Regrettably, since the passage of No Child Left Behind (NCLB) in 2001, education in schools with large Native populations has been negatively impacted due to the emphasis on standardized test results across the country, and for sanctions against schools and teachers who do not show gains in student achievement scores (Klug, 2012).

The education testing movement that began with NCLB (2001) and the movement that followed, including the latest push for charter schools and school choice, are dead as Ravitch (2020) points out. Those who supported these "reforms" were counting on testing, competition, and punishment of students and teachers to raise achievement scores, which proved to be disruptive and damaging to our students. They did not produce the expected gains, while saddling schools/school districts with expensive tests and disparaging their reputations.

In many cases charter schools and private schools receiving vouchers produced worse results due to some of their practices and lack of adherence to a curriculum followed in the public schools (Ravitch, 2020). Ravitch (2020) makes the point—something we all know too well—that "poverty and affluence are the most important determinants of test scores."

> Children and schools need stability, not disruption. They need experienced teachers and well-maintained schools. All children need schools that have a nurse, counselors, and a library with a librarian. Children need time to play every day. They need nutrition and regular medical check-ups.
> All of this is common sense. These are the reforms that work. (Ravitch, 2020)

The poverty rate has been increasing, not decreasing, in this country with over half of the students on free and reduced lunch (Ravitch, 2020). Before the education reform and testing movement, culturally relevant and responsive teaching, or pedagogy, was becoming a reality in many schools and Native American students were making noticeable progress in mastery of school curriculum. In addition, schools were seeing attendance rates increase as more activities and opportunities to engage in Indigenous knowledge activities increased (Klug, 2012).

Due to the "reforms," of the last twenty plus years, public schools in districts and states with small overall populations of Indigenous students (even though particular schools had large populations of Native American students) required that all teachers adhere to the same materials and published textbooks to ensure that students were getting the same information. Teachers could not go back and reteach concepts that students had not mastered. Therefore, students were left to struggle on their own if they were absent for lessons or couldn't understand what was being taught (Klug, 2012).

Working Together for Change in Our Schools

In the following section of this book, we will be discussing areas of childhood development and where we, as teachers, can make a difference with our Indigenous students in both developing resilience and working with them to accomplish their goals of completing high school and beyond. In doing so, we recognize that we have a place in schools and communities that serve our Indigenous populations, schools that need the best teachers and committed teachers.

Regrettably, all too often educators who are dedicated to teaching lower SES and ethnically diverse students are questioned by their peers and families about why they were placed or took jobs in these schools. Weren't they good enough to be in schools for middle-class white students? Is there something wrong with them as teachers? This is due to the racist history that we still share in this country: that only the folks at the top of the economic scale deserve the best teachers, because, after all, those are the people footing the bill for education in this country.

These questions relate to actual practices in public school districts of transferring exceptional teachers to other schools "where they are needed." The thought seems to be that if these teachers can assist lower SES students (i.e., "less capable students") in achieving higher academic test scores, then think of what they could do with our top students.

> I told [the superintendent] that I didn't want to change to another school. I really liked working at [this school]. But they moved me anyway. Year after year I requested to go back to [my first school], but they refused to let me. After a couple of years at [the new school], I finally decided to change school districts. It was apparent that they were never going to let me go back to [my first] elementary school. (F. Anderson, 2020, personal communication)

Teachers must be able to continue in schools where they are making a difference (Klug & Whitfield, 2003). It takes time to build relationships, and if schools always transfer teachers, Native American communities do not have opportunities to really connect with their teachers, which is key to enhancing education for our Native American students in all areas of the country.

REFERENCES

Gecewicz, C. (2018, October 1). "New Age" beliefs common among both religious and nonreligious. Fact Tank: News in the numbers. Pew Research Center. Retrieved from https: //pewrsr.ch/2NR7Bme.

Klug, B. J. (with Pewewardy, C. D.). (2011a, October). "A Study of Factors Influencing High School Completion and Resiliency for American Indian Youth. Preliminary results as of October, 2011." National Indian Education Association Annual Convention. Albuquerque, NM.

Klug, B. J. (with Pewewardy, C. D.). (2011b, October). "My Coach Really Wanted Me: A Study of Factors Influencing High School Completion and Resiliency for American Indian Youth. Preliminary results as of October, 2011." Idaho Association for Physical Education & Sport Science. Pocatello, ID.

Klug, B. J. (2012). Falling from grace: How new government policies undermine American Indian education. In Beverly J. Klug (Ed.), *Standing Together: Indigenous education as Culturally Responsive Pedagogy* (pp. 71–86). Lanham, MD: Rowman & Littlefield.

Klug, B. J. (2013, February). "Children at the Center: A Constellation of Socioecological Factors Influencing Resiliency and High School Completion for American Indian Youth." Association of Teacher Educators Annual Meeting. Atlanta, GA.

Klug, B. J., & Whitfield, P. T. (2003). *Widening the circle: Culturally relevant pedagogy for American Indian children.* New York, NY: RoutledgeFalmer.

No Child Left Behind Act of 2001: Reauthorization of the Elementary and Secondary Education Act of 1965, 20 U.S.C. § 6301 et seq. (U.S.C. 2001).

Noddings, N. (1994). An ethic of caring and its implications for instructional arrangements. In L. Stone (Ed.), *The education feminism reader* (pp. 171–83). New York, NY: Routledge.

Ravitch, D. (2020, February 1). How the "reform" movement has failed America. *Time Magazine, 52*. Retrieved from https://dianeravitch.net/2020/02/01/time-magazine-how-the-reform-movement-has-failed-america/.

Shweder, R. A. (2000). Moral maps, "First World" conceits, and the new evangelists. In L. E. Harrison & S. P. Huntington (Eds.), *Culture matters: How values shape human progress* (pp.158–176). New York, NY: Basic Books.

Chapter Eight

Creating Resilient Students

• *Secrets to Success for Native American Children*

I . . . often think back to boarding school and going, "Maybe tomorrow I could go home, tomorrow I could see my Mom or my Dad or my little brothers or sisters." I remember saying, "Maybe tomorrow we will have a better life." So [to be able to] get through one day, I would break my day in chunks. . . . That is how I was able to get through and accomplish the goals that I've accomplished. . . .

What the boarding school experience did to and for me—there was physical abuse, there was sexual abuse, there [were] other kinds of abuses going on there—and as a young child, I think the greater impact on me was lack of emotional support or emotional connection. . . . I look at my granddaughter, and I cannot imagine having her not be with her family, her support system. And I really was only a few months older than she is now when I was in that boarding school.

And I look at that and I can look at my own reflections of no connection emotionally and having these periods of endurance, and if you will, that endurance also helped me in my life get through some very difficult times, personally and emotionally. . . . When someone said I couldn't do something, I'd say, "Just watch me!" —Ramona Klein, Turtle Mountain Chippewa (interviewed by B. J. Klug, October 2010)

Cross (1998) asserts that for American Indians, children learn how to cope with stressors through "self-talk and by the stories [they] hear about how others have managed" (p. 152). However, many Native American students do not have these opportunities to learn resiliency from family models in their homes for a variety of reasons. Additionally, there are few opportunities to address development of resiliency skills in schools.

As a result, we still have a school Event Dropout Rate (EDR) in Indigenous communities and across the nation where they may be attending urban or suburban schools of 4.4 percent in 2017 (McFarland, Cui, Holmes, & Wang, 2019). This is good news compared to the EDR of 20.8 percent reported in 2007 for Native Americans and typical of many of the prior years reported. While the 2017 EDR appears comparable to that for non-Native students, the Adjusted Cohort Graduation Rate (ACGR) shows that of those who started together in ninth grade was 72 percent for American Indians and Alaska Natives compared to 89 percent for white students, with a high of 91 percent for Asian/Pacific Islanders (McFarland, Cui, Homes, & Wang, 2019).

When you compare these indicators, this suggests that some of the American Indian and Alaska Native student populations are dropping out for some time, but may be acquiring their GEDs or returning later to complete their high school educations. The Averaged Freshman Graduation Rate (AFGR) for those who started together in ninth grade ranged from a high of 93 percent in Nebraska and Wisconsin, to lows of 74 percent in South Carolina, 74 percent in Alabama, 73 percent in Louisiana, 72 percent in New Mexico, 71 percent in Georgia, and 68 percent in Mississippi and Nevada (McFarland, Cui, Holmes, & Wang, 2019). These are all states with low SES or concentrated populations of low SES, and higher populations of Native Americans.

For the Native American students in the 16–24 age range, the status dropout rate (students who have not registered for school to complete graduation) for the years 2013–2017 were high for Indigenous populations compared to white populations. A sample shows Alaska, with 5.5 percent for white and 11.9 percent for Indigenous students; Kentucky, with 6.6 percent for white and 13.8 percent for Indigenous students; Kansas, with 5.5 percent for white and 10.9 percent for Indigenous students; Louisiana, with 9.6 percent for white and 16.6 for Indigenous students; Colorado, with 6.0 percent for white and 13.8 percent for Indigenous students; Montana, with 7.5 percent for white and 18.2 percent for Indigenous students; Idaho, with 6.0 percent for white and 13.3 percent for Indigenous students; and Mississippi, with 7.5 percent for white and 18.2 percent for Indigenous students (McFarland, Cui, Holmes, & Wang, 2019).

While we may never know the reasons that individual Native American students choose not to complete their high school degrees, we do know that for a period of time during the "testing craze" following the passage of NCLB in 2001, that half of the states in the United States required students to take some sort of exit exams (Gewertz, 2017/2019). Now the number is approximately thirteen states that still necessitate these exams for graduation (Gerwitz, 2017/2019). Other reasons may have to do with taking care of family members, leaving no time to attend school, pregnancy, or for reasons unknown.

While the high school graduation rates for Native American students have officially increased in the last few years, we still are not accounting for the number of Indigenous students who drop out of school before they are counted in ninth grade; many of these students are dropping out during their middle school years.

If school counselors and teachers are non-Native, they may use the reasons that are typically cited by the dominant culture as justification to stay in school, namely to have good jobs and make good salaries; or they may cite additional reasons for staying in school such as the fact that prisons are filled with high school dropouts as shown by the National Dropout Prevention Center's (n.d.) research. While these rationalizations may make a difference to non-Native students in their struggle to stay in school, they may not have any impact on Native students whose cultural values do not include a high priority on individual wealth acquisition.

While the skills involved in creating resiliency within people and cultural groups appear to involve a constellation of school, home, and community factors, it does appear that there is reason to believe that educators can teach some of these skills to students and also create the types of environments that are supportive of American Indian students' success (Hupfeld, n.d.).

Doing so could result in a lowering of the dropout rate for Native students. The newest revision of the Elementary and Secondary Education Act of 1965 is known as the Every Student Succeeds Act (ESSA; 2015) which concentrates on: (a) using growth in achievement as a measurement of success by using multiple measures; (b) emphasizing the need to provide education that is relevant for the needs of all students; (c) creating positive school climate and developing the socioemotional skills of students; (d) generating and maintaining strong ties with families and communities; (f) increasing the trust levels among schools, families, teachers, and students; and (g) strengthening student readiness for college and careers.

There is renewed recognition that educational institutions are not simply places for the transmission of knowledge. They act as small communities where schools operate as organic systems which include not only teaching and evaluating students but caring about the welfare of our students. This means that schools must also attend to the socioecological needs of students as part of their missions, not apart from their missions.

To be an effective culturally relevant teacher for Aboriginal students involves more than simply learning a set of techniques to follow. It involves working with children's natal communities, understanding cultural practices, beliefs, traditions, and learning about their histories. It involves developing skills to support students in becoming more resilient and willing to take chances within the school environment. To be able to do these things requires that we become willing to share power in our schools with Indigenous communities, something that educators have not regularly been want to do. The benefits of doing so, however, far outweigh the initial discomfiture that we experience in doing so.

Darling-Hammond, Bae, Cook-Harvey, Lam, Mercer . . . & Stosich (2016) include recognition of student self-efficacy and growth into self-directed learners as a goal for future student success beyond school. This requires changing the testing mind-set that has dominated school "reform" movements for the last 40 years to that of once again promoting a positive school climate and having teachers who are concerned with the development of the whole child.

Socioecological Factors to Examine in Relation to Students' Academic Lives

Additional measures that now need to be considered with the ESSA (2015) are those in the areas of Social-Emotional Learning and Student Participation. Some of this evidence can be supplied through compiling suspension/expulsion rates, numbers of chronic absenteeism, and culture/climate surveys from students, staff, and parents. For English Language Learners (ELLs), the rate of their progression as well as redesignation rates must be supplied (Darling-Hammond, et al., 2016). For American Indian and Alaska Natives, being able to assess the strength of ties between schools with Native families and communities is essential, as well as having the inclusion of Native cultures and languages in the school curriculum.

In other words, schools are not simply institutions in the mesosystems of students' lives: we cannot ignore the tremendous impact that they have on the entire lives and future lives of our students. Those who comprise the educational macrosystem in this country, state and national boards of education as well as educational researchers and policy directors, are finally acknowledging the fact that caring for the whole child is necessary. This emphasis is something that has been lost during the push for "school choice" with vouchers and Charter schools, and of trying to revise and privatize our schools since the 1980s to the present (Ravitch, 2020).

Just as the "factory" or industrialized approach to education in the first half of the twentieth century viewed students as "products" to be prepared for the workforce (Collins, 2000), so has this last period focused on schools as representing a "market" in the economy, one that would pay off for investors: The public in terms of students prepared for work, but mainly the upper-class investors in companies that serve the "industry" of schools. While the growth between rich and poor in this country has been steadily increasing, neoliberals—those who espouse that what is private is good and what is public is bad—

> argue that making the market the ultimate arbiter of social worthiness will eliminate politics and its accompanying irrationality from our educational and social discussions. Efficiency and cost-benefit analysis will be the engines of social and educational transformation. Yet among the ultimate effects of such 'economizing' and 'depoliticizing' strategies is actually to make it even harder to interrupt the growing inequalities and resources and power that so deeply characterize this society. (Apple, 1998, p. 199)

Human Capital, Social Capital, and Cultural Capital in Schools

The field of economics has yielded terminologies, or metaphors, which allow us to understand the constructs that apply to education in terms of exchange theories: one person has what another person needs or wants, who then proceeds to make an exchange with the first person for what is needed. This is the essence of social exchange theory: teachers and students develop relationships similar to what would be found in communal societies where participants give and receive without the need to think about recompense (Clark & Jordan, 2002).

These communal relationships are very strong and build upon the human capital that members bring with them into society. For education, the term human capital refers to the abilities and knowledge teachers bring with them to educate students as well as what children bring with them to school. Students' human capital depends on the cultural capital provided to them by their families, or inherited cultural capital (Bourdieu, 2011).

Cultural capital will be different for various populations, especially diverse or underrepresented populations in our country (Bourdieu, 2011). Examples of "embodied" cultural capital are belief systems, mores, ethics, values, and practices. Embodied cultural capital is complemented by "objectified" cultural products, such as artwork, music, dances, and writings produced by group members (Bourdieu, 2011).

Cultural capital is maintained through ties with others, whether at the micro-, meso-, or exosystem levels, specified as "Social Capital" (Bourdieu, 2011). Most often, these ties in education are found within the mesosystem level where opportunities for creating trust among schools, teachers, administrators, and families or communities are essential.

All of us are born without ties to outside individuals or groups, and we must therefore become socialized into all of our future roles in society and learn the common norms and rules which govern us (Fukuyama, 2000). Social capital consists of shared informal values or norms that allow groups to develop trust. Trust requires honesty and reliability of group members and is in action when members of groups act in cooperation with each other (Fukuyama, 2000).

Fukuyama (2000) states that historical traditions are an important source of rules and norms for societies, no matter the country of origin. These spontaneously generated rules and norms do not appear to work well in communities of over ten thousand. Conflicts can arise when cultural groups who have different hierarchical rules and norms as well as spontaneously generated rules and norms—some of which have been established over thousands of years—come into contact. This is the case between Western Europeans and Native American societies beginning during the period of European conquest in the Americas and continuing today.

Families are the source of developing social trust, by first producing a "radius of trust" (Fukuyama, 2000, p. 99) within the family that then is extended to other members of the society.

Developing a radius of trust in schools for Native American students does not take place automatically. Instead, it requires that teachers understand the traditions of the particular Indigenous communities where they are situated. It requires respect for Native beliefs and practices, understanding that these have existed for millennia.

Developing a radius of trust in schools requires action on the part of teachers to have high expectations of all students. We need to consider the students in terms of the human and cultural capital they bring with them to school. We must also attend to what we have learned about resilience, and how resilient students are more "endowed" with the abilities to continue to accomplish their aims even in light of negative events in their lives. This means that we, as educators, must become healers in our classrooms for Aboriginal children: paying attention to their needs and incorporating what Noddings (1994) has termed as an "ethic of caring" in what we do and how we teach children in schools (Whitfield & Klug, 2003).

THE ADVERSE CHILDHOOD EVENTS STUDY AND STUDENT TOXIC STRESS

New research is continually shining light on areas of physical and mental health that impact our lives positively or negatively. Psychological, physical, or sexual abuse; street drug use; alcohol abuse; spousal violence; criminal activity; mental health issues/suicide; mother absenteeism/desertion; and incarceration of a family member are all factors that were examined on a large-scale, nationwide study of the relationship between childhood experiences and the likelihood of adult development of physical illnesses and disease or mental health problems (Felitti, Anda, Nordenberg, Williamson, Spitz, Edwards, & Marks, 1998).

The conclusions of this comprehensive study of Adverse Childhood Experiences (ACE) by the eight members involved nationwide in the study were the following:

> Because adverse childhood experiences are common and they have strong long-term associations with adult health risk behaviors, health status, and diseases, increased attention to primary, secondary, and tertiary prevention strategies is needed. These strategies include prevention of the occurrence of adverse childhood experiences, preventing the adoption of health risk behaviors as responses to adverse experiences during childhood and adolescence, and, finally, helping change the health risk behaviors and ameliorating the disease burden among adults whose health problems may represent a long-term consequence of adverse childhood experiences. (Felitti et al. 1998, p. 254)

What is called "toxic stress"—when children experience four or more of the identified adverse events in their lives—we now know leads to chronic stress overload for them. This stress affects the way they can attend, concentrate, and behave appropriately in school and other settings. In later life, this stress could then result in chronic illness and disease, obesity, and mental health problems. One of the findings of the ACE study is that trauma affects more than one generation and it may become encoded in our genes, being passed on from one generation to the next, without some type of intervention as explained next.

Toxic Stress and Epigenetics in Translation for Indigenous Societies

LeManuel "Lee" Bitsoi (Navajo), a PhD Research Associate in genetics at Harvard University, commented on the relationship between toxic stress and health, and passing this on to future generations: "Native healers, medicine people and Elders have always known it and it is common knowledge in Native oral traditions" (Pember, 2015). Epigenetics—the study of factors that influence gene expression—is making connections between adverse experiences and historical trauma, which then becomes translated into intergenerational trauma (Mukherjee, 2016). Pember (2015) cites Sotero, an expert in this area, that intergenerational trauma is produced in the following way:

> In the initial phase, the dominant culture perpetuates mass trauma on a population in the form of colonialism, slavery, war or genocide. In the second phase the affected population shows physical and psychological symptoms in response to

the trauma. In the final phase, the initial population passes these responses to trauma to subsequent generations, who in turn display similar symptoms. (Pember, 2015)

While most of us have experienced some trauma in our lives, it used to be that we were told to "suck it up," that this was life and we had to deal with it. Unfortunately, medical researchers have found that the trauma does not go away but becomes absorbed into our bodies (Mukherjee, 2016).

In terms of Indigenous peoples in this country, the additional trauma of having children taken away to boarding schools without families' knowledge or permission not only marked Native community members, but disrupted traditions, understandings of languages, cultural knowledge, and practices. The sadness and accompanying traumatic stress are still felt in communities today (Trahant, 2018).

Later, where boarding schools were more connected to Native communities and families, and especially if grandparents and parents supported decisions to send children to them, this trauma does not appear to be as significant as shown in this interview excerpt with Karen Gayton (Swisher) Comeau, who grew up in a small, mostly white community. Karen attended a public school on the reservation and later an Indian boarding school as noted below:

> It was a public school; I was the only Indian kid in the whole school. It was a very small school. I went to school there 10 ½ years. The last two years of high school I went to school in Fort Yates, which is the Indian school, Bureau school. Half of my fifth-grade year I went to Fort Yates. So I guess two and a half years I went somewhere else. . . . At that time, the public school I had gone to was very small, no real advantages in terms of sciences or anything like that . . . [and] I was a good student. . . . I realized, probably at 13, that I really wanted to meet more Native kids than I knew. I still had my white friends, of course, and they're lifelong friends. But I also recognized at that young age all by myself that there [were] more advantages going to a bigger school . . . plus I had become more acquainted with some of the Native kids. I definitely knew who I was . . . but I just wanted to be around more Native kids.
>
> It never entered my mind to drop out of high school. In fact, I loved high school. I had a great time. It was like, there were several of our friends that dropped out, but there was a whole bunch of us, who, whatever the motivation was, it was strong to keep us in school. . . .
>
> We just had a 50th class reunion this summer. . . . It was really interesting because this is a federal on-reservation boarding school, and so we had dormitories. . . . Many of us who were together this summer remembered this one teacher who was our senior English teacher. And he recognized that we had not had a good background in English. He spent just about every night having extra

classes for students, because he said, "You have got to know some stuff before your graduate." And it became kind of a fun thing to do. He was really dedicated . . . I think he saved a lot of us. —Karen Gayton (Swisher) Comeau, Standing Rock Sioux (interviewed by B. J. Klug, October 2010)

Karen followed in her mother's footsteps and became a teacher, later receiving her doctoral degree in education. Karen identified with being American Indian and was determined to improve education for Indigenous students through her teaching.

One of the results of the HGP was to explore many more aspects of the genome than we could have done previously, again due to advances in technology. Through the work of geneticists, we now know that genes, located on chromosomes, also carry additional chemicals that are involved in encoding essential information needed for the survival of individuals. If we remember that almost every cell in our body carries our genetic information, when trauma is experienced in one area of the body, it becomes embedded in almost all of our genetic information when trauma and response to trauma are encoded on the genes (Mukherjee, 2016).

This is what is referred to as epigenetics: the science of the influence of our environments on our bodies and how chemicals record these responses on genes. "[The gene] imprints and erases chemical marks on itself in response to alterations in its environment—thereby encoding a form of cellular 'memory'" (Mukherjee, 2016).

Consequently, each human genome has a great many mutations or gene variations. This explains the differences that exist even with identical twins, who start their lives with identical genomes but whose genomes change in response to their environmental experiences, sometimes even in the womb.

This also explains how trauma becomes encoded in our bodies and is carried on through subsequent generations as studies of traumatized populations have shown. Children who were in utero or born after traumas experienced by their mothers will carry that trauma with them even though they, themselves, did not experience the trauma (Mukherjee, 2016).

It appears that excessive trauma causes a difference in gene expression due to the production of glucocorticoids, hormones that cause the genes that handle stress in the brain's hippocampus to switch off (Mukherjee, 2016). The events in our current point in history that contribute to toxic stress for children are identified as abuse of all kinds, abandonment, violence within families, incarceration of family members, and food or housing insecurities (Felitti et al., 1998; Redford, 2016).

Research shows that Native Americans have high rates of ACE scores, which can account for depression, posttraumatic stress disorder (PTSD), and physical illnesses. Understanding that historical trauma (HT) is passed down through the genes may explain some of the differences found in Native families and communities with their perceptions of boarding schools and white man's education as being bad or as contributing knowledge that made positive impacts in Native students' lives.

We find that students who experience toxic stress due to home factors or what they are undergoing in school or outside of their homes have more limited abilities to handle life's challenges. In school, this becomes expressed in behavior problems, attention problems, and negative coping mechanisms for children and adolescents (Felitti et al., 1998; Redford, 2016).

Students can be more explosive; are usually less tolerant of others or what others say or do to them; have higher rates of absenteeism; may have shorter attention spans; may be afraid of taking on new learning challenges; may be more likely to fail or have poor grades; and are more likely to drop out of school. On the other hand, those who experience their education as a positive experience, even counting the extra work that may be needed as shown in the interview with Karen above, are much more likely to carry that positive attitude forward into their future lives.

Colonization and the Production of Historical and Intergenerational Trauma

With new research on toxic stress and the short- and long-term effects on people, there has been a patent creation of awareness that intergenerational trauma is real. For Indigenous populations, it is a result of the HT experienced by American Indians and Alaska Natives over the past five hundred years.

This stress did not end for Indigenous peoples after the colonial period. Countless documents verify the ongoing killing, raping, pillaging, kidnapping, and enslavement of Aboriginals by Europeans and Euro-Americans during the past, all of which continues today in different areas of the country, some under the heading of "human trafficking."

In our postcolonial society, racial biases, prejudices, and the ravaging and killing of Native people, especially women, is an ongoing problem. When these events occur, the whole Native community is aware of what has happened, and our Indigenous children in schools are affected by the news. Couple this with possible trauma experienced in some homes from which our children come, and the recipe for increasing problems at school results.

This is not to say that all Native American families experience all types or any of the above traumatic events. Experiencing toxic stress is not limited to one population, but is experienced by many children in all areas of the country and ethnic groups. Nevertheless, we can't ignore the devastation, genocide, and racist acts perpetrated against Indigenous populations in this country. All of these have contributed to intergenerational trauma and historical trauma, which we see in Native American communities both on and off reservations today.

Lasting Effects of Intergenerational and HT

Many Native communities that experienced the results of intergenerational trauma within families have high numbers of those involved in negative behaviors resulting from toxic stress. As with Aboriginal and other students, we see the results of toxic stress with those who decide to drop out of school, join gangs, or participate in negative behaviors such as being involved with drugs and alcohol abuse (Martin & Halperin, 2006).

In addition, the adjusted suicide rate for Native American adolescents is the highest for those ages of 15–24. In 2017, the rate was 39.7 for Indigenous males and females per one hundred thousand of all races in the United States compared to 9.9 per one hundred thousand of other ethnic groups, with that of adolescent Native American males three times the rate of others (Substance Abuse and Mental Health Services, 2017).

Brave Heart (2003) has identified the following additional responses to HT experienced by Native American youth: survivor guilt, depression, PTSD symptoms, psychic numbing, hypervigilance, low self-esteem, internalization of ancestral suffering, intense fear, disassociation, dreams of massacres, and anger. Students, especially young Native American males, may be reluctant to seek help from school counselors as they do not know what would be the result of those visits (Freedenthal & Stiffman, 2007).

School staff experience the results of intergenerational trauma and HT with students in terms of negative behaviors exhibited at school in classrooms and on the playgrounds (Loukas, Ripperger-Suhler, & Horton, 2009). It is important to identify what the cause (problem) is of the effect (the bad behavior) to name it and address dealing with both areas for students instead of going the usual route and taking disciplinary action without investigating causes, many of which are those underlying contributions to student toxic stress.

An important suggestion made in the recent films about resilience and schools is for teachers to change their ways of responding when students act up or become violent in schools. Instead of asking, "What's wrong with you?" Educators need to be asking, "What happened to you?" In this way, students can name their problem, and by doing so, can refocus their energies instead of constantly ruminating about their situations. If counseling is needed, problems can be addressed in the safety of the school environment (Resilient Idaho: Hope after Trauma, 2019).

The work of Elias (2003) is cited in the research by Garn, Kulinna, Cothran and Ferry (2010) as a possible framework for addressing negative behaviors proactively through teaching social and emotional learning as part of the school curriculum. In this model, students develop competencies related to interpersonal and intrapersonal skills such as self-awareness, cooperation, emotional self-regulation, communication, and empathy towards others through a student-centered program. This program has worked in many schools, but if used with Aboriginal populations, it would need to be adapted to particular Native American expectations.

Some models have worked in schools to address Native American suicide rates and substance abuse that have been successful (Lechner, Cavanaugh, & Blyler, 2016). Clearly, it is essential for education professionals to provide a sense of security in schools for the time that our Native American students are with us, and many times, after they leave us (BigFoot, 2013).

Lowe, Riggs, and Henson (2011) recommend ways to work with Tribal nations to involve them first in identifying the problem to be solved, and then working together as a team to identify solutions to these problems. Though they are working from a health perspective, this is a good example of working across institutional boundaries to solve problems that affect Indigenous students in both their health and education. It is important to work with Native American communities to address some of these problems and develop unique solutions with school partnerships.

Addressing Toxic Stress and Its Results in Schools

We know that there is a relationship between toxic stress and resiliency: the more toxic stress, the less resilient our students are. There is new information, though, about how nurturing and teaching children strategies can combat this problem with our youth, and how schools can be involved in this effort (Meichenbaum, n.d.; Resilient Idaho: Hope after Trauma, 2019). While there are resilience programs that are shown to be effective in schools, an Indigenous component should be included for Native American students.

We know that "Resilient youth respond differently to trauma, stress, and adverse conditions. The research suggests that school can facilitate resiliency in a number of ways," (Thornton & Sanchez, 2010). We need to understand that in schools with large Indigenous populations, we must work with Tribal representatives to be able to bring back the cultural values related to health. These include physical, mental, emotional, and spiritual healing; care for everyone in the community; service to the community in terms of working together to keep the land and water healthy; and emphasizing pride in Native identity (Suina, 2016).

Navajo health educator Michelle Suina (2016), who provides health services in Navajo communities, states that getting back to the core Navajo teachings—about the values and practices of spirituality, community, family and children, healthy eating provided by traditional foods, being involved in hard work for the good of the community, and incorporating traditional breastfeeding for babies—is imperative to bringing healthy lifestyles back to Indigenous communities. There needs to be a shift from the Western medical model of focusing on "prevention, detection, and treatment of disease" to one of "healthy minds, bodies, spirits, and heart" (Suina, 2016, p.74). We note, by extension, this is true for other Aboriginal communities.

THE NATIVE AMERICAN MEDICINE WHEEL

The circle is a sacred symbol in Native American epistemology. Everything in nature is round; there are no squares or rectangles to be found. Therefore, the "sacred hoop" embodies the world, life, the cycles of nature, the sun, the moon, the stars, and more. The circle is reflected in the dances of Native Americans performed during powwows and festivals, always going in the direction of east to west; and the circle is used in other sacred ceremonies.

The Native American Medicine Wheel is a figure well known in Indian country (see Figure 8.1). While it is not a symbol that has traditionally been utilized by every Tribal nation, it can be found in the majority of areas across the country. This sacred symbol incorporates the circle and is sometimes just referred to as "the wheel." It represents the wholeness in which Indigenous peoples perceive the world, and how everything is interrelated both within one's life and own bodies.

The Medicine Wheel is an ancient symbol. The most famous Medicine Wheel on land is that of the Bighorn Medicine Wheel in Wyoming, now included in the National Register of Historic Sites as Medicine Wheel/Medicine Mountain Historic Landmark. It is situated within the Crow Tribal territory, and people from other Tribal nations have reported that their people traveled to it for ceremonial use

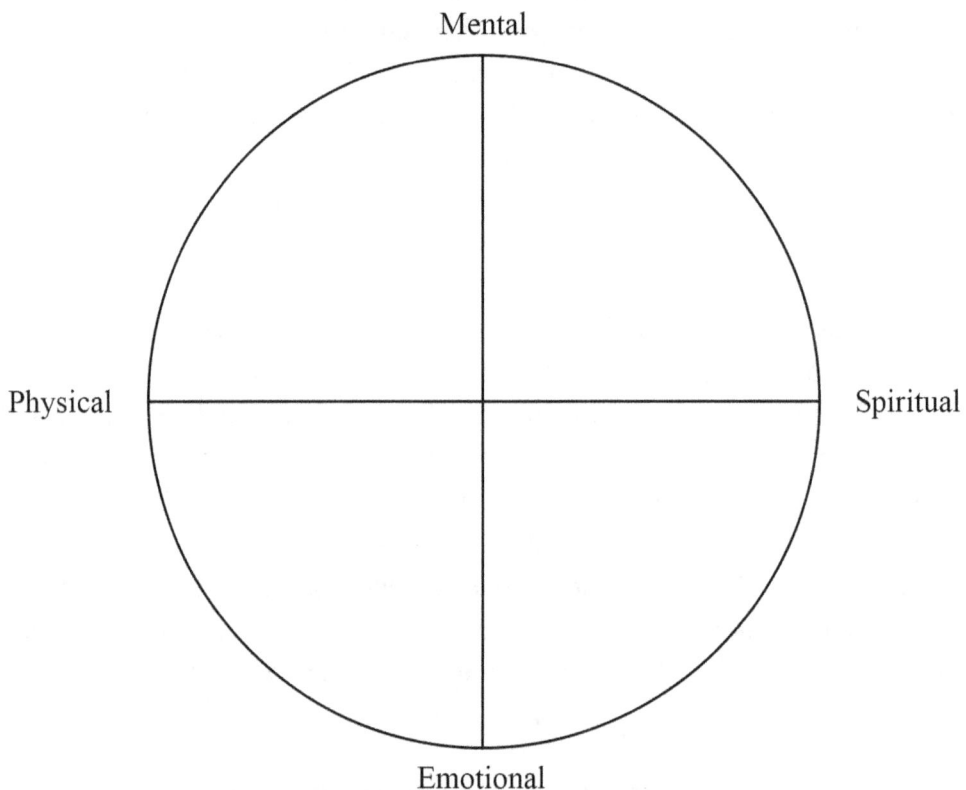

Figure 8.1. Representation of a Native American Medicine Wheel. The Medicine Wheel is a sacred symbol for Indigenous cultures in the U.S. and Canada. This symbol is a reminder that all of life and our perceptions of life are interrelated, and that one area impacts the other areas positively or negatively. It is also a reminder of the holistic nature of physical being, and that if one area is impacted negatively, the other areas are impacted negatively, too. The symbol is presented many times with a number of eagle feathers (also considered sacred) hanging from the bottom according to particular Tribal nation teachings. This symbol should not be appropriated and/or replicated by non-Native Americans.

(Chapman, 2019; Medicine Wheel, n.d.; Trenholm & Carly, 1964). Scientists have found that pillars of the wheel align to astrological events, similar to other sites of Medicine Wheels found throughout the Americas, such as that of the Majorville Wheel in Alberta Canada, which has been dated to 3200 BCE (Medicine Wheel, n.d.).

In Native American epistemology, land and spirituality are linked together. That is one of the reasons that Indigenous peoples fought so hard to retain their lands and keep them from white encroachment. Their lands are their places of worship. One hundred and fifty Medicine Wheels have been found in Wyoming, South Dakota, Montana, Saskatchewan, and Alberta Canada (Chapman, 2019).

Today, the Medicine Wheel embodies ancient traditions of healthy lifestyles and attention to each area of Native Americans' beings. Four is a sacred number in Indigenous communities, and one can see that in Figure 8.1, the Native American Medicine Wheel is divided into four equal parts. There are several alternate ways that people refer to the Medicine Wheel, as the Four Directions, Four Winds, Four Grandfathers, or Four Buffaloes.

To fully understand the wheel, educators need to know that Native peoples do not mean the word "medicine" in the same way as Western cultures. Indian peoples used a word similar to medicine to describe their sacred ways of healing as well as encompassed all aspects of their lives. Europeans then translated the word into English as "medicine." However, the word for Native American peoples holds a meaning far greater than just pharmaceuticals or physician visits. The wheel is a holistic symbol relating to people's mental, physical, emotional, and spiritual systems.

For non-Natives who are Christians, it may be difficult to see the sacred hoop that encircles the four areas, since the first thing noticed is the cross in the middle (Klug & Whitfield, 2003). The cross with equal sides is a symbol used extensively as well in Aboriginal iconography for thousands of years. When examining Figure 8.1, we see that—in general—the direction of north is associated with the color white, the gift of fire, and mental activity: gaining knowledge about the world, intellect, self-concept, memories, and experiences in life.

Continuing, east is associated with the color red, the spirit and spirituality, and the gift of the earth: which people need to take care of and protect. South is linked with the color yellow, the gift of air, and emotion: how we feel about ourselves, our self-esteem, and empathy for others. Lastly, west is coupled with the color black, the gift of water, our physical beings, and our relationships with plants, animals, and other living things. To remain healthy, we need to appreciate and attend to all of these areas as each one impacts the others positively or negatively.

As educators, we can see this readily when children struggle in school, then develop negative physical symptoms, low self-esteem, and lack of energy or connections with the Creator. They become out of balance and may not respect all areas of life when this happens. We also see this when Indigenous students experience toxic stress and its effects.

The wheel is a powerful reminder that as educators we are not only teaching children's brains: we also must act as healers in our classrooms (Whitfield & Klug, 2004), attending to the areas of children's well-being impacted by how they are feeling about themselves and/or their abilities in the classroom. While not all Indigenous nations utilize the iconography of the Medicine Wheel, this teaching is very important and incorporated in the admonition to follow the "Red road" to live a respectful, good life.

Another way to express this is the Navajo expression to "walk in beauty." Again, this refers to the significance of being in balance in all areas of our lives, not to the Western concept of the word "beauty" as physical attractiveness. All of the areas in the Medicine Wheel are addressed within Indigenous students' human socioecological microsystems and mesosystems.

Pewewardy (1998; 2002) reminds us that when teachers and Indigenous students work together and keep in mind the Medicine Wheel, school becomes less of an institution and more of a community concerned with the needs of all of its members. A positive atmosphere results where all members aspire to work together and the Native American values of cooperation, sharing, humility, and care of each other are incorporated along with learning self-efficacy (Yazzie-Mintz, 2007).

In classrooms where the Medicine Wheel made by Native Americans is displayed, whether as a painting, print, or as a physical object, we have found that Indigenous students respond well as this aspect of their culture is present in the classroom. In the same way, in Navajo classrooms where signage reflects the message to "walk in beauty," students feel assured that this environment is not so "foreign" from that of their communities.

In some schools, murals depicting American Indian or Alaska Native themes are found to decorate hallways, libraries, or the outside areas of schools as at Puente de Hózhǫ' in northern Arizona. We have seen hallways decorated with scenes from traditional legends in schools with large populations from particular tribes, such as at Fort Hall Elementary School in Fort Hall, Idaho. A group of Indigenous students attending one of the BIA facilities transformed their bare and shabby environment by painting murals under the guidance of the National Indian Youth Leadership Organization (Lopez & Hall, 2007).

Some schools choose to decorate hallways with patterns particular to the different Tribal nations attending the schools, such as was done in the Indian Community School in Milwaukee, Wisconsin, in their former downtown educational building location. The Shoshone-Bannock Jr.-Sr. High School in Fort Hall, Idaho, also uses many Indigenous patterns in its building and architecture. This is one way to incorporate the mental, emotional, physical, and spiritual realms for students in schools.

Another area to address in schools is that of preventing drug and alcohol abuse, which can start very early and especially affect students' abilities to perform well academically and maintain an interest in schools. Drumming is considered sacred medicine and it is appreciated as a way to build cultural identification, self- and group-expression, and meditative activity (Dickerson, Robichaud, Teruya, Nagaran, & Hser, 2012). Providing a Native American Drumming club, directed by an Indigenous leader, is one way that schools could work with communities to strengthen cultural identity and steer Indigenous youth into positive ways to build their resistance to engaging in harmful activities.

In schools that are language immersion schools, such as Rough Rock Community School in Chinlé, Arizona, Kaiapuni schools in Hawaii, and Chief Tahgee Elementary Academy in Fort Hall, Idaho, one will also find not only the teaching of Indigenous languages but also cultural artifacts and the teaching of traditional cultural arts and crafts. Many times, traditional performance arts such as singing and dancing are included within the curricula, knowing that these are important ways to address language learning as well as to strengthen children's beings as addressed through the Medicine Wheel.

WHERE WE ARE NOW IN UNDERSTANDING EDUCATION FOR AMERICAN INDIAN STUDENTS

[Humans] become socialized into a whole series of roles and identities—Catholic, worker, deviant, mother, bureaucrat—defined by a complex series of norms and rules. These norms bind communities together and are tightly reinforced by them, sharply limiting the kinds of choices people can make about their lives. (Fukuyama, 2000, p. 104)

Most of the time, social capital is overlaid with rules and norms that control the types of behaviors expected of individuals in their various roles. Consequently, while we promote the ideal of freedom for individuals, in reality, we are constricted from doing exactly what we want by the rules and norms of our micro-, meso- and macro-societies. In this way, chaos can be controlled and people are inhibited from perpetrating atrocities on other citizens.

Formal education confirms citizens with rights to participate in the greater society at certain levels where formal academic attainment is a key to admittance. We've come far in understanding the importance of adding culturally relevant teaching and languages into the curriculum for Native American students. This is due in large part to research focusing on best practices in American Indian Education conducted under Clinton's 1998 Executive Order 13096 and listening to recommendations by Tribal officials and educators with expertise in teaching Indigenous students as espoused in Clinton's Executive Order 13175 (2000).

This mandate was to establish regular contact with Tribal nations to provide "meaningful education" for American Indian and Alaska Native students. During the initial period of NCLB (2001), members of American Indian and Alaska Native communities thought that the legislation would result in great changes in education for their children. One of the reasons for this was because of the required disaggregating of student test scores according to race as well as focusing on the types of education, teachers' abilities to educate, and materials and schools that students were attending (Klug, 2012).

Unfortunately, because of all of the additional demands put into place through the NCLB (2001) initiative, culturally relevant teaching was left behind in state efforts to homogenize curriculum to ensure that all schools served up the same curriculum meeting the same standards as that for all students throughout the state. Bush's Executive Order 13336 (2004) to prepare Indigenous students to meet the requirements of NCLB included teaching heritage languages. However, rarely was anything done because of the conflict with the NCLB mandates for public school systems.

The Executive Order 13175 (2000) directive was again taken up in 2010 by the Obama administration. This was done following a 2009 study of the conditions in education for American Indian and Alaska Native students, which detailed the dismal results of NCLB (2001) for Native American students.

As stated by U.S. Secretary of Education Arne Duncan in the Introduction to the *Report of the Consultations with Tribal Leaders in Indian Country*, "We have to dramatically improve the quality of education in Indian country and for Native American students, whether they live on reservations or not" (Tribal Leaders Speak: The State of American Indian Education, 2010; 2011, p. 1). This statement acknowledges one of the greatest obstacles in Native American education: that there is not just one entity responsible for teaching Native American students. The great majority—estimated in 2005–2006 at 92 percent of our Indigenous students—attend local public schools.

This resulted in Obama's Executive Order 13592, Improving American Indian and Alaska Native Educational Opportunities and Strengthening Tribal Colleges and Universities (2011). With this understanding in mind, we know how important it is for our non-Native public school educators, the majority of whom are white, middle-class females, to embrace the concept of culturally relevant teaching or pedagogy. We recognize how important it is for our Indigenous students to have the support of their families and teachers, especially concerning developing their resilience (Wolpow, Johnson, Hertel, & Kincaid, 2016).

In the next chapter, we will continue to address the importance of working closely with Native communities to promote the mental, spiritual, physical, and emotional welfare of all our Indigenous students. We will present culturally appropriate ways to do this with our students, necessary to complete their goals of graduating from high school and for their lives afterward.

REFERENCES

Apple, M. W. (1998). Education and new hegemonic blocs: Doing policy the 'right' way. *International Studies in Sociology of Education, 8* (2), 181–202. DOI: 10.1080/0962021980020021.

BigFoot, D. S. (2013). *Childhood Trauma Series in Indian Country.* Indian Country Child Trauma Center on Child Abuse and Neglect. Norman: University of Oklahoma Health Sciences Center. Retrieved from https://43ejbalotx5n1btits42mnsv-wpengine.netdna-ssl.com/wp-content/uploads/2013/06/Trauma-Series-in-Indian-Country_3.pdf.

Bourdieu, P. (2011). The forms of capital. In A. R. Sadovnik (Ed.), *Sociology of education: A critical reader* (2nd ed.; pp. 83–96). New York, NY: Routledge.

Brave Heart, M. Y. (2003). The historical trauma response among natives and its relationship with substance abuse: a Lakota illustration. *Journal of Psychoactive Drugs, 35* (1), 7–13. Retrieved from https://www.ncbi.nlm.nih.gov/pubmed/12733753.

Chapman, F. (2019, April 10). Medicine Wheel/Medicine Mountain: Celebrated and controversial landmark. *WyoHistry.org.* Wyoming Historical Society. Retrieved from https://www.wyohistory.org/encyclopedia/medicine-wheel.

Clark, M. S., & Jordan, S. D. (2002). Adherence to communal norms: What it means, when it occurs, and some thoughts on how it develops. In W. G. Graziano & B. Laursen (Eds.), *Social exchange in development* (pp. 3–26). San Francisco, CA: Jossey-Bass.

Collins, W. J. (2000). *Race and twentieth-century American economic history.* Cambridge, MA: The National Bureau of Economic Research. Retrieved from https://www.nber.org /reporter/winter06/collins.html.

Cross, T. (1998). Understanding family resiliency from a relational view. In H. I. McCubbin, E. A. Thompson, A. I. Thompson, & J. E. Fromer (Eds.), *Resiliency in ethnic minority families: Vol. 1. Native and immigrant American families* (pp. 143–58). Thousand Oaks, CA: Sage.

Darling-Hammond, L., Bae, S., Cook-Harvey, C. M., Lam, L., Mercer, C., Podolsky, A., & Stosich, E. L. (2016). *Pathways to New Accountability Through the Every Student Succeeds Act.* Palo Alto, CA: Learning Policy Institute. Retrieved from http://learningpolicyinstitute.org/our-work/publications-resources/ pathways-new-accountability-every-student-succeeds-act.

Dickerson, D., Robichaud, F., Teruya, C., Nagaran, K., & Hser, Y-I. (2012). Utilizing drumming for American Indians/Alaska Natives with substance use disorders. *American Journal of Drug Alcohol Abuse, 38* (5), 505–510. Doi: 10.3109/00952990.2012.699565.

Every Student Succeeds Act of 2015, Reauthorization of the Elementary and Secondary Education Act of 1965, 20 U.S.C. § 6301 *et seq.*, Pub. L. 114-95. Retrieved from https://www.congress.gov/114/plaws/publ95/PLAW-114publ95.pdf.

Executive Order 13096, 1998 American Indian and Alaska Education.

Executive Order 13175, 2000 Consultation and Coordination with Indian Tribal Governments.

Executive Order 13336, 2004 American Indian and Alaska Education.

Executive Order 13592, 2011 Improving American Indian and Alaska Native Educational Opportunities and Strengthening Tribal Colleges and Universities.

Felitti, V. J., Anda, R. F., Nordenberg, D., Williamson, D. F., Spitz, A. M., Edwards, V., Koss, M. P., Marks, J. S. (1998). Relationship of Childhood Abuse and Household Dysfunction to Many of the Leading Causes of Death in Adults: The Adverse Childhood Experiences (ACE) Study. *American Journal of Preventative Medicine, 14* (4), 245–58. DOI: https://doi.org/10.1016/S0749-3797(98)00017-8.

Freedenthal, S. & Stiffman, A. R. (2007). "They might think I was crazy": Young American Indians' reasons for not seeking help when suicidal. *Journal of Adolescent Research, 22* (1), 58–77. DOI.10.1177/0743558406295969.

Fukuyama, F. (2000). Social capital. In L. E. Harrison & S. P. Huntington (Eds.), *Culture matters: How values shape human progress* (pp. 98–111). New York: Basic Books.

Garn, A. C, Kulinna, P. H., Cothran, D. J., & Ferry, M. (2010). An examination of social and emotional behavior skills with American Indian elementary students: Issues of measurement, gender, grade, and culture. *Journal of American Indian Education, 49* (3), 24–40.

Gerwertz, G. (2017, February 17/ 2019, April 9). Which states require an exam to graduate? An interactive breakdown of states' 2016–2017 testing plans. *Education Week*. Retrieved from https://www.edweek.org/ew/section/multimedia/states-require-exam-to-graduate.html.

Hupfeld, K. (n.d.) *Resiliency skills and dropout prevention*. Denver, CO: ScholarCentric. Retrieved from www.scholarcentric.com/image/pdf/resiliency.../SC_WP_FNL.pdf.

Klug, B. J. (2012). Falling from grace: How the latest government policies undermine American Indian education. In B. J. Klug (Ed.), *Standing together: American Indian Education as Culturally Responsive Pedagogy* (pp. 71–86). Lanham, MD: Rowman & Littlefield.

Klug, B. J., & Whitfield, P. T. (2003). *Widening the circle: Culturally relevant pedagogy for American Indian children*. New York, NY: RoutledgeFalmer.

Lechner, A., Cavanaugh, M., & Blyler, C. (2016, August 24). Addressing Trauma in American Indian and Alaska Native Youth. Washington, DC: Mathematica Policy Research. Reference Number: 4014. Retrieved from https://www.icctc.org/AIANYouthTIC%20(1).PDF.

Lopez, A., & Hall, M. (2007). Letting in the sun: Native youth transform their school with murals. *Reclaiming Children and youth, 16* (3), 29–35.

Lowe, J., Riggs, C., Henson, J. (2011). Principles for establishing trust when developing a substance abuse intervention with a Native American community. *Creative Nursing, 17* (2), 68–73.

Loukas, A., Ripperger-Suhler, & Horton, K. (2009). Examining temporal associations between school connectedness and early adolescent adjustment. *Journal of Youth Adolescence, 38*, 804-812. DOI 10.1007/s10964-008-9312-9.

Martin, N., & Halperin, S. (2006). Whatever it takes: How twelve communities are reconnecting out-of-school youth. Washington, DC: American Youth Policy Forum. Retrieved from www.aypf.org/publications/WateverItTakes/WIT_nineseconds.pdf.

McFarland, J., Cui, J., Holmes, J., & Wang, X. (2019). Trends in High School Dropout and Completion Rates in the United States: 2019 (NCES 2020-117). U.S. Department of Education. Washington, DC: National Center for Education Statistics. Retrieved from https://nces.ed.gov/pubsearch.

Medicine Wheel/Medicine Mountain. (n.d.). *Wikipedia*. Retrieved from https://en.wikipedia.org/wiki/Medicine_Wheel/Medicine_Mountain_National_Historic_Landmark.

Meichenbaum, D. (n.d.). *How educators can nurture resilience in high-risk children and their families*. Teach Safe Schools. Retrieved from http://www.TeachSafeSchools.org.

Mukherjee, S. (2016). *The gene: An intimate history*. New York, NY: Scribner.

National Dropout Prevention Center/Network. (n.d.) *Top 5 reasons to stay in school*. Clemson, SC: Author. Retrieved from http://www.dropoutprevention.org/resource/family_student/reasons.htm.

National Indian Education Association. (n.d.). *Native education 101: Basic facts about American Indian, Alaska Native, and Native Hawaiian education*. Washington, DC: Author.

No Child Left Behind Act of 2001: Reauthorization of the Elementary and Secondary Education Act of 1965, 20 U.S.C. § 6301 *et seq*., Pub. L. 107–110.

Noddings, N. (1994). An ethic of caring and its implications for instructional arrangements. In L. Stone (Ed.), *The education feminism reader* (pp. 171–183). New York, NY: Routledge.

Pember, M. A. (2015, May 28). Trauma may be woven in the DNA of Native Americans. *Indian Country Today*. Indian Country Today Media Network. Retrieved from: https//:indiancountrytodaymedianetwork.com/2015/05/28/trauma-may-be-woven-dna-native-americans-160508.

Pewewardy, C. D. (1998). The holistic Medicine Wheel: An Indigenous model of teaching and learning. *Winds of Change, 14* (4), 28–31.

Pewewardy, C. (2002). Learning styles of Native American/Alaska Native students: A review of the literature and implications for practice. *Journal of American Indian Education, 41* (3), 22–56). Pdf. Retrieved from https://pdfs.semanticscholar.org/93d8/333518b61671c5b5fb9692b9b45c18f69c04.pdf.

Ravitch, D. (2020). *Slaying Goliath: The passionate resistance to privatization and the fight to save America's public schools*. New York, NY: Knopf.

Redford, J. (with N. Burke-Harris; Dirs.). (2016). *Resilience: The biology of stress and the science of hope*. KPJR Films. Retrieved from https://kpjrfilms.co/resilience/.

Resilient Idaho: Hope after Trauma. (2019). *Idaho Resiliency Project.org*. Retrieved from https://www.pbs.org/video/resilient-idaho-hope-after-trauma-sptebc/.

Substance Abuse and Mental Health Services Administration. (2017). *Suicide Clusters within American Indian and Alaska Native Communities: A review of the literature and recommendations*. HHS Publication No. SMA17-5050. Rockville, MD: Center for Mental Health Services, Substance Abuse and Mental Health Services Administration. Retrieved from http://store.samhsa.gov/SMA17-5050.pdf.

Suina, M. (2016). Reflections of a Pueblo Indian Health educator: Weaving Pueblo worldview into health education. *Journal of American Indian Education, 55* (3), 72–90.

Thornton, B., & Sanchez, J. E. (2010). Promoting resiliency among Native American students to prevent dropouts. *Education, 131* (2), 455–464.

Trahant, M. (2018). Indian country remembers trauma of children taken from their parents. *Indian Country Today*. Retrieved from https://www.indiancountrytoday.com.

Trenholm, V. C. & Carly, M. (1964). *The Shoshones: Sentinels of the Rockies*. Norman: University of Oklahoma Press.

Tribal Leaders Speak: The State of American Indian Education, 2010. (2011). *Report of the Consultations with Tribal Leaders in Indian Country*. U.S. Department of Education, Office of Elementary and Secondary Education, Office of Indian Education, White House Initiative on Tribal Colleges and Universities: Washington, D.C. Retrieved from http://www2.ed.gov/about/inits/ed/indianed/consultations.report.pdf.

Whitfield, P. T. & Klug, B. J. (2004). Teachers as "Healers": A 21st Century possibility? Or necessity? *Multicultural Perspectives: The Official Journal of the National Association of Multicultural Education, 6* (1), 43–50.

Wolpow, R., Johnson, M. M., Hertel, R., & Kincaid, S. O. (2016). *The heart of learning and teaching: Compassion, resiliency, and academic success*. Olympia, WA: Office of Superintendent of Public Instruction. Retrieved from https://www.k12.wa.us/sites/default/files/public/compassionateschools/pubdocs/theheartoflearningandteaching.pdf.

Wu, G., Feder, A., Cohen, H., Kim, J. J., Caleron, S., Charney, D. S., & Mathé, A. A. (2013). Understanding resilience. *Frontiers in Behavioral Neuroscience, 7*. PMC3573269. Retrieved from https://www.ncbi.nlm.nih.gov/pmc/articles/PMC3573269.

Yazzie-Mintz, T. (2007). From a place deep inside: Culturally appropriate curriculum as the embodiment of Navajo-ness in classroom pedagogy. *Journal of American Indian Education, 46* (3), 72–93.

Chapter Nine

Educational Collaborations with Native American Communities

_____ School District was the one that I attended K through the first week of my 9th grade year, and it's a public school on the _____ Reservation. I left after one week my freshman year and transferred to _____, another public high school on the _____ Reservation, and a lot of that was because of the issues and challenges and the race relations: the unstable race relations among the community.

[The school district was a member of a group] who asserted that the _____ tribe had been diminished and that the _____ tribe no longer existed. . . . There were just a lot of Native kids and not a lot of them graduating from high school. And so [the assertions about the tribe], that impact carried on into the classrooms with kids. . . . And in that 8th grade year I actually presented to the school board [about] why I thought that [what they were doing] was wrong. And the following year, [nothing changed]. And I just decided that I was going to quit school.

[My parents tried to find another school] when we got a call back from the superintendent at _____ saying, "We've done some internal movement, but we can get her here." Little did I know down the road that the principal of the high school was very well aware of my basketball skills and abilities and said, "You know, we can make some room. We'll do whatever it takes." And so I ended up going to _____, academically performed very well. Graduated with a 3.0 from high school, and was very active. I was student body AC representative, I was the senior class president . . . and homecoming queen. There was just not that social and economic hierarchy in that community. —Mary Jane Oatman (WakWak), Nez Perce (Interviewed by B. J. Klug, December 2010)

Even as a student, Mary Jane was a leader and a strong defender of her Tribal nation. The fact that her school district and some of the administrators and staff could turn against her people was very disturbing to her, and she tried to reach out and correct their misperceptions. Luckily she was able to find allies in her new school from which she graduated.

Teaching is a moral act (Sanger & Osguthorpe, 2009; Stengel, 2013). While this statement is simple, it is profound: As educators we are obligated to find the best way to reach all of our students, no matter what our students' ethnicities and cultures. As a nation, we have to move beyond the hegemonic idea that we can support only a monocultural system that exclusively privileges and validates Western-European values, practices, and knowledges.

> Perhaps nothing has so clarified the inadequacy of traditional social science scholarship as the advance of minority interests in this [twentieth] century. As minority groups have gained power, their self-assertion has compelled the dominant culture to recognize frames of reference. *The historical bondage to a single, monolithic cultural perspective runs counter to that dimension of the classical-liberal view of education which values understanding and adaptation of multiple perspectives as the key to a fuller and more mature intellect. And it cherishes a diverse and many-sided understanding of perennial issues as the very key to human liberty.* But modern liberalism has privileged another strain of classical liberalism, that in which the cultural products of classical societies have become canonized as "culture." (Tozer, Violas, & Senese, 1993; italics mine)

For many years, it was taken for granted that some of our students in schools would just drop out, and there was nothing that could be done to prevent this from happening. We know better now, and we also understand that those same students who may become dropouts possess knowledge that will make a difference in our world today. The cost is too high to allow any child to become victim to an educational system that only cares about majority student success.

CULTURAL DIFFERENCE AND CRITICAL THEORIES

Social scientists determined through many different studies of ethnically diverse cultures that one of the main reasons for the school failure of diverse student populations was due to cultural mismatches, not cultural deficits as promoted previously. At this time, educators and representatives of those populations, along with allies, began to search for ways to change the status quo in schools. As stated by Tozar, Violas, and Senese (1993):

> The transition from cultural deficit theories to cultural difference theories marks a significant passage in the social sciences. It represents a transition from a fixed frame of reference to multiple frames of reference. Anthropologists and linguists, disgraced by their willing endorsement of imperialism, nationalism, and

cultural jingoism leading up to the world wars, have since acquired a respect for human culture in all its splendid variety. This view allows for a richer, more appreciative sense of the human cultural panorama. Other social scientists have followed suit. (p. 308)

Of course, moving to this position in schools ignited the backlash from conservative neoliberals in this country with the resultant intent to close public schools and replace them with private and charter schools (Berliner, 2014; Berliner & Biddle, 1995; Ravitch, 2020). This movement began after the desegregation of schools in the South with the rise of more fundamental Christian schools and movement of white people from core cities to the suburbs (Blakeslee, 1978–79).

As discussed earlier in chapter 6, by creating false narratives of failing schools and failing teachers neoliberals completely undermined and maligned public education and professional educators. By then creating a one-size-fits-all system of teaching, curriculum, and testing, these business people and large corporations have actively attacked our most valued treasure of free education: one that promises to develop full citizens possessing the knowledge and force of habit enabling them to be creative and critical thinkers (Ravitch, 2020).

At this writing, we are not quite out of the woods in terms of this thinking with national tests and state-administered standardized tests to ensure that everyone learns the same set of facts and limited thinking processes. However, we are finally reaching a turning point where those in authority are beginning to recognize the folly of these approaches and the damage being done to students and communities as a result (Ravitch, 2020).

Hopefully, in this turnaround, we will be able to return to effective means of teaching all students, recognizing that the growth of our children's intellects, and not political intrigues, are the most important mission that our schools have. Key elements in this effort to successfully teach our American Indian and Alaska Native students are the communities in which we teach.

Due to various evaluation systems used to judge teacher competency, including the efforts that are still in place of blaming teachers and administrators for students' low standardized test scores as a result of NCLB (2001), many teachers are reluctant to reach out to others for fear that they will be judged as less prepared or able to teach. This is a barrier to being open to working closely with Indigenous peoples in creating culturally relevant teaching or pedagogy supported by the National Indian Education Association (NIEA; n.d.).

We need to remember that our first priority is always our students, and that anything we can learn about their Native ways of learning, values, and belief systems will only enhance our understandings of how to teach them. We can never know everything there is to know about each of the American Indian and Alaska Native societies. Instead, we can learn some general information concerning cultural values, practices, and belief systems, and then it is our job to learn more about the particular Tribal nations from which our students hail. For this to be successful it requires that we take the first steps toward including families and community members in our planning for our curricula within our classrooms.

We already have a model for doing this. When Head Start was first proposed for children from poverty areas so they could begin to learn at an early age the "school knowledge" they needed to know by the time they reached America's Kindergartens and first grades, it was considered a radical idea. At that time with the cultural deficit theory, it was believed that culture was immutable, something that just happened and was as much a part of genetics as one's hair and skin color.

Three developmental psychologists were on the team to address the issue of how to make low-income children more successful in school. Of these three—Urie Bronfenbrenner, Mamie Clark, and Edward Zigler—Bronfenbrenner, of whom you already know, made the point that to be successful, programs needed to include families and community members responsible for raising children, a revolutionary idea at the time. As we now know, this is the cornerstone of what has made Head Start so successful (Paquette & Ryan, 2007/2015).

Integrating Indigenous Cultures, Knowledge, and Ways of Learning and Knowing into Our School Systems

Edgerton (2000) states that no society can know everything about its neighbors, environmental considerations, or its institutions, and people solving new problems quite often cannot make decisions based on logical thinking. This is true of highly secularized societies as well as small societal groups—many focus on solving a few problems and ignore the rest.

There is an overall reluctance of people to change, and when they do make change, economists refer to them as "minimal" and with the least risks. Traditional practices may be continued mostly because they work without people delving into why they work. The logical reason undergirding the workable solution becomes lost in the process (Edgerton, 2000).

While Edgerton (2000) was referring to greater cultural societies, we have to recognize that educational institutions themselves are small societies, and as such, they have their own cultures. Educators have our ways of doing what has worked for the education of dominant-culture students and assimilated students in the past, and without direction, will flounder in trying to implement directives concerning integrating Native American histories and cultures into the curriculum.

Culturally relevant/responsive teaching has grown out of the cultural difference and critical theory traditions. It represents the recognition that children need to see themselves in their schools and their textbooks. Because so much white, Anglo-Saxon culture is represented in schools, we need to provide equal representations of the heroes and sheroes of other ethnically diverse populations and their accomplishments that have made our country a better place for all.

We understand that because so much of American Indian and Alaska Native histories have been pushed underground, many non-Native teachers are fearful of making mistakes regarding what to teach and how to teach about our Indigenous populations (Sabzalian, Morrill, & Edmo, 2019; Schneider, Allender, Berta-Ávila, Borunda, Castro, Murray,& Porter, 2019; Stanton, Carjuzaa, & Hall, 2019). Educators need to be assured that it is not their fault that they have not learned the truth about Native peoples in this hemisphere, but that we can now open ourselves up to this knowledge for the sake of our students, ourselves, and our relationships with Aboriginal communities.

Euro-Americans will face the prospect of dealing with "white guilt" as they present this information as well as the fear of rejection by Native Americans. This is only natural, and while many white people may dismiss this guilt by saying they weren't responsible for what happened, doing so is not helpful. A simple, "I'm sorry for what happened to your people," tells listeners that you understand what happened to them, a first step in the healing process and a beginning for forming trust with Indigenous communities.

As educators, many times we are reluctant to admit that we do not know about what really happened to Native peoples or that we do not know enough about their cultures. Due to the different traditions of relating historical events, many times Indigenous populations are surprised that many non-Natives do not know about what happened to Native Americans, much less particular information relating directly to their own Tribal nations.

We can be honest with our Aboriginal allies and acknowledge that we would like to learn more about them. By our recognizing the full citizenship of Aboriginal students and communities in this country, and the need to enlighten all people about Native communities as the first peoples of this country, we won't be as hesitant to approach Native Americans as collaborators with us. In doing so, educators are taking the first step to opening themselves to new knowledge. The reward will be in the way Native communities extend their trust toward educators, knowing that we want to know about them.

Stanton, Carjuzza, and Hall (2019), found that in school districts where superintendents and principals supported the Montana IEFA, the results of teachers' efforts were very positive with all of their students. A door was opened in many communities for Indigenous students to share their knowledge with their teachers and classmates. On the other hand, where there was not much guidance from those in positions of leadership at different levels, including teacher education, non-Native teachers and non-Native preservice teachers struggled and resented what they were supposed to learn and know to teach (Stanton, Carjuzaa, & Hall, 2019).

Other difficulties concern the passage of initiatives and laws in different states to include Native American histories and knowledge in state-required standards for education, but not the funding to adequately prepare teachers for implementing these initiatives or laws, as was the case at first with Montana's IEFA (Stanton, Carjuzaa, & Hall, 2019). Because of this, materials were not developed to assist teachers in classrooms with the information they needed to teach, nor were any efforts made to provide professional development for teachers in this area, or collaborations with American Indian Tribal Nations.

Needless to say, little has been done in these states. Sockbeson (2019) speaks of the situation in Maine, which was the first state to pass such legislation. She was a tribal representative for the Wabanaki Studies Commission (WSC) for the implementation of the Wabanaki Studies Law (WSL). The WSC continued for only two years after the law was passed and nothing had been done since. Unfortunately, non-Native children still play games on the playground of "Kill the Indians," not recognized by teachers nor administrators in this area as racist and cruel.

In other states, Native American communities have been more fully involved with creating materials to be used in schools, such as California, where Native American nations had been almost erased from the history of the state (Schneider et al., 2019). California Indians have been trying to correct the official history of the state for the last fifty years by changing the narrative from focus on the Missions—which only affected approximately 9 percent of the population—and the Gold Rush era, which became one of the greatest threats to California American Indian Nations, though this information has not been part of the official narrative for student curricula (Schneider et al., 2019).

Instead, both of these historical occurrences were glorified in social studies materials, according to Schneider et al. (2019). Through creating the California Indian History Curriculum Coalition (CIHCC), a group of K–12 educators, historians, university professionals, and American Indian representatives from different tribal Nations at all levels, curricula and resources for use in California schools have been developed in conjunction with the California Department of Education.

These materials provide a much greater depth of knowledge of Aboriginal peoples in California, creating more understandings and respect among all of the ethnically diverse groups in the state.

In addition, there are regular conferences and professional development opportunities that are provided to all California educators so that Native American histories, cultures, and practices can be integrated into educational curricula and taught accurately in schools across the state. This support, provided by the CIHCC, creates a successful model for providing the changes needed in thinking in schools and the appropriate materials to do so (Schneider et al., 2019).

In the Alaska Standards for Culturally Responsive Schools (1998) that were adopted by the Assembly of Alaska Native Educators on February 3, 1998, standards were created for five groups involved in Alaska's schools: (a) students, (b) educators, (c) schools, (d) curriculum, and (e) communities. Representatives of Alaska Native nations were involved in developing the standards at all levels, and recognition of the involvement of their communities for the successful implementation of these standards was essential.

Area E of the Standards for Communities explicitly states that: "a culturally-supportive community assists teachers in learning and utilizing local cultural traditions and practices" (Alaska Standards, 1998, p. 23). It then goes on to state that:

A community that meets this cultural standard:

1. Sponsors a cultural orientation camp and community mentoring program for new teachers to learn about and adjust to the cultural expectations and practices of the community;
2. Encourages teachers to make use of facilities and expertise in the community to demonstrate that education is a community-wide process involving everyone as teachers;
3. Sponsors regular community/school potlucks to celebrate the work of students and teachers and to promote on-going interaction and communication between teachers and parents;
4. Attempts to articulate the cultural knowledge, values and beliefs that it wishes teachers to incorporate into the school curriculum;
5. Establishes a program to ensure the availability of Elders' expertise in all aspects of the educational program in the school. (pp. 23–24)

This set of standards is in addition to promoting active involvement of teachers, parents, families, and elders throughout the community in schools and in community events, using the local environment as another curricular resource. This includes availing educators of departmental resources such as education, game and fish, culture and language, Tribal museums, health, and more to promote cross-cultural interactions and moving American Indian and Alaska Native education from the margins of educational curricula to the center where it belongs.

Notice that a place is given for community potlucks: The sharing of food is an important ritual of Indigenous cultures and other cultures around the world. It is a way of coming together that sets the stage for peaceful interactions with each other and acts as a social protector for participants. For schools, having food available for different events such as conferences with teachers, powwows, special presentations, and graduations, bestows an atmosphere of goodwill and that we are all working together for the benefit of our children.

It is important to remember that under the American Indian Religious Freedom Act of 1978 (AIRFA), Congress reversed the prior actions of suppression of Native American religious practices to convert American Indians, Alaska Natives, and Hawaiian Natives to Christianity. This act restored the rights to practice sacred cultural ceremonies, protect sacred sites, and exercise this right without interference from governments.

Ceremonies in which Native Americans are involved always begin with a prayer usually said by a Tribal elder, a practice allowed in schools as part of this legislation in the recognition of the intertwining of the sacred within every aspect of Native students' and communities' lives (AIRFA, 1978). Respectful listening of these prayers is expected by non-Natives during these occasions.

As stated earlier, in contrast to the ways that schools traditionally operated in the early part of their histories as entities separate from the rest of society, we have to be more inclusive of Native American communities (as well as other ethnically diverse communities) in terms of educating all children in our nation's schools (Anthony-Stevens, 2017; Castagno & Brayboy, 2008; Hammerness, Darling-Hammond, & Bransford, 2005; Klug & Whitfield, 2003). In particular, we need to move away from the one-size-fits-all curriculum and standardized testing that is taking such a toll on students, teachers, school districts, and communities.

Teaching Native American Languages in Schools

Many Indigenous languages have been lost due to colonization and genocidal actions on the part of the government and rapacious Europeans and Euro-Americans. In the process, much cultural knowledge was taken from the world. Languages are the most necessary ingredient in helping us understand cultures and to the life of cultures, and each time we lose a language, we lose much needed cultural knowledge (Hinton and Hale, 2013). There is a saying that, "Every time we lose an Elder, we lose a library," which explains the importance of language to Native American cultural lives.

Many linguists have dedicated their careers to the revival of languages in different parts of the world. Their practices have led to changes within societies where languages were lost in terms of regaining important cultural practices and knowledges (Hinton & Hale, 2013), and thereby contributing to the overall mental or physical health and well-being of these groups of people. The Bilingual Education Act of 1968 was passed in order to ensure that Native American languages would not completely die out, an effort to undo the damage to Indigenous societies and cultures by the English-only policies of American Indian education.

Due to discussions in Congress, a transitional view towards teaching Native American languages was adopted over a maintenance view with an emphasis on learning English. This impacted the amount of funding which was allotted to schools for bilingual education. Eventually, though, it was recognized that students who came from various language backgrounds did better in school and in English when they had their first languages taught and reinforced in school.

Part of the reason for this is that young children need to master the grammar of home languages before they can easily master additional languages. In many instances, children were speaking a mixture of English and their natal languages, which impeded their abilities to comprehend and understand the structure and "deep meaning" of either language.

In this country, it was once thought that young children would be confused by having more than one language in the home. However, in Europe and other countries around the world, it is not uncommon for young children to be exposed to and speak three or more languages. We know now from studies of the brain that children actually "grow" their brains when they learn a second language (Osterhout, Poliakov, Inoue, McLaughlin, Valentine, Pitkanen, Frenck-Mestre, & Hirschensohn, 2008; Posit Science, n.d.).

Loss of language is due to the dislocation of communities, their subjugation to other powers, and the loss of prestige of their mother tongues when forced to speak dominant languages only (Fishman, 1991). This includes the loss of traditional communal society traditions of caring and sharing with other members of their societal groups when the dominant power is individualistic and competitive in nature.

There were 136 language groupings of Native American languages still alive toward the middle of the 1990s (Crawford, 1995). Of these, forty-seven were spoken by fewer than one hundred people and an additional twenty-two were spoken by less than two hundred people. The Darwinian idea of survival of the fittest does not apply to languages and should be dismissed when used to discuss the importance of language revival and revitalization efforts (Crawford, 1995; Hinton & Hall, 2013).

The Native American Languages Act (NALA) of 1990 and 1992 affirm the need to teach heritage languages in our schools. The Esther Martinez Native American Languages Programs Act, as well as the Reauthorization Act passed recently in December 2019 are to support "language nests" where full immersion in Native languages can occur.

There is always controversy in some Tribal nations about teaching Native American languages to those who are non-Natives. For the most part, though, there is recognition that to be able to teach languages in schools, non-Native allies and Indigenous peoples need to work together (Fillerup, 2011; McCarty, 2002; 2012; Romero-Little & Blum-Martinez, 2012). Simms (2003) states that recent efforts have been aimed at working to revive Indigenous languages in communities and homes, otherwise students stop using their languages when schools are not in session.

Peter, Hirata-Edds, Feeling, Kirk, Mackey, and Duncan (2017) have observed that even when there are programs in place to use Native languages-only in full immersion programs, children will resort to using a mixture of both English and Native languages in the process of learning. Especially important is the proportion of verbs to nouns in many Indigenous languages in comparison to English and being able to master this grammatical information.

In other languages, such as Shoshoni, verbs do not carry any "time-stamp" information, so speakers and readers make inferences as to when events took place. Additionally, there are no plurals for nouns in the same way as English, but there are different suffixes to add depending on if the noun is in the subjective or objective case. There are phonemes, or sounds, that are made in Shoshoni but not in English and vice versa, as happens with other Indigenous languages and languages around the world (Gould & Loether, 2002). We can understand why language-learning takes time and how difficult the reverse is true when learning English in our schools for Indigenous speakers.

McCarty (2012) details information about the successes of several types of language immersion programs from those that only use foreign language approaches to those that use structured English immersion programs. McCarty's analysis has led to the conclusion that programs must have high student expectations from teachers and rich content with interwoven language and cultural information throughout the curricula to be the most successful. These programs contribute the most to student self-identity and pride in being American Indian and Alaska Natives, resulting in a strong sense of self-efficacy, contributing to higher achievement levels.

McCarty (2012) uses a case study of Puente de Hózhó, a trilingual language immersion program that allows the option of following a Diné/English or Spanish/English program for the students attending this school cofounded by Michael Fillerup. The idea is to present language-learning in an enrichment environment where ethnically diverse Diné (Navajo) and Latinx students could thrive. The goal is for students to become fluent in Navajo and English or Spanish and English. Navajo children are given an enriched Diné language curriculum taught by fluent Diné teachers beginning in Kindergarten, and gradually add more English into the program through the later grades. The same occurs in the Spanish/English program.

Teachers in both programs regularly plan lessons and activities together, and students have responded well to their teachers' high expectations and enriched curricula (McCarty, 2012). The test scores of students who have been involved with the program for the longest time have been superior to those in English-only programs. This model has been duplicated in other areas of the country, such as the Chief Tahgee Elementary Academy in Fort Hall, Idaho.

No matter what type of program is offered in schools for Indigenous language development or maintenance, as educators we need to support our students and each other in what they are learning, being proud of them and their abilities to succeed (Kipp, 2000; Matthews, 1996). In so doing, we are providing strong messages about their capabilities throughout their efforts to master curricula and to make sense of their worlds (Freire, 1994; Macedo, 1994), knowing that they will become poised to make contributions in the future to their families, communities, and the greater society.

Nonverbal and Verbal Behaviors

There are some important differences in terms of verbal and nonverbal behaviors and cultural values between Native American and Western European cultures that unless known will have negative impacts upon our Indigenous students and their learning. Note that the following are generalizations, and children who are more on the end of assimilation as opposed to traditionalism in their cultural practices may act differently in classrooms.

We have already mentioned eye contact, which is also very important when teachers meet American Indian and Alaska Native grandparents and relatives: do not expect or force them to give eye contact to you as this is not appropriate. Additionally, a "soft" handshake extended to students' family members is appreciated. Do not take offense if someone opts not to take your hand: different Tribal nations may have alternative ideas about what is or is not appropriate.

Another area that we do not address well in teacher education programs is that of voice control. We all know teachers who are very loud and strident in their classrooms. This behavior is very inappropriate in Aboriginal societies. Instead, a soft voice that can still be heard by projecting to the back of the classroom is more effective. We have found that if students are not attentive, teachers should wait silently while students, in their self-monitoring, realize they need to be listening. Nonverbal cues for listening can be given as a last resort, such as holding one's hand clost to an ear, signaling students should be listening. Singing a song in transitions, or using a rhythmic clap to get attention, are additional effective means to use in classrooms.

For more traditional children, it is best to stand at the side in the front of the class instead of full-face forward which is confrontational to many Indigenous students. Teachers need to circle the room to check for students' misunderstandings, working side-by-side with children and speaking in a soft voice to them. Non-Native teachers have to become accustomed to more silence in the classroom. In some Native American cultures, children are taught that words are sacred and shouldn't be wasted. Therefore answers may be very short, and students may be reluctant to elaborate on what they have already said.

In most Indigenous communities, children are taught not to make themselves look better than others. In the classroom, we have to remember this. Do not "spotlight" children by calling on them by name, as again, this can be confrontational, resulting in refusals to answer questions or giving the wrong responses so no one will be embarrassed if they don't know the answers. If a question or solicitation of ideas is needed, state this out loud and if children volunteer to answer, a nonverbal pointing of your head or chin in their direction will allow them to answer, as pointing a finger is not culturally appropriate. Make sure that students know that they are helping everyone in the class understand concepts, not that you are judging them.

Effective Teaching Practices with Native American Students

Along this line, having students work together through cooperative learning is especially important as everyone has a chance to make contributions to their group endeavors (Little Soldier, 1989). Many times children will teach others in their groups or will ask you as the teacher for clarification for the whole group. In this way, no one child is being signaled out in the group.

Competition by individual children is discouraged, but team competition is allowable as children are working together for a purpose. Sports play an important role in Aboriginal communities, and students are encouraged to participate. Having Elders or community members come in to teach some of the Native American games played when they were young is a wonderful way to bring the community into the school.

Incorporate multiple intelligences (MIs) in your classrooms and assignments. Howard Gardener (1983; 1999) first brought the idea of many ways of being smart to the fore in the 1980s. The MIs that he has identified are linguistic, logical-mathematical, spatial, bodily kinsethetic, musical, interpersonal, intrapersonal, and added later, aesthetic (spirituality). His work has complemented that of Swisher and Deyhle (1992), which emphasizes that American Indian and Native Alaskan students are primarily visual, creative, hands-on, and holistic learners who learn much from the stories of their ancestors. If one examines these learning styles, we can easily see the relationship with Gardner's MIs (1983; 1999), including the area of spirituality.

We have found that while working with Indigenous populations, we need to capitalize on each child's strengths. At the same time, we need to be sure that we are not overgeneralizing to the extent that we think that all Native American students learn in the same ways (Cleary & Peacock, 1998; Peacock, 1997). Clearly, there have been many examples of American Indian students who have succeeded well in traditional Western-oriented classrooms over the centuries. Unfortunately, that percentage is very low in comparison to those who have not.

The one constant that has been found over and over—perhaps more with children who are not fully assimilated—is the importance of holistic learning grounded in real experiences. For example, a second-grade child was struggling with the concept of "adding up" as a form of subtraction that was being presented by the teacher as a lesson in the student's textbook.

This Native American student is very gifted in the area of mathematics but was unable to grasp this particular concept. Large groups of ten were represented by figures that looked like big bumps, and ones by figures that looked like little bumps. Finally, in naming the figures as mountains and hills (representative of the locale where she lives), this young girl was able to grasp the concept very efficiently. Instead of the child being punished for not grasping the information, simply asking her to name what she was seeing made all the difference in empowering her to find the answers for this assignment.

Zull (2002) speaks of how the brain changes as it is learning, and how important it is to engage as many parts of the brain when teaching as possible. Similar to Indigenous learning philosophies, he promotes learning first by engaging students in concrete experiences, then reflecting on the experience, followed by making a hypothesis about what they learned or thought, and then going through a period of active testing of their ideas. This is how we capitalize on how the brain learns by making neuronal connections called "networks," pulling information together from different areas of the brain, a process based in our very biology (Zull, 2002).

Since Zull's work first appeared in 2002, other authors such as Jensen (2005) and Hardiman (2003) have come forth with their teaching methods based on how the brain learns. We know now that we need to have activities in schools that engage both sides of the brain. This means that we must bring the arts and physical education back into our schools and integrate them into our teaching and learning activities (Dewey, 1916; Klug & Whitfield, 2011).

Vygotsky (1978)—a cognitive psychologist whose focus was on maximizing students' cognitive growth (thinking, memory, comprehension, theorizing, and application of knowledge) as communities of learners through use of language, teacher reflection, and activities—proposed that learning had to be purposeful and should move students through their Zone(s) of Proximal Development (ZPD). By this he meant that we needed to take children from the point of their knowledge when instruction is begun and guide them through to what they needed to know by working collaboratively with their teachers and peers, using language as a way to socially mediate instruction (Putney, 2012; Vygotsky, 1978).

We can notice a common theme emerging here of the importance of having students work together to acquire "school knowledge," bringing in concrete experiences and then having students talk about, reflect upon, and theorize about these experiences without the pressures of always having to search for "right" answers. In working together, children are on the same level and can bring forward what they already know when presented with different concepts to learn about in their classrooms, as well as using the language for purposeful means.

THE RELATIONAL WORLDVIEW AND ITS APPLICATION TO INDIGENOUS EDUCATION

The relational worldview is a conception that all of the world and our beings are connected and interrelated. That is why Native peoples have been great natural scientists and environmentalists. Children are taught from early on to pay attention to and remember what they see around them. As stated by Cajete (2000),

> Native cultures talk, pray, and chant the landscape into their being. This is the animating power of language inherent in the spoken word that connects the breath of each person to the breath of the world. Native languages invest their homeland with their presence through active verb-based processes of "talking the land," that is naming its places, singing its virtues, and telling its stories. Native languages are highly descriptive of natural places and pay special attention to the way the event or place they are describing is in a perpetual state of motion. The verb-based nature of Native languages is also connected to the Native cosmological assumption that we live in an interrelated living world in perpetual creative motion. Native languages echo the natural reality of a universe that is alive and creative. (p. 184)

Nowhere is the conflict between Western ideas of education and Native American ideas seen in such contrast than in the area of science and its related disciplines. The Scientific Revolution in Europe took place at the end of the Renaissance period approximately from the years of 1543 CE–1700 CE, creating tension between the Roman Catholic Church and those who were first making "scientific" discoveries. Up until this point, the Bible, as we discussed, was used for all truth. As a result, anyone who made statements that were not supported by biblical texts was considered to be a heretic and punished severely, even by burning at the stake.

This scientific revolution occurred simultaneously with the rise of the merchant class and craftsmanship as the new economic system of capitalism began to emerge (Singh, 1987). While nobles and intellectuals still ruled overall and spoke and wrote in Latin, a new group of individuals exploring the world became connected to universities along with expert machinists and craftsmen who could develop the instruments for them to do so, such as the telescopes, microscopes, and many more inventions previously unknown to people.

The new "scientific method" of stating a theorem and then making experiments to prove or disprove the proposition became the rule for anything considered scientific (Singh, 1987). During this Age of Enlightenment, anything that couldn't be proven through experimental observation was held as untrue. All of this extended to knowledge produced in other parts of the world and belief systems of ethnically diverse populations.

In this way, the belief systems of Native populations in the Americas were discounted as so much superstition, along with such concepts as the power of prayer and other Christian and non-Christian belief systems. Today, the scientific method is still privileged in our educational systems. However, due to the advances of technology since the 1400s, we are finally able to understand that much of what Native peoples knew to be true about the earth and the cosmos is true.

Atoms are in perpetual motion. The earth is not static, and we can use computer technology to predict earthquakes; examine the floor of our oceans; understand changes made over millions of years of the earth's existence; and fly to places in the world we could never have imagined to examine what is happening with the melting of the sea ice that is currently on-going.

In other words, science is not as limiting and fact-driven as it once was but can be seen as having potentialities of which we have previously been unaware and were told to generations of Native Americans through their stories and legends. These stories are the metaphors that Native peoples use to connect with the cosmos and also to lead ethical and moral lives. An important difference between Indigenous populations and European populations, though, is that man is neither superior to all of creation, nor has dominion over all of creation, as is pronounced in the Bible.

Therein lies the rub: For Indigenous populations, man is part of creation and does not have special standing above the rest of creation. Aboriginal populations, their ethics, and morals include how people treat the whole of the cosmos, the whole of creation. That means the recognition that all things have life, and we should not wantonly make use of the gifts given to us by the Creator.

> There's a powerful feeling at our most sacred places, such as the medicine wheel in the Bighorn Mountains. My grandfather told stories about how the medicine wheel used to be much taller than it is now. But people took rocks from the wheel, maybe to take that feeling with them. We need to have respect, not just for Indian sacred sites, but for every place. (Yellowtail, n.d.)

Western-European science is finally beginning to catch up to what Native peoples have always known: The earth is made up of systems, and what happens to one part of the system impacts other parts of the system, which then impact more of the systems. Not having enough rain, for instance, or having wind that dries out the earth, impacts the ability to grow food, which impacts the ability to feed large populations, which then impacts the health and survival of nations, and on and on.

Historical traditions are an important source of rules and norms for societies, no matter their countries of origin (Fukuyama, 2000). Incest taboos appear to be common to human populations. Religious rules and values not originating within formal religions are another source of informally generated rules and norms. And then there are biologically grounded norms. These deal with taking care of the common or shared spaces of communities. Taking care not to deplete fishing resources in rivers and oceans to ensure enough for all and continuation of fish species is an example of this. These spontaneously generated rules and norms appear to work well in communities of less than ten thousand (Fukuyama, 2000).

Conflicts can arise when individuals or groups who have different hierarchical rules and norms as well as spontaneously generated rules and norms—some of which have been established over thousands of years—come into contact. This is the case between Western Europeans and Native American societies beginning during the period of European conquest in the Americas and continuing today.

A way of capitalizing on the relational worldview in schools is to use thematic approaches toward education for our Indigenous students. One of the things that we are reminded of is that while we are planning lessons and units for our students, we want to be aware of how to connect students' "prior knowledge" as explained by Vygotsky (1978)—or as Piaget in 1954 called this, their "schemata" (Wadsworth, 1996)—neurologically to what they are learning as explained by Zull (2002). We also want to move our students from always relying on us, as their teachers, to provide all the pedagogy they need to make these connections to that of "andragogy," a way of engaging interest in their learning as adult life-long learners (Samaroo, Cooper, & Green, 2013).

With a thematic approach, teachers supply the pedagogy when choosing an overall theme, and addressing that theme across multiple subject areas with several types of activities. We need to remember to include some type of real object or experience to begin the process of activating the students' neurological networks, also described as providing a pre-experience to assess students' prior knowledge as suggested by Zull (2002).

By interweaving subject areas with this theme we are "deepening" Indigenous (and other) students' knowledge of curricula areas. By incorporating the arts and other MIs (Gardner, 1983; 1999) throughout our thematic units, and building on students strengths, we are moving our Native American students more toward andragogy and life-long learning, a condition we want to promote for all of our students (Klug & Whitfield, 2011).

For older students, thematic learning requires working collaboratively with other teachers in the middle school and high school grades. For Native American students, their histories and cultural teachings can be integrated into the process, and communities may be able to assist with providing information particular to what is being studied.

We celebrate the convergence of family, home, and teachers as positive factors constituting the necessary ingredients for resiliency, culturally relevant teaching or pedagogy, and strengths-based education together to bolster education for Native

American youth. This includes teacher understandings of Indigenous knowledge and strengths in such areas as biology and mathematics. We must understand and respect Native peoples and their ways of doing so that our classrooms provide safe places for our Indigenous students to learn. By providing the support students need in schools, we celebrate them and with them as they reach their goals.

REFERENCES

Alaska Standards for Culturally-Responsive Schools. (1998). Fairbanks, AK: Alaska Native Knowledge Network.

American Indian Religious Freedom Act of 1978, Public Law 95-341, 42 U.S.C. § 1996.

American Indians/Alaska Natives. (2004–2005). *Focus on series*. National Education Association. Washington, DC: NEA Human and Civil Rights.

Anthony-Stevens, V. (2017). Cultivating alliances: Reflections on the role of non-Indigenous collaborators in Indigenous educational sovereignty. *Journal of American Indian Education*, 56 (1), 81–104.

Berliner, D. (2014). Effects of inequality and poverty vs. teachers and schooling on America's youth. *Teachers College Record*. Retrieved from https:www.tcrecord.org/PrintContentID=16889.

Berliner, D. C., & Biddle, B. J. (1995). *The manufactured crisis: Myths, fraud, and the attacks on America's public schools*. Cambridge, MA: Perseus Books.

Bilingual Education Act of 1968, Public Law 90-247, Title VII of the Elementary and Secondary Education Act of 1965.

Blakeslee, J. (1978–1979). White flight to the suburbs: A demographic approach. *Focus: Institute for Poverty Newsletter*, *3* (2) 1.

Cajete, G. (2000). *Native science: Natural laws of Interdependence*. Santa Fe, NM: Clear Light.

Castagno, A. E., & Brayboy, B. M. J. (2008). Culturally responsive schooling for Indigenous youth: A review of the literature. *Review of Educational Research*, *78* (4), 941–93.

Cleary, L. M., & Peacock, T. D. (1998). *Collected wisdom: American Indian education*. Boston, MA: Allyn & Bacon.

Crawford, J. (1995). Endangered Native American Languages: What is to be done and why? (Rev. ed.). *Bilingual Research Journal*, *19* (1). Special issue on Indigenous Language Education and Literacy. Retrieved from http://www.languagepolicy.net/archives/endanger.htm.

Dewey, J. (1916). *Democracy and education: An introduction to the philosophy of education*. New York, NY: Macmillan.

Edgerton, R. B. (2000). Traditional beliefs and practices—Are some better than others? In L. E. Harrison & S. P. Huntington (Eds.), *Culture matters: How values shape human progress* (pp. 126–40). New York, NY: Basic Books.

Education and Socioeconomic Status. (n.d.). American Psychological Association. Retrieved from https://www.apa.org/pi/ses/resources/publications/education.

Esther Martinez Native American Languages Programs Reauthorization Act of 2019–2020, Public Law No: 116-101.

Fillerup, M. (2011). Building a "bridge of beauty": A preliminary report on promising practices in Native languages and culture teaching at Puente de Hózhó Trilingual Magnet School. In M. E. Romero-Little, S. J. Ortiz, T. L. McCarty, & R. Chen (Eds.), *Indigenous languages across the generations—Strengthening families and communities* (pp. 145–164). Tempe: Arizona State University Center for Indian Education.

Fishman, J. A. (1991). *Reversing language shift: Theoretical and empirical foundations of assistance to threatened languages.*Clevedon, England: Multilingual Matters.

Freire, P. (1994). Introduction. In D. Macedo, *Literacies of power: What Americans are not allowed to know.* Boulder, CO: Westview Press.

Fukuyama, F. (2000). Social capital. In L. E. Harrison & S. P. Huntington (Eds.), *Culture matters: How values shape human progress* (pp. 98–111). New York, NY: Basic Books.

Gardner, H. (1983). *Frames of mind: The theory of Multiple Intelligences.* New York, NY: Basic Books.

Gardner, H. (1999). *Intelligence reframed: Multiple Intelligence in the 21st Century.* New York, NY: Basic Books.

Gould, D. & Loether, C. (2002). *An introduction to the Shoshoni language: Dammen Daigwape.* Salt Lake: University of Utah Press.

Hammerness, K., Darling-Hammond, L., & Bransford, J. (with Berliner, D., Cochran-Smith, M., McDonald, M., & Zeichner, K.). (2005). How teachers learn and develop. In L. Darling-Hammond & J. Bransford, *Preparing teachers for a changing world: What teachers should learn and be able to do* (pp. 358–89). New York, NY: Jossey-Bass.

Hardiman, M. M. (2003). *Connecting brain research with effective teaching: The Brain-Targeted teaching model.* Lanham, MD: Scarecrow Press.

Hinton, L., & Hale, K. L. (2013). *The green book of language revitalization in practice.* New York, NY: Academic Press. (Originally published 2001).

Jensen, E. (2005). *Teaching with the brain in mind* (2nd ed.). Alexandria, VA: Association for Supervision and Curriculum Development.

Kipp, D. (2000). Commitment to language-based education. In M. Benham & W. Stein (Eds.), *Indigenous educational models for contemporary practice: In our mother's voice* (pp. 62–69). London: Lawrence Erlbaum.

Klug, B. J., & Whitfield, P. T. (2003). *Widening the Circle: Culturally relevant pedagogy for American Indian children.* New York, NY: RoutledgeFalmer.

Klug, B. J., & Whitfield, P. T. (2011). A Mind with a view: Education through the kaleidoscopic lenses of the arts. In C. J. Craig & L. F. Deretchin (Eds.), *The role of teachers and teacher educators: Part II. ATE Annual Yearbook XVIII* (pp. 160–78). Lanham, MD: Rowman & Littlefield Education.

Little Soldier, L. (1989). Cooperative learning and the Native American students. *Phi Delta Kappan, 7* (2), 161–163.

Macedo, D. (1994). *Literacies of power: What Americans are not allowed to know.* Boulder, CO: Westview Press.

Matthews, M. (1996). Vygotsky and writing: Children using language to learn and learning from the child's language what to teach. In L. Dixon-Krauss (Ed.), *Vygotsky in the classroom: Mediated literacy instruction and assessment* (pp. 93–131). New York, NY: Longman.

McCarty, T. L. (2002). *A place to be Navajo—Rough Rock and the Struggle for self-determination in Indigenous schooling.* Mahwah, NJ: Lawrence Erlbaum.

McCarty, T. L. (2012). Indigenous languages and cultures in Native American school achievement: Promising practices and cautionary findings. In B. J. Klug (Ed.), *Standing together: American Indian education as Culturally Responsive Pedagogy* (pp. 97–119). Lanham, MD: Rowman & Littlefield.

Native American Languages Act of 1990, 25 U.S.C. § 3000 *et seq.*, (U.S.C. 2000). Public Law 101-477, Title I of the Elementary and Secondary Education Act of 1965.

National Indian Education Association. (n.d.). *NIEA Talent Management Best Practices.* Retrieved from https://www.niea.org/national-education-initiative-project.

No Child Left Behind Act of 2001: Reauthorization of the Elementary and Secondary Education Act of 1965, 20 U.S.C. § 6301 *et seq.*, Public Law 107–110.

Osterhout, L., Poliakov, A., Inoue, K., McLaughlin, J., Valentine, G., Pitkanen, I., Frenck-Mestre, C., & Hirschensohn, J. (2008). Second language learning and changes in the brain. *Journal of Neurolinguistics, 21* (6), 509–21. Retrieved from https://www.ncbi.nlm.nih.gov/pmc/articles/PMC2600795/. doi: 10.1016/j.jneuroling.2008.01.001.

Peacock, T. (1997). Ways of learning: Teachers perspectives on American Indian learning styles. *Tribal College: Journal of American Indian Higher Education, 8* (3), 36–39.

Peter, L., Hirata-Edds, T., Feeling, D., Kirk, W., Mackey, R., & Duncan, P. T. (2017). The Cherokee Nation Immersion School as a translanguaging space. *Journal of American Indian Education, 56* (1), 5–31.

Posit Science. (n.d.). *Brain Connection.* Retrieved from. https://brainconnectionbrainhq.com / 2001/01/27/how-the-brain-learns-a-second-language/.

Putney, L. (2012). Collectively Transformative Pedagogy: Enhancing educational opportunities for Native American students. In B. J. Klug (Ed.), *Standing together: American Indian education as Culturally Responsive Pedagogy* (pp. 13548). Lanham, MD: Rowman & Littlefield Education.

Ravitch, D. (2020). *Slaying Goliath: The passionate resistance to privatization and the fight to save America's public schools.* New York, NY: Knopf.

Romero-Little, E., & Blum-Martinez, R. (2012). In retrospect, revitalizing the Chochiti language— A proposal for community re-engagement in collective spirit and mutual respect. *Journal of American Indian Education, 51* (3), 95–103. Special Issue: The Native American Languages Act of 1990/1992—Retrospect and Prospects.

Sabzalian, L., Morrill, A., & Edmo, S. (2019). Deep organizing and Indigenous studies legislation in Oregon. *Journal of American Indian Education, 58* (3), 34–57.

Samaroo, S., Cooper, E., & Green, T. (2013). Pedandragogy: A way forward to self-engaged learning. *New Horizons in Adult Education and Human Resource Development, 25* (3). Retrieved from https://doi.org/10.1002/nha3.20032.

Sanger, M., & Osguthorpe, R. (2009). Analyzing the Child Development Project Using the Moral Work of Teaching Framework. *Journal of Moral Education, 38* (1), 17–37.

Schneider, K., Allender, D., Berta-Ávila, M., Borunda, R., Castro, G., Murray, A., & Porter, J. (2019). Native Californians and allies changing the story of California history. *Journal of American Indian Education, 58* (3), 58–77.

Simms, C. P. (2003). Tribal languages and the challenges of revitalization. *Anthropology & Education, 36* (1), 104–106.

Singh, V. (1987). Why did the Scientific Revolution take place in Europe and not elsewhere? *Indian Journal of History of Science, 22* (4), 341–53. Retrieved from https://insa.nic.in/writereaddata/UpLoadedFiles/IJHS/Vol22_4_7_VSingh.pdf.

Sockbeson, R. (2019). Maine Indigenous education left behind: A call for anti-racist conviction as political will toward decolonization. *Journal of American Indian Education, 58* (3), 104–29.

Stanton, C., Carjuzaa, J., & Hall, B. (2019). The promises, purposes, and possibilities of Montana's Indian Education for All. *Journal of American Indian Education, 58* (3), 78–104.

Stengel, B. (2013). Teaching moral responsibility: Practical reasoning in a pedagogical "Wonderland." In M. N. Sanger & R. Osguthorpe (Eds.), *The moral work of teaching and Teacher Education: Preparing and supporting practitioners* (pp. 44–50). New York, NY: Teachers College Press.

Swisher, K. & Deyhle, D. (1992). Adapting Instruction to Culture. In J. Rehyner (Ed.), *Teaching American Indian students* (pp. 81–95). Norman, OK: University of Oklahoma Press.

Tozer, S., Violas, P. C., & Senese, G. B. (1993). *School & Society: Educational practice as social expression.* New York, NY: McGraw-Hill.

Vygotsky, L. (1978). *Mind in society: The development of higher psychological processes.* Cambridge, MA: Harvard University Press.

Wadsworth, B. (1996). *Piaget's theory of cognitive and affective development* (5th ed.). New York, NY: Longman.

Yellowtail, J. (n.d.). Brochure. Crow Agency, MT: Apssalooke Tours.
Zull, J. E. (2002). *The art of changing the brain: Enriching the practice of teaching by exploring the biology of learning*. Sterling, VA: Stylus.

Chapter Ten

Celebrations

Shared Success Is Success for All

I was a National Merit semifinalist. I attended college at Cornell University. There were fifty-two fraternities there. I was only invited to join one fraternity because everyone thought our family was really African American! . . . This was 1961. I had grown up without awareness of differences in the kids back then. . . . So this is how I became aware of prejudice in college.

My wife and I went to teach in Africa after college. When I returned, I was upset by the way my grandfather could never talk about being Indian or prejudice. Then I learned about the eugenics project in the Northeast in Vermont. This project was regarded as a model by Germans where they sterilized Indians as part of a larger effort to control Indian populations. The Indian Health Service was notorious for sterilizing women without their permission. This is part of our hidden history: a lot has been covered over and not publicized. . . .

The importance of contemporary American Indian writers is that the stories need to be told. This contributed to my wanting to be a writer. Knowledge is empowering. Even history that is painful may be powerful. It's OK "being a dirty Indian," as some have called us. . . .

Factors [that allowed me to overcome obstacles] include having the ability to keep on going, not to give up. If you think it's hopeless, it will be. I was small, but a wrestler. I was in wildlife management. I took a poetry course and the professor concluded that I was not supposed to be in his class. I loved poetry and I loved to write. The professor tore my work up in front of the class. But I kept attending class. I kept writing. And finally the professor admitted I could write poetry. He has become a huge supporter of me and my writing. . . .

[My advice to Native American youth is this]: I was a championship wrestler and now I'm a championship writer. Don't give up—don't let them convince you that you can't do something. . . . I had a martial arts instructor who taught physical competence. This is related to the warrior ethic. I see this as being a good thing, as being able to protect the people.

There is bullying. We live in a color conscious society and need to have respect. Respect for others means the need to be respectful to ourselves. — Joseph Bruchac, Nulhegan Abenaki (Interviewed by B. J. Klug, September 2010)

By the 1970s, American Indians and Alaska Natives had the capabilities of launching litigation as a way to protest and abrogate unjust laws and legislation that interfered with their abilities as sovereign nations to make their own laws and have their own governments. The political and real battles beginning with the American Indian Movement (AIM) in the 1950s and 1960s in time translated into pride in being Native Americans once again (Treuer, 2019).

The number of American Indian legal scholars increased, and both the Native American Rights Fund and the Indian Law Resource Center were crucial in this effort. During this period, the Supreme Court recognized "more than 120 decisions handed down since the 1950s that touched on tribal affairs, Indian rights, and Indian sovereignty" (Treuer, 2019, p. 384). As Treuer (2019) explains, the fact that there are three systems of sovereignty in the United States, the U.S. government, state governments, and Tribes, had been ignored since the early 1800s, and this legitimacy of sovereignty included the prerogative to have gaming as part of the right to regulate Tribal nations' civil laws.

Gaming on Tribal reservations and lands has allowed Tribal nations the opportunities to become involved in the modern technological world. The laws regarding gaming for American Indian Nations include the provision that 60 percent of the monies generated must be used for Tribal development (Klug, 2002). With this provision, along with wealth generated that directly benefits families, changes have come about on many reservations in terms of conservation of resources, development of infrastructure, and program developments that benefit Tribal members directly such as job training, education, and language revitalization and culture programs.

There have been many spinoffs from the gaming industry that have the potential to positively impact Tribal nations, including local employment opportunities, advertisement for visiting venues held on local reservations, demands for Indian-made goods from local and tourist visitors to casinos, and impacts on school funding in local communities. The impetus for more Indigenous youth to complete high school and go on to some form of higher education is due in part to requirements necessary for advanced employment opportunities in local Tribal entities.

All of these are reasons to celebrate changes that are occurring in many local Tribal communities. One of the most laudable results of increased availability of funding for Tribal governments is the effort of many Tribal nations to invest in language and culture preservation so that Native cultures can survive in global economies. The teachings and understandings of Native peoples who have taken care of the earth and its resources over the millennia are particularly pertinent as communities are faced with climate changes due to negative forces resulting from industrialization and abuses of Mother Earth.

Many Tribal nations are involved in efforts to bring back regional native species of plants and animals whose populations have dwindled because of negative impacts on their environments. When Aboriginal students are made aware of these efforts, they witness firsthand how their values of taking care of the earth are being employed in modern societies and their communities. We need to make explicit for our Native students the deep connections between what they are learning in school (academic knowledge) and the types of knowledge they learn as tribal members, connecting both types of knowledge for the future of their Tribal nations.

While the government supplies some funding to Tribal nations, this funding is always the first to be cut by Congress when times are lean. The funding itself is minimal and does not take care of the many needs on reservations. At this point, there are 246 Tribal nations with 500 casinos, mainly in the West. They employ 296,000 individuals, and the money from gaming has allowed the tribes to increase funding for law enforcement, schools, scholarships, daycare programs, and cultural programs (Smith, 2020).[1] Many gaming tribes assist other non-gaming Tribal nations with their needs, since many of those are located in remote rural areas.

> Sovereignty isn't only a legal attitude or a political reality; it has a social dimension as well. The idea and practice of sovereignty carries with it a kind of dignity—a way of relating to the self, to others, to the past, and to the future that is dimensionally distinct. . . . [My mother's] early struggles and the continuing struggles of Indian people across the country exist alongside, and are bound up in, what it means to be Indian. But to be Indian is not to be poor or to struggle. To believe in sovereignty, to let it inform and define not only one's political and legal existence but also one's community, to move through the world imbued with the dignity of that reality, is to resolve one of the majority contradictions of modern Indian life: it is to find a way to be Indian and modern simultaneously. (Treuer, 2019, p. 389)

REVIVAL OF NATIVE AMERICAN PRACTICES

One of the most encouraging things that educators can do as part of the microsystems of our Indigenous students is to attend events held throughout the year in Native American communities. By doing so, we are sending nonverbal messages to Aboriginal communities that we want to know more about them and their traditional practices. Teachers will find that children and families will want to talk to them in those places when they may have been reluctant to meet teachers at school. Participating in these events demonstrates good faith that can exist between schools and Native American communities.

Dancing, Singing, and the Powwow Traditions

We can celebrate with Indigenous peoples during the powwow season as they perform the dances, prayers, and ceremonies that occur throughout the day and into the wee hours of the next morning. Dancing has always been a form of prayer to the Creator by Native Americans.

One of the dances performed by women and girls is known as the Jingle Dance. An Ojibway man's granddaughter was seriously ill and not thought to be able to live very much longer. In a dream, the grandfather learned that if young girls and women would make "bells" to sew on their regalia, one for each day of the year, and perform the dance he described, his granddaughter would be cured. The jingles sound like rain, the cleansing water needed to cure anyone. This dance happened, and the man's granddaughter was cured (Native Pride Dancers, 2018).

While the different dances may vary somewhat from Tribal nation to nation, they are all shared within Indigenous communities. The dress for the Jingle Dance, though, belongs to the Ojibway or "Anishinaabe" (Native Pride Dancers, 2018). The men's Eagle Dance is also a powerful prayer dance. Groups such as Native Pride Dancers perform for audiences around the country and the world to educate non-Natives about the powwow dances and their meanings. It is important to remember that the beautiful regalia, or outfits, of the dancers are not to be called "costumes," just as you would not call priestly vestments "costumes," or Jewish, Protestant, or Mormon regalia "costumes."

If powwows are advertised, then they are open to the public. In schools where a large number of Indigenous students attend, there will usually be powwows held during the fall or spring of the year. In classrooms with non-Native and Native students, it is wise to have students watch videos produced about different types of powwow dances and their meanings (available on YouTube) so that they can understand what they are seeing and act respectfully. The seasonal powwow dancing, horse relays, traditional games played, and parades all bring together Native American and non-Native communities. They showcase Indigenous ways, religion, and help keep tribal languages alive.[2]

Name Giving

The Religious Freedom Restoration Act (1993) gave Indigenous communities the right to restore their ceremonies which had been so important to Aboriginal survival throughout the millennia. As the government had "given" different reservations to various Christian denominations, Christianity and Native spirituality are sometimes joined. In some communities, the ceremonies involving name-giving have been revived and students will speak of getting "their Indian names." When we hear this, we should not inquire about the students' new names as this is a private, sacred part of their lives, but we can congratulate them.

In some Aboriginal communities, members would receive different names throughout their lives and then be called by the last names given. One thing that we need to note is that while students may have nicknames given to them by family, we should never shorten their first names, such as calling a person named Henry "Hank" or think that Hank's name is really Henry. The same goes for a name like Elizabeth shortened by educators to "Betsy" or "Betty." In other words, we need to be sensitive to what parents/families prefer to have their children called, and not be afraid to ask them to tell us their preferences.

A Native last name does not always translate well into English. For instance, "Afraid of Bear," may not mean that someone's ancestor was afraid of bears, so we need to be sure that we do not make assumptions that this would be the case. Bears are renowned for their power, so the original name may have been in honor of the bear's physical or spiritual power.

Animals form an important part of the Native American pantheon, and different animals are renowned and revered in different Indigenous communities. Animals are considered to be brothers in Aboriginal epistemologies, or ways of knowing. Trickster animals, creatures, or gods teach people what not to do and the repercussions, or punishments, for being bad or not listening.

While coyote is a trickster in many Tribal nation traditions, raven is the trickster along the West Coast in Oregon, Washington, and the Aleuts in Alaska; turtle, hare (cottontail, rabbit), and Skeleton Man (Hopi) are tricksters in some of the interior Tribal nations; along with mink, hare, and a host of others in the East and throughout the country ("Native American Tricksters of Myth and Legend," n.d.). Native American legends are considered to be sacred and we can think of them as

Indigenous equivalents to the Bible with their messages about good living, values, and morals.

Graduation from Schools

As stated earlier, more Indigenous students are graduating now from our schools in general; in some Native communities, that is still not the case for a variety of reasons. Unfortunately, due to NCLB (2001), we find that many schools have gone back to dis-empowering literacy practices by using "canned" programs that stress Standard English and phonetic knowledge of word pronunciation, not reading for comprehension and writing for self-expression. Because of testing, Standard English has been privileged in schools (Edelsky, 2006; Janks, 2010).

However, we cannot stress enough that children's first languages are their home languages, which need to be recognized by teachers. They, too, provide legitimate power to communicate, analyze problems, and allow for abstract thinking. By simply repeating information in Standard English, we can teach children how to "code switch" between Standard English and one of the many forms of American Indian English (AIE) or Red English. One way to do this without demonizing AIE is to tell the children that in school, we use "school" English, but on the playground, it's all right to use their "home" English.

Meanwhile, we need to ensure that our literacy practices are not a way to continue what Freire (1981) refers to as "pedagogy of the oppressed," where children are only allowed to learn facts, rules, and little that has any meaning to them. We must be able to teach children to use their literacy practices for meaningful activities connected with their lives, communities, and interests in the greater world. This means ensuring that schools have libraries with a variety of books and authors available, especially books written about and by Native American authors.

One of the ways that ethnically diverse authors have resolved issues of privileging one form of rhetoric over others is by writing the main text in Standard English, while including dialects as part of what their characters would say. African American writer Virginia Hamilton was one of the first authors to do this in her children's books. Spokane/Coeur d'Alene author Sherman Alexi also does this, as well as some other American Indian authors. Janks (2006) makes a point that bringing in diverse dialects/languages in the classroom requires planning and searching for appropriate materials. Otherwise, the effort fails and our students are poorer for not having these experiences.

Inviting Indigenous Community Members into Urban/Suburban Schools

Many educators may feel that it is inappropriate to invite Indigenous family and community members into schools or as members of school boards, and if they asked, Indigenous people would decline their invitation anyway.

> Any view of AI/AN student achievement is incomplete without acknowledging that the passing down of knowledge and skills between generations of native peoples predates the arrival of Europeans and the imposition of governmental control of Indians' education. The current relationship between American Indians and public education is strained due to a history of federal control. After centuries of forced assimilation, the U.S. government, 70 years ago, shifted policy to allow Indian education to preserve and maintain native language and culture while building academic achievement. The strength of the earlier policy and weak enforcement of the latter approach have done its damage. (American Indians/Alaska Natives, 2004–2005, p. 1)

We need to remember that for Indigenous peoples, everything is built on relationships. Teachers are part of Aboriginal students' microsystems traditionally, and as such, we can build those relationships. But it takes effort to do so, and a willingness to step out of our comfort zones. It takes educators' readiness to do more than send home notes from schools. We have to find ways through potlucks, family evening programs, and attending community events to form relationships with the families of our students. If we can remember that extended families are very important in the lives of our Indigenous students, we will also know that our efforts will be recognized within our Indigenous communities. Then we can begin the process of working together for the sake of our Aboriginal children.

As we endeavor to have accurate Native American representation in our schools, and as the majority of American Indians/Alaska Natives are living in urban areas across the country, it is important to ensure that they are part of our school communities. One of the difficulties in urban area schools is that the majority of students may not even be aware of the existence of Indigenous peoples in their midst, or they may only have ideas of Native Americans as stereotypes (Bizzaro, 2015).

This is especially true in areas where students have not had contact with "real Indians" or have but don't recognize it. If Native Americans are living in the vicinity or Native families are attending these schools, we need to have the courage to ask them to come and speak to our students about themselves or their families and give them recognition in our schools. In this way, they know that they have a place in our urban societies as well, and our non-Native students' thinking can be positively influenced as well.

We have found that by inviting Indigenous authors to speak in local schools as well as schools located on a nearby reservation, that all of our students have had the opportunity to engage with contemporary Native American authors and artists. Not only does this make a difference for our Indigenous students, but also for their peers as they see literacy as a gift for all cultures and peoples. Additionally, non-Native students' respect for Aboriginals grows in this way and our Native American students are imbued with pride in who they are and what they can accomplish.

Confronting the "Self-Made Man" Mythology in This Country

In 2012, David Berliner asked the following:

> What does it take to get politicians and the general public to abandon misleading ideas, such as, "Anyone who tries can pull themselves up by the bootstraps," or that "Teachers are the most important factor in determining the achievement of youth"? Many ordinary citizens and politicians believe these statements to be true, even though life and research informs us that such statements are usually not true.

This idea—that people can rise from rags to riches with integrity, hard work, and determination to conquer all obstacles—was promoted in dime-store novels for boys written by Horatio Alger in the 1800s. Part of that mythology includes getting an education, and of course being dedicated to God, as Alger was a graduate of Harvard Divinity School. Alger's novels were very popular in offering hope to the oppressed that this dream could be accomplished completely on one's own, a rare phenomenon (Merriman, 2005).

In his book, *Outliers: The Story of Success* (2008), Malcolm Gladwell explores the idea that success is always a matter of people's superior intellect or other superior traits. What he has found is that we have to examine the lives of successful people to find out what has made them successful: Their cultures, families, generations, and experiences in their young lives.

Gladwell (2008) discovered that these outliers didn't get to be the people they are through chance alone, but through a combination of opportunities presented to them at the right time in history under the right circumstances, and with the right coaching. He found that it takes ten thousand hours of practicing a particular task to become a master of anything. That means children have to have the right tools to follow their passions as well as being born under the right circumstances to become an "outlier" or huge success at anything.

Gladwell (2008) gives the example of one school in the Bronx that outshines others and attempts to turn unequal circumstances of poverty around for students. He found that not only did the school day begin earlier in this "miracle school," but they also ended later in the day. Everyone enrolled in the school played in the orchestra. They had afterschool activities, and they held school for half-days on Saturdays.

One mathematics teacher showed how he worked with students on one problem for twenty minutes, engaging students in discussion while doing so, and asking if there was only one way to get the right answer. The teacher explained to Gladwell (2008) that the extra time allowed gave students more time to be relaxed and to learn more deeply as he could answer their questions, explain for a longer period if necessary, and go over information in different ways if the students still had questions.

This particular school provided a three-week summer session in July. The school has turned the lives of impoverished children around and given their graduates many opportunities to continue forward. As Gladwell (2008) states:

> We are so caught in the myths of the best and the brightest and the self-made that we think outliers spring naturally from the earth. . . . But that's the wrong lesson. . . . To build a better world we need to replace the patchwork of lucky breaks and arbitrary advantages that today determine success—the fortunate birth dates and the happy accidents of history—with a society that provides opportunities for all. (p. 268)

This message has a ring to it for all educators involved in Native American education: The arts and physical education are part of culturally relevant teaching for our Indigenous students. We must add the arts and physical education back into our schools. Our schools need to become true places of educating the whole child again, and children need to be able to learn to master many different sign—or communication—systems in addition to those connected with literacy and mathematics.

Indigenous peoples incorporate many different types of sign systems in their artwork, whether in paintings, jewelry, pottery, beading, carvings by Inuit, or traditional rug-making patterns by Navajo weavers. They incorporate sign systems in their music: The songs that are sung, the beat of the drum, and the messages in the notes of their traditional flutes. These cultural arts need to be allowed into the curriculum again, as this becomes another way of connecting our schools with our

Native American communities. As part of teaching these traditional arts, children learn the history of their people and the use of material culture to meet Indigenous needs. They become the future, the seventh generation awaited with so much prayer.

The power of the arts to contribute to understanding the strength of Native American languages and symbols as ways of evoking deep cultural meanings for their Tribal nations cannot be underestimated. Elders can be invited to come into classrooms as "teacher partners" and talk about their experiences in sharing their traditions with the students.

By focusing on strengths-based education for Indigenous students with support from families, grandparents, and teachers together—in other words, active engagement by the figures in our Aboriginal students' human socioecological models—we can positively influence the futures of our Native American students. As educators, we do this by opening our hearts and our school doors to our Aboriginal families and communities.

CHANGING IMAGES OF AMERICAN INDIANS

We can celebrate that we live in an era of changing ideas about American Indians/Alaska Natives. Credit is being given to them for the many gifts that have positively impacted how we live today (Keoke & Porterfield, 2001; Weatherford, 1988). A great number of the foods and pharmaceuticals which we use today have come from the Americas, as well as inventions; they've provided practical ways of increasing crop yield through crop rotations, terracing hillsides and mountainsides, and using fertilizers from bat and bird droppings. Indigenous peoples used plant cuttings rather than just broadcasting seeds, which allowed them to control the genetics of the desirable plants long before experiments in the Western world (Weatherford, 1988).

We can be proud that we live in a country formed under a different type of government than the monarchies of Europe: a union that was proposed by the Iroquoian chief Canassatego who, in July 1744, advocated that the young confederacy follow the League of Iroquois model. Canassatego was speaking to the Indian-British assembly in Pennsylvania and explained that it was too difficult to deal with so many separate governmental entities, and that it would be easier if the colonists united as the Iroquois had (Weatherford, 1988). Benjamin Franklin appears to be the first to take up this idea seriously, examining the effectiveness of this long-standing political practice operating in the Americas which unified disparate Tribal nations through diplomacy.

We can rejoice that there is more information online now about Indigenous peoples and that truths about what has happened in the Americas during the last five hundred years plus are available to us. There are more accurate accounts accessible in the forms of films and books, such as the book by David Grann (2017) that addresses the actual numbers of Osage families negatively affected by events in Oklahoma during the beginning of the oil boom period, and that of Claudio Saunt's 2020 book that shows how Indigenous lands were taken through "legal means" to dispossess American Indians of their wealth.

In examining these issues, we can realign our perceptions of American Indians and Alaska Natives and perceive our students and their families and communities for the people they truly are, prying out the master narrative in this country from its racially based promulgations to a narrative that makes evident the dominant-culture views of the past. In this era, we recognize that false chronicles of Indigenous peoples were politically contrived. This was done to hide the true character of Native Americans and what was being practiced by Europeans and Euro-Americans to diminish their presence throughout the hemisphere.

The Nature of Language Use and Metaphor

Language used for political power is very potent (Pugh, Ovando, & Shonemann, 2000). It can be used to hide the true intentions of political leaders and others, as happens many times with employing the use of metaphors. Because the metaphor sounds good, as in the "Blue Skies"—legislation that increased air pollutants in the environment—people do not question the intent, or ulterior motive, of what is being proposed. Such is the power of metaphor that it acts like a switch to power off our brains from investigating more. "When a speaker's utterance intimidates the audience, it's because its content triggers certain thoughts and emotions in the audience. The psychological dynamics run their course" (Lepore & Stone, 2010). In other words, by using a metaphor that sounds "innocent," our cognitive facilities process it as so unless there is further investigation.

When the phrase, "A Nation at Risk," was first used, it was baffling to educators who heard it. Using the metaphor of something at risk implies that there is a real and present danger. Consequently, the emotions of the public were pulled in to respond to a crisis in American education. Teachers' emotions were engaged as educators felt they were being wrongfully attacked. For the last forty years, educators have been under a cloud as they worked their hardest to teach children of all ethnicities and socioeconomic levels, and there has been a loss of many great teachers due to continued attacks on teachers, schools, and the educational profession.

There has been search after search for magical answers to change the achievement tests' status quo, and there are none. For one thing, as pointed out earlier, every time the level of "average" is statistically calculated for assessment results, the bell curve is altered up or down changing the middle of the curve. The higher the test scores, the higher "average" becomes. Average is an ephemeral concept akin to performing a dance that never ends.

Our nation is not at risk, but the will to adequately fund our schools and teacher salaries at the levels they need to be *is* at risk by the movement to privatize education (Ravitch, 2020). By using powerful metaphors, neoliberals and their political allies have learned how to manipulate the world and the consensus of powerful élites into believing that their neoliberal view of education is the correct one. For example, before the era of charter schools, neoliberals first attacked the way reading was being taught in schools in the 1980s and 1990s (Edelsky, 2006). At this time, multicultural literature was introduced into basal reading programs, and comprehension was considered the key to truly understanding the content of what was being read.

The National Reading Panel was convened in 1997 with the supposed target goal of revealing which type of instruction produced the best "results" in reading. The panel members, doctors, and lawyers (with one reading specialist who eventually left the panel as members would not listen to her) were told to restrict their research to quantitative, or experimental, studies only and not to consider qualitative studies. As a result, only five of over forty different reading skills analyzed were given the "green light," increasing heavy phonics instruction and introducing reading words quickly into the curriculum for grades K–12 (Report of the National Reading Panel, 2000). Gone was the idea of reading for pleasure and increasing knowledge (Edelsky, 2006).

There was an active warfare campaign mounted against teachers of reading and those concerned with multicultural education:

> Blacklists in California that prevented state funds from being used for professional development that mentioned invented spelling, cueing systems or whole language, and that blackballed consultants whose bibliographies cited Ken or Yetta Goodman, among others; the secrecy surrounding high-stakes tests; a government-imposed victory for phonics; and the corporate media-created "Reading Wars" should now be seen retroactively in the light of that tradition of McCarthyism. (Edelsky, 2006, p. 14)

In addition to wanting to put forth the agenda of NCLB (2001) with its emphasis on extreme testing for the benefit of the corporations involved, as well as eliminating the arts and other programming, the neoliberal agenda includes eliminating social justice initiatives in this country. This is and has been funded mainly through "dark money" funneled into the hands of politicians who then are obligated to carry out the wishes of these powerful individuals (Klug, 2018; Mayer, 2016).

Since 2016, there have been renewed attacks by hate groups across the country on those who are different from themselves (Southern Poverty Law Center, 2020). The people involved in hate groups make disparaging remarks about our Indigenous students and others of color. As such, educators need to be very careful when we hear unflattering descriptions of ethnically diverse populations as language can make something appear to be real that is not as discussed above (Lakoff & Johnson, 1980).

In his book, *Blink* (2005), Malcolm Gladwell points out that the brain processes information very quickly: "It works out contingencies and relationships and sorts through the mountain of information we get from the outside world, prioritizing it and putting flags on the things that demand our immediate attention" (p. 19). Because of this, we make unconscious decisions based on past information we've been told about those who are different from ourselves. For example, in border towns by reservations, it is still not uncommon to hear college students talk about being told by their families that if they stepped onto reservation lands, the Indians would kill them.

Unless a person is committing a crime, the probability of this happening to a non-Native is very low—in fact, the number of non-Natives who are prosecuted for crimes against Native Americans is still very low, a real problem in Indian country. The point is, we can make false judgments about others based on misleading or contrived information. As educators, we can counter negative narratives about Aboriginal students in our schools by using positive descriptions to describe who they really are and how they are making their dreams come true. We can do this in concert with our American Indian families and communities.

Science, Technology, Engineering, and Mathematics for Native American Youth

We're beginning to realize the advantages for utilizing resources for online and alternative learning in remote areas of the country. While having real teachers in the classroom is the most important tool for education, offering supplemental learning to American Indian students through alternative enhancement programs can also bring many benefits to these students. One program that has seen results is a program operating in San Juan County in Utah.

San Juan County covers 7,933 miles and is located in Utah's Canyons area. A little over three thousand students are served in this area. Students are primarily from Ute, Shoshoni, Navajo, and other Tribal nations. During the past five years, the AIS Boarding School has operated under the auspices of the American Indian Services to provide opportunities for Indigenous students interested in science, technology, engineering, and mathematics (STEM) careers to come together and learn during the summer months. Students are enrolled in activities to help them develop the academic skills they will need for different areas and to expose them to a host of these types of careers (Moody, 2019).

Students stay at the boarding school during the week and then return by bus to their homes on the weekends, thereby shortening the time that they are away from their families. Thereby, Aboriginal students maintain family ties and can be involved in home activities taking place on the weekends while they are still learning and developing career goals that will enhance their future abilities to contribute to their families and communities.

Native students involved in the program have stated that it makes a difference in their regular classrooms during the school year as they can relate the information that they learned during the summers to what they are being taught in the classroom. In this way, the program is enhancing what Piaget calls students' schemata, their schema in more than one area (Wadsworth, 1996)—or what Vygotsky (1978) refers to as their prior knowledge that they bring with them—in the area of STEM that prepares them for academic achievement in the classroom, while enhancing their motivation to learn about STEM areas (Moody, 2019). Private donations have made this program available to Indigenous students.

It will be exciting to see if there are other programs developed similar to this one that can influence even more of our Native American students. It is commendable that this program does not separate students from their communities, but maintains these bonds.

POSITIVE MOVEMENTS FORWARD FOR INDIGENOUS COMMUNITIES

There is a renewed desire in this country to portray the true nature and accomplishments, skills, artistic endeavors and cultures of Indigenous peoples in the United

States. This has been a welcome change, with examples given below of trying to right previous wrongs and misperceptions of Native American peoples.

Military Recognition

The highest per capita percentage of all ethnically diverse groups in the United States who have served in the military are Native Americans. In 1994, Congress legislated that a memorial be built honoring the approximately 156,000 Native Americans and Alaskan Natives who have served in the U.S. military through all the wars of the United States.

Having more knowledge about how Native American Code Talkers made a difference in both World War I and II (Barnes, 2010) has given Americans a new vision of the importance of Indigenous peoples and their languages. However, while the legislation was passed and the memorial was to be sited by the Smithsonian's Museum of the American Indian, no money was actually appropriated for the monument. The Warriors Circle of Honor was completed in 2020 due to fundraising that was permitted by legislation in 2013 (Ault, 2020).

Genetic Testing

The opportunity for more Americans to learn about their genetic heritage has allowed numerous individuals to learn about their Native American roots, revealing secrets hidden for generations. In some families, the surprise has been overwhelmingly positive, as in this response: "I was really excited when I learned that I had Native American connections!" (D. Martin, 2020, personal communication).

For this individual, knowing her genetic history answered numerous questions that had never been discussed within the family. Living in an urban community, she witnessed her grandmother's essentially raising her uncle's children, again a Native American cultural practice. Having this genetic information has opened up dialog among her siblings concerning their heritage, including their physical features.

Ms. Martin did not know that she could be blond and blue-eyed and still have American Indian heritage. It is not uncommon to see blond, blue-eyed American Indians as well as African American, Asian, or Latinx American Indians. The results for the 2020 Census—which has fifteen different ethnicities listed so that those of multiple ancestries can claim their heritages, plus a category of "other"—will give us a much better understanding of the ethnic makeup in this country.

Some individuals have been told that they are Native American, but this information does not show up with the current genetic testing. It is important to realize that numerous Tribal nations in the United States discourage their members from having genetic testing. This is based on the fear that there will be a new genocide launched against Native Americans through their genes.

Consequently, it is imperative to realize that there are other ways to authenticate Native American ancestry through photographs, census rolls, the Dawes Rolls, and information that has come down through families. Given the history of racism against American Indians in particular, secret family stories of Native American ancestry can be believed, especially if there is evidence of practicing Indigenous traditions.

Reclaimers

There are those who are "reclaimers," people who have enough family information in terms of letters, census roll information, or other documents proving their ancestry. In some cases, they have been able to use this information to pursue being considered for enrollment in particular Tribal nations (Fitzgerald, 2007).

This has been an issue especially for those who were adopted out of their natal communities. The Indian Child Welfare Act (ICWA) of 1978 was passed due to the high number of Native American children who had been kidnapped and "sold" to adoption agencies, or had been adopted out without knowledge of their Tribal nations.

Prior to ICWA (1978), a person could simply take Indigenous children and claim neglect or abuse was taking place in homes without any substantiation and court adoptions would take place. There was complicity between the courts and social welfare systems that allowed these adoptions to occur. In addition, some churches placed Native American children in white households to be raised.

Children are the hope for the future and are cherished in Native American communities. These practices caused great heartbreak for Indigenous families, as we can readily understand, and the children were raised without knowing about their Native heritages. Many of these adoptees have found their way back to their natal communities. Whether they stay or go, their returns are always greeted with excitement and relief that family members have been found.

Acknowledgment of Boarding School Abuse

The recognition and acknowledgment of abuses in the boarding schools (as well as abuses by members of organizations) has made a difference in the lives of survivors and their moving forward in their lives. Through Talking Circles and other types of programs on Native American reservations and in Native American organizations in cities, people are beginning their journeys of recovery from abuse (Reinschmidt, Attakai, Kahn, Whitewater, & Teufel-Shone, 2016).

This process may best be expressed by Fontaine (2010), a member of Canadian First Nations, who experienced abuse in a Canadian religious residential school:

> Someone once said that the hardest wounds to recognize and identify are those that go back to the distant past of our childhoods. We sometimes no longer remember the wounds, or who or what caused them. All that remains are the rigid behaviours and defensive reactions stirred up by the slightest offence. We continue to feel these childhood misfortunes at an unconscious level throughout our lives. (p. 188)

Elimination of October 12 as Columbus Day

The proposal to commemorate Christóbal Colón (a.k.a., Christopher Columbus) was made in the early part of the twentieth century by Italian Americans. They did not have knowledge concerning the records of the atrocities committed by the "Conquistadors," or "Explorers," which had been hidden away from public view (Puglisi, 2018). One movement we can celebrate is eliminating Columbus Day from our calendars as it signals the physical and cultural genocide which has taken place in the Americas over the past five hundred years. More and more communities and states are now celebrating "Indigenous Peoples' Day" instead.

Native American Humor

While we don't discuss humor much in Native American education, Indigenous peoples have a wonderful sense of humor and irony that catches people off-guard. They have used humor to off-set many of their trials. As David Treuer (2019) notes:

> By 1992 Indians were strong enough—not symbolically but really—to resist [the dominant culture of this country]. This strength was a result of physical adaptability (no longer would disease single us out), political savvy (no longer would we fight alone), and hard-won knowledge of what we were up against. Just as the Lakota, Comanche, Nez Perce, and other Plains tribes had adopted the horse and the gun and made them their own, so, too, did modern Indians take the tools that could have spelled our end (English, technology, Western education, and wage labor) and make them ours. As my cousin Scott likes to say, *Indians don't waste what we kill: we use all parts of the computer.* (p. 412)

As earlier, Sherman Alexi and other contemporary Native American writers bring their humor into their writings, such as in the Alexi's book and the film by the same name, *Smoke Signals*, which gives folks an opportunity to laugh about too-true reservation conditions.

All Colors Will Come Together

Thomas Banyacya, the late Hopi prophet, stated in an address given at Idaho State University in 1993 that he had been taught that the Hopi had prophesized thousands of years ago that people of all colors, red, black, white, and yellow, would come together again as one in the Americas. We see that this is happening today, especially in countries such as Brazil with a high population of inter-ethnically comingled people, and we see this more in the United States. As we conclude this writing, it is important to go back to what we learned about our genetic connections as a species, that we are more alike than different, and that color is a function of biological environmental adaptation.

In the words of Native Americans, we are all brothers. We are connected to all life on our planet and universe. As such, we celebrate that we are all related. It is up to us to collaborate with Indigenous communities to prepare our Native American and non-Native students for lives where they are able to respect the great diversity of human beings, cultures, animals and plants, and become part of the future keepers of our world and the environment.

Survivance is a synonym for "survival." Used in the context of American Indians and Alaska Natives, Anishinaabe writer Gerald Vizenor uses this word as a combination of survival plus resistance, an indication of the strength of the Americas' Indigenous peoples (cited in Bizzaro, 2015). Students must recognize each other's gifts and interrogate the mainstream cultural stereotypes still present in visual, audio, and written works, together with on the playing fields of many sport teams which treat Indigenous peoples as characters in a great theatrical work whose parts are to be eliminated at the end.

The U.S. is beginning its pathway toward healing, with recognitions of great contemporary Native Americans among us, including retired senator and artist Ben Nighthorse Campbell, Northern Cheyanne; Congressional Representatives Sharice Davids, KS (Ho-Chunk, WI); Deb Haaland, NM (Laguna Pueblo with Jemez Pueblo heritage); Yvette Herrell, NM (Cherokee); Markwayne Mullin (Cherokee, OK); and Tom Cole (Chickasaw, OK). Ms. Joy Harjo, Muscogee Creek, an accomplished author and musician, became our twenty-third U.S. poet laureate in June 2019, the first American Indian to hold this title.

Many Indigenous groups are poised once more as the powerful Tribal nations they were prior to the coming of Europeans. We celebrate a new era of equal educational opportunities for all of our Aboriginal students, and our working to build on their strengths in our classrooms. There is not one formula for doing so; rather, success will depend upon the type of school and where schools are located. All schools, though, at a minimum should actively engage students in learning about the true histories of Indigenous peoples, especially of the Tribal nations in their vicinities.

In reservation areas, educators should actively engage with Tribal nation departments of education in order to connect with human and material resources that can be utilized in schools, including accessing various departments such as Game and Fish which could provide activities for students in connection with their Nation. In urban areas, schools can readily acknowledge the need to accommodate not just learning histories of Aboriginal peoples but also engaging in learning about the arts, Native ways of connecting with science and mathematics as well as technology, and if possible, having elders come into the schools to teach these areas.

If there are Native Americans who are shareholders in school districts, educators must actively seek to have their participation in schools and on school boards. All states should strive to have Indigenous representation at the state departments of education and/or on their state school boards to advance Native American education in schools within states. This can be done with having committees on Indigenous education as is done in several states, but funding must follow planning to integrate this education within schools. This also means that there needs to be funding allocated for personnel to assist with doing so for school districts.

This will be a relatively small cost as we invest in the lives of Indigenous students, helping them to realize their strengths and achieve their dreams. There are many materials that have already been developed by Tribal nations as well as by various state departments of education that can also be utilized in these endeavors. Tribal nations have prepared these materials specifically with the idea that they would be utilized in schools to teach students about their heritage. There are also materials available on the World Wide Web that can be accessed for integration with subject areas for all grade levels (see Appendix B for a sample of resources for teachers).

Thank you for being part of the journey to make the dream of dynamic culturally relevant education for Aboriginal students come true. We hope that you will take the knowledge gained from this book with you as endeavor to make change for Aboriginal students and their peers wherever you are teaching or involved in making policy decisions. While we can't promise the initial journey will be an easy one, we can promise it will be a fruitful one for all of our Indigenous and non-

Indigenous students, families, and communities. This includes our success as educators as we witness the achievements and positive growth and development in all areas of the Medicine Wheel for our students.

REFERENCES

Agoyo, A. (2020, May 7). Coronavirus relief funds finally going out to Indian Country after long wait. *Indianz*. Retrieved from https://www.indianz.com/News/2020/05/07/coronavirus-relief-funds-finally-going-o.asp.

American Indians/Alaska Natives. (2004–2005). *Focus on series*. National Education Association. Washington, DC: NEA Human and Civil Rights.

Ault, A. (2020, November 10). Native American veterans receive a place of their own to reflect and heal. *Smithsonian Magainze*. Retrieved from https://www.smithsonianmag.com/smithsonian-institution/native-american-veterans-receive-place-their-own-reflect-and-heal-180976247/.

Banyacya, T. (1993). "Hopi Spiritual teachings." Address given at Idaho State University. Pocatello.

Barnes, I. (2010). *The historical atlas of Native Americans*. New York, NY: Chartwell Books.

Berliner, D. C. (2012). Effects of inequality and poverty vs. teachers and schooling on America's youth. *Teachers College Record*. Retrieved from http://www.tcrecord.org/PrintContent.asp?ContentID=16889.

Bizzaro, R. C. (2015). Foreword—Alliances and community building: Teaching Indigenous rhetorics and rhetorical practices. In L. King, R. Gubele, & J. R. Anderson (Eds.), *Survivance, sovereignty, and story: Teaching American Indian rhetorics* (pp. xi–xiii). Boulder: University Press of Colorado.

Edelsky, C. (2006). *With Literacy and justice for all: Rethinking the social in language and education* (3rd ed.). Mahwah, NJ: Lawrence Erlbaum.

Egerstrom, L. (2020, April 18). Tribes and nearby communities take huge hits from COVID-19 casino shutdowns. *The Circle: Native American News and Arts*. Retrieved from http://thecircle-news.org/environment/tribes-and-nearby-communities-take-huge-hits-from-covid-19-casino-shutdowns/.

Fitzgerald, K. J. (2007). *Beyond White ethnicity: Developing a sociological understanding of Native American Identity reclamation*. Lanham, MD: Rowman & Littlefield.

Fontaine, T. (2010). *Broken circle: The dark legacy of Indian residential schools. A memoir*. Toronto: Heritage House.

Freire, P. (1981). *Pedagogy of the oppressed*. New York, NY: Continuum.

Gladwell, M. (2005). *Blink: The power of thinking without thinking*. New York, NY: Back Bay Books.

Gladwell, M. (2008). *Outliers: The story of success*. New York, NY: Back Bay Books.

Goodkind, N. (2021, January 12). Supreme Court to review whether or not Mnuchin failed to distribute COVID relief to Native Americans swiftly enough. *Fortune*. Retrieved from https://fortune.com/2021/01/12/supreme-court-native-americans-covid-relief-mnuchin-cares-act/.

Grann, D. (2017). *Killers of the Flower Moon: The Osage murders and the birth of the FBI*. New York, NY: Penguin Random House.

Indian Child Welfare Act of 1978, 25 U.S.C. §1901 et seq. (U.S.C. 2000).

Janks, H. (2010). *Literacy and power*. New York, NY: Routledge.

Keoke, E. D., & Porterfield, K. M. (2001). *Encyclopedia of American Indian Contributions to the World: 15,000 Years of Inventions and Innovations*. New York, NY: Checkmark Books.

Klug, B. J. (2018). Social justice in the United States. *Journal of the World Federation of Associations for Teacher Education* (ISSN 2520-632X). Available from https://www.worldfate.org.

Klug, B. J. (2002). Case XVII: Gambling as a source of funding for schools. In N. L. Quisenberry & J. D. McIntyre (Eds.), G. Duhon (Case Studies Author), *Racism in the classroom: Case studies* (pp. 118–21). Olney, MD, and Reston, VA: Association for Childhood Education International and Association of Teacher Educators.

Kraus, R., Hilsendager, S. C., & Dixson, B. (1991). *History of the dance in art and education* (3rd ed.). Englewood Cliffs, NJ: Prentice-Hall.

Lakoff, G., & Johnson, M. (1980). *Metaphors we live by*. Chicago, IL: University of Chicago Press.

Lepore, E., & Stone, M. (2010). Against metaphorical meaning. New Brunswick, NJ: Rutgers University. Topoi DOI 10.1007/s11245-009-9076-1.

Mayer, J. (2016). *Dark money: The hidden history of the billionaires behind the rise of the radical right*. New York, NY: Doubleday.

McLean, N. (2017). *Democracy in chains: The deep history of the radical right's stealth plan for America*. New York, NY: Penguin.

Merriman, C. D. (2005). Horatio Alger: Rags to riches. *The Literature Network*. Jylic, Inc. Retrieved from http://www.online-literature.com/horatio-alger/.

Moody, S. (2019, July 18, 5:50 PM MST). San Juan County boarding school exposes students to STEM careers. TV News broadcast. Retrieved from https://ksltv.com/418167/san-juan-county-bcounty-boarding-school-exposes-students-to-to-stem-careers/?fbclid=IwAR28aDbRbzFaQ1BtX16rKj-1fc5xghYXp4OtVAZFlsbMygRTupGwceu5dtY.

National Reading Panel. (2000). Report of the National Reading Panel: Teaching children to read: an evidence-based assessment of the scientific research literature on reading and its implications for reading instruction. Bethesda, MD: U.S. Department of Education.

Native American Graves Protection and Repatriation Act of 1990, 25 U.S.C. §3001 et seq. (U.S.C. 2000).

Native American Tricksters of Myth and Legend. (n.d.). Native Languages of the Americas: Preserving and promoting American Indian languages. Retrieved from http://www.native-languages.org/trickster.htm.

Native Pride Dancers. (2018, January 9). Millennial Stage, Kennedy Center. Retrieved from https://www.youtube.com/watch?v=jpR5H9zu_4k.

No Child Left Behind Act of 2001: Reauthorization of the Elementary and Secondary Education Act of 1965, 20 U.S.C. § 6301 et seq. Public Law 107–110.

Pugh, S., Ovando, C. J., & Shonemann, N. (2000). The political life of language: Metaphors in writings about diversity in education. In C. J. Ovando & P. McClaren (Eds.), *The politics of multiculturalism and bilingual education: Students and teachers caught in the crossfire* (pp. 2–21). New York, NY: McGraw-Hill.

Puglisi, P., Dir. (2018). *Columbus in America* (Documentary). Pug Media: Zinne Education Project. Retrieved from https://www.zinnedproject.org/materials/columbus-in-america-2.

Reinschmidt, K. M., Attakai, A., Kahn, C. B., Whitewater, S., & Teufel-Shone, N. (2016). Shaping a "Stories of Resilience Model" from urban American Indian Elders' narratives of historical trauma and resilience. *American Indian/Alaska Native Mental Health Research*, 23 (4), 63–85.

Religious Freedom Restoration Act of 1993, Public Law No. 103-141, 42 U.S.C. § 2000bb through 42 U.S.C. § 2000bb-4.

Saunt, C. (2020). *Unworthy Republic: The dispossession of Native Americans and the road to Indian territory*. New York, NY: W. W. Norton.

Smith, A. V. (2020, April 10). Casino closings in Indian country hit core tribal services. *High Country News*. Retrieved from https://www.hcn.org/articles/covid19-casino-closures-in-indian-country-hit-core-tribal-services.

Southern Poverty Law Center. (n.d.). *Hate and Extremism*. Retrieved from https://www.splcenter.org/issues/hate-and-extremism.

Treuer, D. (2019). *The heartbeat of Wounded Knee: Native America from 1890 to the present*. New York, NY: Riverhead Books.

Vygotsky, L. (1978). *Mind in society: The development of higher psychological processes*. Cambridge, MA: Harvard University Press.

Wadsworth, B. (1996). *Piaget's theory of cognitive and affective development* (5th ed.). New York, NY: Longman.

Weatherford, J. (1988). *Indian givers: How the Indians of the Americas transformed the world*. New York, NY: Fawcett Columbine.

NOTES

1. During the COVID-19 pandemic, Congress passed the CARES Act for small businesses with $8 billion for Tribal nations. However, Tribal nations were actually forced to file a lawsuit against Secretary of the Treasury Steven Mnuchin before funds were finally released to them with the first payments of 60% of the allotted monies received on May 6, 2020 (Agoyo, 2020), long after other citizens and entities had received their funding from the Act. The remaining 40% was distributed in June, though a portion was held back by Mnuchin and a suit now scheduled to come before the Supreme Court regarding these actions (Goodkind, 2021). Analysts at Meister Economic Consulting found that impacts from Tribal nations' casino closures on the U.S. economy totaled $4.4 billion in lost economic activity. Along with that came $631 million lost in taxes and revenue to federal, state, and local governments, and 728,000 Native and non-Native people out of work (Egerstrom, 2020). Gaming has become the "tax base" for Indian country since the federal government is not involved in assisting Tribal nations with revenue-development activities as a matter of course, though there may be grants that can be applied to for this purpose.

2. As an aside, dancing was part of the Christian tradition until it was outlawed by priests as being "sinful." The processions held in churches today are remnants of these dances (Kraus, Hilsendager, & Dixon, 1991).

Short Biographies of Those Providing Quotations

Ms. Tana Atchley Culbertson (Klamath Tribes) Tana grew up on her father's ancestral land. However, because the Modoc tribe was the second tribe to be federally terminated (1954), their land base was not returned when they were restored. Because there were no schools in the area where Tana lived, she and her sister and brothers had to be driven to school which was an hour's drive each way. She was determined to finish her education and graduated from high school followed by acquiring her college degree and taking advanced graduate classes. Tana has developed programs in Native American youth development and career education both in higher education and in tribal settings. She currently is the Co-Director/Director of Network Coordination for the Willamette River Network.

Dr. Joseph Bruchac (Nulhegan Abenaki) Joseph grew up in upstate New York, in Greenfield Center, and was raised traditionally by his grandfather. He is the author of over 170 books for children and adults featuring American Indians. Many of his books focus on famous and not-so-famous American Indians who have made important contributions to their Tribal nations and society at large, teaching others about Indigenous accomplishments. Joseph holds a doctoral degree in Comparative Literature, and speaks to Native American and non-Native student audiences around the country, captivating them simultaneously with playing his native flute. Joseph also composes songs and music for the Indian flute, makes recordings, and has video presentations on YouTube.

Dr. Karen Gayton (Swisher) Comeau (Standing Rock Sioux) Karen Gayton (Swisher) Comeau followed in her mother's footsteps teaching at elementary public schools and a BIA school. She served as a principal for four years and then pursued her doctoral degree in Educational Administration. Karen determined to improve education for Indigenous students through her teaching, research, and work in administration at Huron College in South Dakota; the University of Utah; and Arizona State University (ASU). She directed the Center for Indian Education at ASU and was editor of the *Journal of American Indian Education*. Karen served as President of Haskell Indian Nations University in Lawrence, Kansas, from 1996–2006, then President of Sitting Bull College in Rapid City, North Dakota.

Dr. Ed Galindo (Yaqui) Ed survived his Special Education for low-level students experience; after the school followed procedures for testing students' IQs, they found he qualified for the gifted program! In the way of Indian humor, he introduces himself to those he meets for the first time as "Special Ed." He spent many years teaching science in a BIE Junior-Senior High School, during which he involved his students in protection of native animal populations and had them involved with NASA. He is currently a faculty member at the University of Idaho, Associate Director for Education and Diversity for the NASA Idaho Space Grant Consortium, and an affiliate faculty member at Idaho State University (Biology) and at Utah State University (Physics).

Dr. Ramona Klein (Turtle Mountain Chippewa) While Ramona encountered problems many Indian Boarding School students describe, she is a strong survivor. Ramona eventually left the boarding school she was attending before her graduation. As a single mother, she then completed her GED. Ramona then obtained her bachelor's degree in education and became a teacher. Eventually, she returned to the university where she completed her master's degree and her Doctorate in education. Ramona taught at the university level in teacher education before becoming a full-time educational consultant to schools with American Indians. She is sought after by many school districts and BIE schools trying to improve their programs for Indigenous students.

Ms. Mary Jane Oatman (Wak Wak) (Nez Perce) Mary Jane has been a strong voice for American Indian education throughout the years. She held the position of Idaho Coordinator for Indian Education in 2007 and was a member of the Tribal Education Departments National Assembly. In 2008 she was selected to the board of the National Indian Education Association and elected as secretary. Mary Jane was nominated to be a member of the National Advisory Council on Indian Education under the Obama Administration in 2010. She was President of the National

Indian Education Association in 2010–2011. Later, Mary Jane returned to Idaho where she has been taking law classes and working on projects for the Nez Perce tribe.

Mr. Jason Pretty Boy (Standing Rock Sioux, North and South Dakota) Jason's family comes from the Rock Creek (Bullhead) and Wakpala district, and is descended from the Good Plume and Pretty Boy tiospaye of the Oglala Lakota Nation. He was raised on a cow-calf operation in Southern Idaho and attended local public schools. Jason was the director for KISU public radio in Pocatello, Idaho, and the host for the morning news. He attended the College of Business at Idaho State University where he received several honors for his leadership abilities and work with other Native American students. He then moved to Boise, Idaho, where he graduated from Boise State University. Jason has worked with nonprofits for most of his career with occasional forays into Native American education and mass media.

Mr. Harlan McKosato (Sac and Fox) Harlan became very successful in his life, considered an Indigenous icon as host and producer of "Native America Calling" on National Public Radio, among other positions. It was Harlan's passion to always bring the current issues affecting Indian country and Alaska to the forefront through the medium of radio. In this way, opinions of Aboriginal and non-Aboriginal people throughout the country and North America could be voiced and grievances addressed. Challenging the status quo in Indian country and working for positive change in the United States was an important part of his role. Harlan recently passed on July 21, 2020, after making many contributions to Indigenous peoples and paving the road for young journalists. He was fifty-four.

Appendix A

Important Legislation for Indigenous Education

Bilingual Education Act of 1934.
Bilingual Education Act of 1965, 20 U.S.C. § 7401 *et seq.* (U.S.C. 2000).
Childhood Education and Development Act of 1989 (under the Elementary and Secondary Education Act of 1965).
Civil Rights Act of 1964, 42 U.S.C. § 1901 *et seq.* (U.S.C. 2000).
Economic Opportunity Act of 1964, 42 U.S.C. § 2701 *et seq.* (U.S.C. 2000).
Education of All Handicapped Children Act of 1975, 20 U.S.C. § 1400 *et seq.* (U.S.C. 2000). Pub. L. No.: 94–142.
Education of Mentally Retarded Children Act of 1958 (Public Law 85–926).
Elementary and Secondary Education Act of 1965—Amendment of 1995 Addressing American Indian Education specifically.
Elementary and Secondary Education Act of 1965—Title I of Improving America's Schools Act of 1994.
Elementary and Secondary Education Act of 1965, 20 U.S.C. § 6301 (U.S.C. 2000).
Esther Martinez Native American Languages Programs Reauthorization Act of 2019–2020, Public Law No: 116-101.
Every Student Succeeds Act of 2015, Reauthorization of the Elementary and Secondary Education Act of 1965, 20 U.S.C. § 6301 *et seq.*, Pub. L. No.: 114-95. Retrieved from https://www.congress.gov/114/plaws/publ95/PLAW-114publ95.pdf.
Executive Order 13096 American Indian and Alaska Native Education 63, Fed. Reg. 154, 1998.
Executive Order 13175, 2000 Consultation and Coordination with Indian Tribal Governments.
Executive Order 13336, 2004 American Indian and Alaska Education.
Executive Order 13592, 2011 Improving American Indian and Alaska Native Educational Opportunities and Strengthening Tribal Colleges and Universities.
Goals 2000: Educate America Act of 1994, Pub. L. No.: 103-227.
Higher Education Act of 1965, 20 U.S.C. § 1001 *et seq.* (U.S.C. 2000).
Indian Civil Rights Act of 1968 (ICRA), 25 U.S.C. § 1301-1304 (ICRA).
Indian Education Act of 1972, 20 U.S.C. § 3385 *et seq.* (U.S.C. 2000).
Indian Reorganization Act of 1934, 25 U. S. C. § 461 *et seq.* (U.S.C. 2000).
Indian Self-Determination and Education Assistance Act of 1975, 25 U.S.C. § 450f. (U.S.C. 2000).
Individuals with Disabilities Education Act of 1997. 20 U. S. C. § 1400 *et seq.*, Pub. L. No.: 101–476.
Johnson-O'Malley Act of 1934, 25 U.S.C. § 452 *et seq.* (U.S.C. 2000).
National Literacy Act of 1991, Pub. L. No.: 102–73.

Native American Languages Act of 1991, 25 U.S.C. § 2901 *et seq.* (U.S.C. 25) Pub. L. No: 102–24.

No Child Left Behind Act of 2001: Reauthorization of the Elementary and Secondary Education Act of 1965, 20 U.S.C. § 6301 *et seq.*, Pub. L. No.: 107–110.

School Dropout Prevention and Basic Skills Improvement Act of 1990, Pub. L. No.: 101–600; H.R. 5140.

Termination Policy 1953–1968. (1980). Partnership with Native Americans. Retrieved from http://www.nativepartnership.org.

World Language Advancement and Readiness Act of 2019, H.R. 1094.

Appendix B

Resources for Teachers

This is just a small sampling of the available resources, with new books, DVDs, and programs being added every year. Hopefully this will provide you with places to start to add to your curriculum.

Alaska Native Knowledge Network. (2011). *Curriculum Resources*. Website: http://www.ankn.uaf.edu/.
AlterNative: An International Journal of Indigenous Peoples. Begun in 2005 and published by Sage. More at https://journals.sagepub.com/home/alna.Top of Form
Berkhofer, R. F. (1978). *The White man's Indian: Images of the American Indian from Columbus to the present*. New York, NY: Random House.
Bigelow, B., & Peterson, B. (1998). *Rethinking Columbus: The next 500 years* (2nd ed.). Milwaukee, WI: Rethinking Schools.
Bigfoot, M. Y. (n.d.). Childhood Trauma Series in Indian Country. Website https://43ejba1otx5n1btits42mnsv-wpengine.netdna-ssl.com/wp-content/uploads/2013/06/Trauma-Series-in-Indian-Country_3.pdf.
Bruchac, J. Many Native American nations and heroes are featured in over 170 children's and young adult books written by him.
Caduto, M., & Bruchac, J. Series, *Keepers of the earth: Native American stories and environmental activities for children* (Series). Golden, CO: Fulcrum
California Indian Education for All: California American Indian Education Centers. California Department of Education. Website: https://www.cde.ca.gov/sp/ai/re/.
Dennis, Y. W., & Hirschfelder, A. (2010). *A kid's guide to Native American history: More than 50 activities*. Chicago, IL: Chicago Review Press.
Domonoske, C. (2016, June 27). David Bald Eagle, Lakota chief, musician, cowboy and actor, dies at 97. *All things considered*. Washington, DC: National Public radio. Retrieved from http://npr.org.
Education Northwest: Native Education. Education Northwest regularly partners with Tribes and school districts to provide culturally relevant education to Native American students. This website provides information about resources and several articles on Native education in the Northwest including public schools, charter schools, and language immersion schools. Website: https://educationnorthwest.org/areas-of-work/native-education.
Hutchins, A. R. (1974). *Indian Herbalogy of North America*. New York, NY: Random House.
Hutchins, A. R. (1991). *A handbook of Native American herbs*. New York, NY: Random House.

Indian Education for All. (2010, August 4). Montana Education for All. Native American Netroots. Website: http://nativeamericannetroots.net/diary/614.

Indian Land Tenure Foundation. 151 East County Road B2, Little Canada, MN 55117-1523. info@indianlandtenure.org. Website http://www.indianlandtenure.org.

Indian Reading Series. Education Northwest. Website: https://educationnorthwest.org/resources/indian-reading-series.

Indian Tourism Trends for 2020. American Indian/Alaska Native Tourism Association (AIANTA). Website https:www.aianta.org/indian-country-tourism-trends-for-2020/.

Indigenous nations. Many Indigenous nations have developed materials to teach about their histories and cultures. Educators can contact their Education Departments to speak with them about acquiring resources and possible speaker opportunities.

Josephy, A. M. (2015). *The longest trail: Writings on American Indian history, culture, and politics* (Edited by M. Jaffe & R. Wandschneider). New York, NY: Vintage Books.

Keoke, E. D., & Porterfield, K. M. (2001). *Encyclopedia of American Indian Contributions to the World: 15,000 Years of Inventions and Innovations*. New York, NY: Checkmark Books.

Kumelos, R. A. (2016). *Wild wisdom: Animal stories of the Southwest*. Tucson, AZ: Rio Nuevo.

Lajimodiere, D. (2019). *Stringing rosaries: The history, the unforgiveable, and the healing of Northern Plains Indian boarding school survivors*. Fargo: University of North Dakota. (Writings of survivors of their experiences).

Lechner, A., Cavanaugh, M., & Blyler, C. (2016, August 24). *Addressing Trauma in American Indian and Alaska Native Youth*. Washington, DC: U.S. Department of Health and Human Services.

Marvel Comics. (2020). *Indigenous Anthropology*.

Marvel Comics. (2020). *Indigenous Voices #1*. Jeffry Veregge (Port Gamble S'Kallam Tribe), Leader.

Maryboy, N. C., & Begay, D. (2010). *Sharing the skies: Navajo astronomy*. Tucson, AZ: Rio Nuevo.

National Indian Youth Leadership Project. PO Box 2140, Gallup, NM 87305. Includes Native Peace Jam; and the Clearinghouse for Native Service-Learning Information. Website: https://www.NIYLP.org.

Native Circle. (n.d.). Includes information about Indigenous peoples, teacher resources, writings, and collections of materials useful for classrooms. (The New York Public School System has included materials from Native Circle in their Social Studies curriculum update. Co-founded by John Two Hawks, who is available as a speaker.) At http://www.nativecircle.com & http://www.johntwohawks.com.

Native Words, Native Warriors. (n.d.). Includes Native American language use by Code Talkers; information about boarding schools; other matters; lessons and resources. At https://americanindian.si.edu/education/codetalkers/html/chapter2.htmlNative.

Nelson, S. D. Many children's books about numerous American Indian sheroes and heroes written and illustrated by him.

Puglisi, P. Dir. (2018). *Columbus in America* (Documentary). Pug Media: Zine Education Project. Retrieved from https://www.zinnedproject.org/materials/columbus-in-america-2.

Sacred People Foundation. (n.d.). *Native American contributions*. Website: https://www.sacredpeoplefoundation.org/celebs.php.

Talking Feather. This website contains lesson plans and resources for teaching about Native Americans. https://talking-feather.com/home/walk-in-beauty-prayer-from-navajo-blessing/.

Waldman, C. (2006). *Encyclopedia of Native American Tribes* (3rd ed.). New York, NY: Checkmark Books.

Villanueva, E. (2018). *Decolonizing wealth: Indigenous wisdom to heal divides and restore balance*. Oakland, California: Berrett-Koehler. Issued May 2012 C2010BR-12.

Wisdom Tales. On this website there are links for teachers on Native Americans and events. Website: http://www.wisdomtalespress.com/authors_artists-childrens/Joseph_Bruchac.shtml.

World History Timeline. (2019). *Essential humanities*. Retrieved from http://www.essential-humanities.net/history-overview/world-history-timeline/.

NAVAJO CODE TALKERS

Bruchac, J. (2018). *Chester Nez and the unbreakable code: A Navajo Code Talker's story*. Park Ridge, IL: Albert Whitman.

Kawano, K. (1990). *Warriors: Navajo Code Talkers*. Flagstaff, AZ: Northland.

Paul, D. A. (2003). *The Navajo Code Talkers*. Pittsburgh, PA: Dorrance. Originally published 1973.

Turner, J., & Schute, G. (2019). *Navajo Code Talker Manual*. Tucson, AZ: Rio Nuevo.

OTHER

G I Joe: Navajo Code Talker doll. Speaks seven phrases in Navajo and English, plus comes with a laminated list of Navajo Code words.

American Girl Nez Perce doll Kaya

DVDS

Black Indians: An American Story
Great Indian Leaders & Nations
March Point
Navajo Code Talkers: *The Epic Story*
PBS Native America
The Journey of Man

INDIAN LAND TENURE FOUNDATION

For American Indian communities, working with foundations such as the Indian Land Tenure Foundation provides an opportunity to assist Native youth in developing interest in political issues that have relevance to their lives and that of all people in their Native communities. High school students especially need to know that what they are studying can apply and be useful in their futures. By introducing students to laws that directly impact Native peoples, suddenly subjects like history and political science come alive. Resources available for creating lesson plans.

STATE RESOURCES

The **Alaska Standards for Culturally Relevant Pedagogy** have been successfully utilized to do just that. In turn, there are organizations, such as the Alaska Fish and Game, which have created sets of lesson plans addressing real problems such as salmon recovery. Salmon Programs and Resources is an online list of sites containing lesson plans, activities such as field trips and games, descriptions of habitat and what is needed to develop more habitat for salmon, and other fish. For middle schoolers, there is a site that gives information related to dissection of salmon, which includes information about the unique biological needs of salmon.

Alaska Department of Fish and Game. https://www.adfg.alaska.gov/

Alaska Sea Life Organization. Activities can be found at: http://www.alaskasealife.org/uploads/education/curriculum/salmoneducationwebresources.pdf

Ohio: *Project WILD* (1983/2018) is one of the resources that is available not only in Ohio but nationally, and has been approved for use in K–12 grades by the National Science Teachers Association as well as the National Council for the Social Studies. They have already done the work of connecting their lesson plans to the Ohio standards, as well as to other state standards where this curriculum is taught. Reference: Western Association of Fish and Wildlife Agencies and the Council for Environmental Education (1983/2018). Ohio Division of Wildlife. *Education and Outdoor Discovery: Conservation Education/Project WILD* Retrieved from http://wildlife.ohiodnr.gov/education-and-outdoor-discovery/nasp.

National Archery in the Schools Program (NASP): created in Kentucky by Departments of Education and the Fish and Wildlife Services in 2002 to address the needs of 4–12 grade students in terms of physical education. This national program operates in many states and is significant in that it addresses problems with healthy lifestyles for all students as stated below:

The core content covers archery safety, equipment, technique, mental concentration, and self-improvement. The program positively influences student attendance, behavior, self-esteem, confidence, and on task behavior. NASP transcends gender, racial, ethnic, and economic backgrounds and provides an equal learning opportunity to all students by utilizing standardized equipment, training, and implementation. Website: https://www.naspschools.org

Message: To Native American Students Considering College*
From: Tana Atchley, Advisor for Student Affairs & Activities, Portland State University (2010)

If you are considering going to college, you need to find somebody who is going to support you, not just to give encouragement to you. You need someone who knows resources and can help plan out for you. You need a plan that is realistic. This is because you may find that you're supposed to graduate at such and such a time, but if that doesn't happen due to factors beyond your control, you'll still be able to graduate.

You have to have motivation to finish the plan, and if that means taking a semester of summer school, that's all right. But you do need people around you who are resources in terms of funding, support for taking care of family needs, etc. If that is family, if that is a school counselor, if that is a community leader or a big brother or sister, you've got to have somebody around you to support you.

You can't do much without a high school diploma and some sort of education beyond high school. So you need to know what it is that you want to do in your adult life, and then plan how to make that accomplishment come together. It's not going to happen overnight, and there will be times of struggle, but with support, you can make it through. It is not as hard to get through the "hoops" that everyone has to go through when you have a plan and support.

It's not just about money and getting a good job: it's about empowering yourself, being able to understand systems and to know that you are able to bring that knowledge back to your community to benefit everyone. You can advocate for yourself and your community with your knowledge that you can then share with your family, community, and other Tribal members. That's what the ultimate benefit of your education provides.

*Permission is given to readers to share this message with potential Indigenous college students.

Index

Abenaki tribe, 39, 121–122, 205–206
Aboriginal culture before conquest: agriculture, 33–35; families, 32–33; mound builders, 37; pharmaceuticals, 35–36; settlements, 36–37; spirituality, 36; traditions, 31; writ large, 41
Aboriginal societies before conquest: in Great Basin, 40; Maori people, 13; in Mississippi, 37; in Northeast, 38–39; in Plains, 40; population, 31; in Southeast, 40–41; in West, 34, 39. *See also* America's early civilizations
ACE (Adverse Childhood Experiences) research, 166–170
Adjusted Cohort Graduation Rate (ACGR), 162
adoption of Native Americans, 220
Adverse Childhood Experiences (ACE) research, 166–170
Aegean civilization, 21
AFGR (Averaged Freshman Graduation Rate), 162
agriculture: in ancient Rome, 49; early development of, 11–12; language and, 18; of Native Americans before conquest, 33–35; storage of foodstuffs, 34–35
AIE (American Indian English), 147, 210
AIM (American Indian Movement), 125, 126, 206
AIRFA (American Indian Religious Freedom Act), 190
Alaska Knowledge Network (AKN), 138
Alaska Natives. *See* Native Americans/Alaska Natives
Alaska standards and state programs, 189, 236
Alexi, Sherman, 210, 221
Alger, Horatio, 212
Amazonia, 30–31
American Indian Education Act, 126
American Indian English (AIE), 147, 210
American Indian Movement (AIM), 125, 126, 206
American Indian Religious Freedom Act (AIRFA), 190

American primativism, 114
America's early civilizations: Amazonia, 30–31; Andes, 28–29, 76–77; Aztecs, 27–28; Holmberg's mistake about, 22–23; Mesoamerica, 22, 24–27, 76–77; migrations, 22; origins of Native Americans/Alaska Natives, 113–114; Peru, 23–24; Qosqo, 29–30, 76; research revealing rich legacies, 31. *See also* Aboriginal societies before conquest
America's Languages (Commission on Language Learning), 139
ancient Greece, 21, 47–48, 69–70
ancient Rome: beginnings of racism in, 69–70; cultural accomplishments, 49–50; trade and slavery, 48, 50; unrest in, 50. *See also* Roman Empire
Andes, 28–29, 76–77
animals, 209
anthropologists, 108–109
anti-miscegenation laws, 107
Arias, E., xx
arts and culture: cave paintings, 47; films, 235; murals, 176; music, 11, 41, 98, 165, 213; paintings of American Natives, 96; relevance in teaching, 213–214; resilience and, 176–177; rock art, 37; sacredness of legends, 209. *See also* Aboriginal culture before conquest; Medicine Wheels
Asian Clan, 10–11, 17
Athens, 47
atrocities. *See* massacres
Australasian clan and marker, 8–9, 17, 22
Australian Maori peoples, 13
Averaged Freshman Graduation Rate (AFGR), 162
Aztecs, 25–28

Bae, S., 164
balance in life, 176

Barnes, I., 13
basketmaking, 41
behavior problems of children, 171–172
Bering Straight theory, 32
Berliner, D., 128, 212
BIA (Bureau of Indian Affairs), 110, 116, 118
biculturalism, 139. *See also* multicultural movement
Biddle, B. J., 128
BIE (Bureau of Indian Education), 144
Bighorn Medicine Wheel, 173
bilingual education, 101
Bilingual Education Act and amendments, 118, 124
bison, 100
Bitsoi, LeManuel, 167
Blackhawk, N., 78, 99
Black Kettle (peace chief), 98
Black Power movement, 123
Blink (Gladwell), 217
"blood quantum", 119
boarding schools: as 51st state in education regulations, 118; acknowledging abuse within, 220–221; boarding school movement, 104–106, 115; under Indian agents and superintendents, 102–104; Pratt's boarding schools, 104–106; as toxic stress, 168–169
Boas, Franz, 108–109, 116
Boccaccio, 71
books, xii, 136, 210
Brave Heart, M. Y., 171
bread and circuses, 56
Bronfenbrenner, U., 142–146, 145, 147, 151, 186
Bronze Age, 21
Brown v. the Board of Education, 122
Bruchac, Joseph, 121–122, 205–206, 227
buffalo herds, 100
Bureau of Ethnology, 114
Bureau of Indian Affairs (BIA), 110, 116, 118
Bureau of Indian Education (BIE), 144
Bush, President George W., 178

Cahokia community, 37
California gold rush, 98, 188
California Indian History Curriculum Coalition (CIHCC), 188–189
California natives, 114
Canadian natives, 108–109
Canassatego (Iroquoian chief), 214
cannibalism, 72
Caonabo (Taino Indian), 74
Caral (Supe valley), 30
Carjuzaa, J., 188
Carlisle Indian Industrial School, 105
Catlin, George, 96
Cato the Elder, 49
cave art, 47

CDIB (Certificate of Degree of Indian Blood), 119
census information, 87–90, 89, 90, 219
ceremonies. *See* collaboration with communities; traditional ceremonies
Certificate of Degree of Indian Blood (CDIB), 119
Champoux, Rick, 137
Chan Chan (city), 29, 30
charter schools, 157–158, 185
Cherokee: educating children of, 101; losses of, 82; removing from land, 102; Rogers, Will, 115–116; in Southwest, 41; Trail of Tears, 82, 102
Cheyanne peoples, 85, 98, 222
Child, B. J., 106
Chilocco Boarding School, 106
Chimor Empire, 29
Chinese civilization, 21
Chivington, Col. John, 85, 98
Choctaw, 102
Christianity: Doctrine of Discovery, 74, 75; Mary, mother of Jesus, 54; in the Middle Ages, 61, 62–63, 65; origins in Roman Empire, 53–55; Protestantism, 82; Protestant Reformation, 78–79; teaching in schools, 101, 102; treatment of Native Americans and, 74–75. *See also* missions and missionaries
Cicero, 49
CIHCC (California Indian History Curriculum Coalition), 188–189
circles, Medicine Wheels as, 173–176, 174
civilization classification, 19
civil rights: backlash to movement, 133; education and, 123–125, 126–127; rights to sovereignty, 118–119, 206–207; segregation and, 122–123
Civil War, 82
Clark, Mamie, 186
classroom practices: cooperative learning, 194–195; holistic learning with real experiences, 195–196; learning styles, 195; new era of equality in, 222–223; nonverbal communication, 146, 148, 193–194; relational worldviews, 196–199; resources for teachers, 233–237; silence in the classroom, 194; STEM studies, 217–218; thematic lessons, 199. *See also* collaboration with communities
Clemmons, Samuel, 99
Clinton, President William Jefferson, 177–178
Cloud, Henry Roe, 117
Coastal Clan and marker, 8–10, 32
Code Talkers, 219, 235
Cody, Anthony, 129
Cody, "Buffalo Bill", 100
collaboration with communities: cultural mismatches, 184–186; family input, 186; integrating Indigenous cultures into schools, xv–xvi, 186–190; invitations to schools, 211–212;

natural world incorporated into, 196–199; self-made man mythology, 212–214. *See also* classroom practices
college education, support for, 237
collegia (social clubs), 51
Collier, John, 110
Colón, Christóbal (Christopher Columbus), xix, 41, 72–75, 221
Comeau, Karen Gayton (Swisher), 168–169, 227
Commission on Language Learning, 139
communication, 151. *See also* language; nonverbal communication
compulsory education, 121
confrontational stance, 194
Connors, Col., 85
conquest and colonization: cultural differences during, 45; early slavery, xx, 47, 71–72, 74–75; early Spanish settlements, 77–78, 83–84; results of, 84–85; trauma and, 170–172. *See also* Aboriginal culture before conquest; Aboriginal societies before conquest; early European history
conservative movement, 128–129, 133–134
Constantine, Emperor, 54–55
Constantinople, 63, 65
Cook-Harvey, C. M., 164
cooperative learning, 194–195
Cooper's Ferry (Idaho), 7, 9–10, 17, 22, 32
Copper Age, 20–21
Cothran, D. J., 172
cowboy and Indian films, 114
Crick, Francis, 4–5
Critical Theory, 127
Crosby, Alfred S., xxiiin2
Cross, T., 161
Culbertson, Tana Atchley, 227, 237
cultural capital, 165–166
cultural deficit theory, 125–126, 186
cultural difference theory, 128
cultural relativism, 109
cultural relevance: Alaska Knowledge Network (AKN), 138; importance of, 163–164, 186–187; needed in pedagogy, 136–138; role of family and, 138–139; sharing of food, 190; Standards for Culturally Responsive Schools, 189; state programs, 188–189
culture: defined, 19; development of, xxv–xxvi, 18–19; distinction of, xiv–xvi; renewed interest in, 218. *See also* Aboriginal culture before conquest; arts and culture; diversity; dominant culture; righting of wrongs; *specific cultures*
Cuneiform script, 21
curriculum relevancy, 136, 136–138. *See also* classroom practices
Custer, Col. George Armstrong, 99

dances, 208
Danes and Vikings, 63–64
Darling-Hammond, L., 164
Darwin, Charles, 113
Davidson, L., 95
Davis, Loren, 9
Dawes Act, 106–107
day schools, 108
deoxyribonucleic acid (DNA), 4–5
desegregation, 122, 124
Dewey, J., 117
Discovery, Age of, 78–79
diversity: cultural mismatches and deficits, 184–186; distinct cultures and, xiv–xvi; hate groups and, 217; multicultural movement, 126–127, 133, 136; new era of equality, 222–223; in socioecological systems, 144–148, 145, 147, 151. *See also* language
DNA. *See* mitochondrion DNA
Doctrine of Discovery, 74, 75, 79
dominant culture: humor as resistance to, 221; language and, 191; as problematic in classrooms, 137, 141, 163; Western European as, xxv. *See also* socioecological systems
drumming, 176–177
dual citizenship, 147
Duncan, Arne, 178
Duncan, P. T., 192

early civilization: Bronze Age, 21; Copper Age, 20–21; Iron Age, 21; Neolithic period, 20. *See also* ancient Greece; ancient Rome; migration of early humans
early European history, 46–50, 57, 65–66. *See also* conquest and colonization; migration to Americas
East Asian clan, 10
Edgerton, R. B., 186
Edicts of Constantine, 54
EDR (Event Dropout Rate), 162
education of American Indians/Alaska Natives: anthropologists influencing, 108–110; conservative v. progressive, 128–129; Dawes Act, 106–107; day schools, 108; firsthand accounts, 121–122, 123; losing federal funding, 119; Meriam Report, 107–108, 110; in post-Meriam era, 117–118; segregation in, 118; support needed for college, 237; teacher preparation, 120–123; traditional tribal teachings, 117. *See also* boarding schools; classroom practices; missions and missionaries; standardized testing
Education of Mentally Retarded Children Act, 122
Egyptian civilization, 21
elders, 214. *See also* families of Native Americans/Alaska Natives
Elementary and Secondary Education Acts, 134, 163

Elias,, 172
ELL (English Language Learners), 164
El Norte, 83–84
Eltis, xx
English Language Learners (ELL), 164
epigenetics, 167–170
equality, xv, 39, 69–70, 222–223
ESS (Every Student Succeeds Act), 163, 164
Essential Understanding of Tribal Nations, 137–138
Esther Martinez Native American Languages Programs Reauthorization Act, 139
ethic of caring, 166
ethnographers, 13, 109, 116
Etruscans, 48
eugenics, 205
Eurasians, historical perspective, 8, 20–21, 22
European Clan, 11
European explorers and early settlers: prejudice and racism of, 81–82; responding positively to American Indians, 93; settlements in America, 76–81. *See also* conquest and colonization
European scientific method, 197–198
Event Dropout Rate (EDR), 162
Every Student Succeeds Act (ESS), 163, 164
exchange theories, 165–166
executive orders, 177–178
exosystem, 143, 145, 146–148, 147
experience, holistic learning with, 195–196, 218
experiences of Indigenous people. *See* first-person accounts of Indigenous experiences
explorers. *See* European explorers and early settlers
eye contact, 146, 193

families of Native Americans/Alaska Natives: anti-miscegenation laws, 107; before conquest, 32–33; constellations of, 142–146, 145, 147; diversity and, 141–142; grandparents, 149–150, 193, 214; including in curriculum planning, 186; matrilineal and patrilineal communities, 148–151; reclaimers, 220; role of, 138–139; schooling causing separation from, 102–104; social trust built in, 166; support of, 140–141
Feeling, D., 192
Ferry, M., 172
films, 235
first man/woman, 5–6, 13
first-person accounts of Indigenous experiences: background on, 227–229; Bruchac, Joseph, 121–122, 205–206; Comeau, Karen Gayton (Swisher), 168–169; Culbertson, Tana Atchley, 237; Galindo, Ed, 123; Klein, Ramona, 161; Martin, D., 219; McKosato, Harlan, 155–156; Oatman (Wakwak), Mary Jane, 183; Pretty Boy, Jason, 150
Fontaine, T., 221

food, sharing of, 190
Fort Hall (Idaho), 103–104, 176, 193
Franklin, Benjamin, 214
Franklin, Rosalind, 4–5
Freire, Paolo, 210
French settlers in America, 80–81
funding for Tribal governments, 206–207

Galindo, Ed, 123, 228
Galloway, C. G., 81
games as social events, 37
gaming industry, 206–207
Garn, A. C., 172
genes, 167–170, 219–220. *See also* mitochondrion DNA
Georgics (Virgil), 49
Germanic peoples, 57, 58–59
"giveaways", 39
Gladwell, Malcolm, 212–213, 217
Goodman, K., 136, 216
Goodman, Y., 216
Goths of Europe, 52–53, 56–58, 63–64
graduation ceremonies, 210
graduation rates, 162–164
grandparents, 149–150, 193, 214
Grann, D., 215
Great Basin Aboriginal societies, 40
Great Lakes agriculture, 33
Great League/Law of Peace, 38
Greece: ancient world of, 21, 47–48, 69–70; beginnings of racism, 69–70; Greek Orthodox Church, 63; slavery, 47–48
greed, 94–96

Halbert, xx
Hall, B., 188
Hamilton, Virginia, 210
handshakes, 194
Hardiman, M. M., 196
hate groups, 217
health of Native Americans: European invasions bringing disease, 76, 97; healing and medicines, 35–36, 175–177; smallpox, 79. *See also* toxic stress
hegemony, 76, 85, 127–128
Henson, J.,, 172
HGP. *See* Human Genome Project (HGP)
high school graduation rates, 162–164
Hirata-Edds, T., 192
historical traditions: importance of, 166; rules and norms, 198–199. *See also* collaboration with communities; traditional ceremonies
historical trauma (HT). *See* toxic stress
Hohokam people, 36–37
holistic learning with real experiences, 195–196

Holmberg, Allan R., 22–23
Hoopes, M., xx
Horpe, Jim (Wa Tha Huch), 115
HT (historical trauma). *See* toxic stress
human genome, 3–6
Human Genome Project (HGP): about, xix, 4–6; additional research needed for, 13–14; conclusions from, 12–13; migration and, 17–18; trauma encoded on genes, 167, 169–173
human trafficking, 170–171. *See also* kidnappings
humor, 221
hunters in Aboriginal societies, 35

ICWA (Indian Child Welfare Act), 220
identification of tribal members, 119
IEFA (Indian Education for All Act) in Montana, 137–138, 188
Inca peoples, 22, 29–30, 76
Indian Child Welfare Act (ICWA), 220
Indian Civilization Act, 101
Indian Clan (East India), 17
Indian Land Tenure Foundation, 235
Indian Nations at Risk, 130
Indian Relocation Act, 120
Indian Removal Act, 102
Indian Reorganization Act, 118
Indian Self-Determination and Education Assistance Act, 127
Indigenous peoples: about, xxvi; prejudices against, xxi–xxii; teachings, 173. *See also* Native Americans/Alaska Natives; *specific Indigenous tribes*
Indigenous Peoples' Day, 221
individual experiences of Indigenous people. *See* first-person accounts of Indigenous experiences
Indus civilization, 21
Ingalls, G. W., 103
Inquisition, 63, 69–70
intergenerational trauma, 170–172
interviews of school experiences, 140–141
involuntary minorities, 144
Iron Age, 21
Iroquois Confederacy, 81
Islamic world, 64–65

Jackson, President Andrew, 82
Janks, H., 210
Jason Pretty Boy, 150
Jefferson, President Thomas, 96, 113
Jensen, E., 196
Jesus's teachings. *See* Christianity
Jewish citizens in Middle Ages, 69–70
Jim, C., xx
Jim, M., xx
Jingle Dance, 208

Johannsen, Wilhelm, 3
Johnson, Lyndon, 124
Johnson, N., xx
Johnson-O'Malley Act, 117
Johnson v. M'Intosh, 76
Justinian legal code, 60

Kendi, I. X., 69
Kennedy, Robert F., 124, 126
kidnappings, 77–78, 100, 105, 220
King, Martin Luther, Jr., 123
Kirk, W., 192
Klein, Ramona, 228
knights, 61
knowledge, prior. *See* experience, holistic learning with
Kulinna, P. H., 172

Lam, L., 164
land and spirituality, 174
land holdings and Dawes Act, 106–107
language: American Indian English, 147, 210; biculturalism and, 139; bilingual education, 101; as cultural tool, 18; English Language Learners, 164; groupings of heritage languages, 191; immersion programs, 177, 192–193; loss and revival of, 190–193; migration and, 14, 17; power of, 215; standardized reading testing and, 216–217; super-languages, 14; teaching Native languages to non-Natives, 192–193; trilingual language programs, 193
Last Glacial Maximus (LGM), 6–8, 13
Law of the Twelve Tables, 49
Lea, Henry Charles, 70
League of Five Nations, 38
League of Iroquois, 214
learning, theories of, 135–136
legislation, listing of, 231–232. *See also specific laws*
Lewis and Clark expedition, 96
LGM (Last Glacial Maximus), 6–8, 13
Llanos de Mojos, 30–31
Louisiana Territory, 81
Lowe, J., 172
Luhan, Mabel Dodge, 110
Luther, Martin, 78
Luther Standing Bear, 115

Mackey, R., 192
macrosystem, 143–144, 145, 146–148, 147, 157–158, 164
Maine legislation, 188
Majorville Wheel, 174
Manifest Destiny, 96–98
Mann, C. C., xx, 23, 73
Martin, D., 219

massacres: of Pequots, 80, 94; rationale for atrocities, 113–114; in the West, 85, 98–99, 113–114
Massasoit, 79
mathematics lesson, 195
matrilineal and patrilineal communities, 32, 148–151
Maya, 25–27
McCarty, T. L., 192–193
McKosato, Harlan, 155–156, 229
media: books, xii, 114, 136; newspapers with advertised bounties, 107; portrayals of Native Americans, xii, 114; preservation of oral texts, 114; role in racism and prejudice, 93–96, 99–100; social media, 143. *See also* stereotypes; writings
medicine. *See* health of Native Americans
Medicine Wheels, 173–176, 174, 198
Mendel, Gregor, 3
Mercer, C., 164
Meriam Report, 107–108, 110
Mesoamerica, 22, 24–27, 76–77
Mesopotamia, 21
mesosystems, 142–148, 145, 147, 157–158
Metacomet (King Philip), 80
metaphors and stories, 198, 215
Métis peoples, 80
Mexican-American War, 84
Mexico, Spanish conquest of, 77
microsystems, 142, 144–148, 145, 147, 151, 211
Middle Ages: about, 60–62; Christianity during, 61, 62–63, 65; Islamic leadership during, 65; racism in, 69–70
Middle East slavery, 47
Mieschler, Frederick, 5
migration of early humans: to Americas, 9–10, 13, 22; first man/woman, 5–6, 13; gene mutations and, 6–11, 7; summary of, 17–18; theories about, 10, 32. *See also* early civilization
migration to Americas: early humans, 9–10, 13, 22; explorers' response to Native Americans, 93; Holmberg's mistake, 22–23; of Slavs, 64–65; of Vikings, 63–64. *See also* Aboriginal societies before conquest; conquest and colonization; early European history
military recognition, 219
missions and missionaries, 77, 83, 100, 101
Mississippian mound builders, 37
mitochondrion DNA, 5–6, 8–11, 14. *See also* migration of early humans
Moche Empire, 30
Montana Indian Education for All Act (IEFA), 137–138, 188
moral act of teaching, 184
multicultural movement, 126–127, 133, 136
myths about ethnic groups, 4

NAGPRA (Native American Graves Protection and Repatriation Act), 14
names of Native Americans: animal names, 209; Euro-American names compared to, 148, 150; giving, 209; loss of, 105, 106, 108, 151
National Advisory Council on Indian Education, 126
National Defense Authorization Act (NDAA), 140
National Dropout Prevention Center, 162
National Indian Education Association., 185
National Indian Youth Council, 122
National Reading Panel, 216
National School Lunch Act, 118
A Nation at Risk (National Commission), 128–129
"Nation at Risk" phrase, 215
Native American Graves Protection and Repatriation Act (NAGPRA), 14
Native American Indian Languages Act, 128
Native Americans/Alaska Natives: changing attitudes in 1924, 110; current populations, xx; early European encounters with, 70–72, 73–74; theories about origins of, 113–114
Native Hawaiians/Pacific Islanders' census data, 87–90, 89, 90
Navajo peoples: agriculture, 34; Bitsoi ("Lee") on toxic stress, 34; Code Talkers, 219, 235; importance of core teachings, 173, 218; language of, 193; "Walk in Beauty" prayer, xiii, 176; woven goods, 34, 213
NCLB. *See* No Child Left Behind (NCLB)
NDAA (National Defense Authorization Act), 140
neoliberal views, 165, 185, 216–217
Neolithic period, 20, 25
Network for Public Education (NPE), 129
New Age movement, 156–157
Nez Perce, xiv–xv, 9, 183, 221, 228, 235
No Child Left Behind (NCLB): early hopes for, 178; effect on Native Americans, 157–158; effect on teachers, 185; emphasis on testing, 210, 217; exit exams, 162; literacy practices, 210
Noddings, N., 166
Nokus Feke Ematha Tustanaki (Bear Heart), 14
nonverbal communication, 146, 148, 193–194
Normal Schools, 120–121
Northern Asians and American Indian Nations, 13
nostalgia, 114
NPE (Network for Public Education), 129
numbers as sacred, 175

Oatman (Wakwak), Mary Jane, 183, 228
Obama, President Barack, 178
Ogbu, J. U., 144
Ohio's *Project WILD*, 236
Olmecs, 25
On Agriculture (Cato the Elder), 49
On Duties (Cicero), 49

On the Origin of Species (Darwin), 113
oral histories, 13
Oregon Trail, 97, 98
organizations of American Indian scholars, 116
origins of Native Americans/Alaska Natives, 113–114. *See also* Aboriginal societies before conquest; early civilization; mitochondrion DNA
Outing Programs, 104–105, 107. *See also* boarding schools
Outliers (Gladwell), 212–213

Pachakuti (Incan ruler), 29
Pacific Coastal Aboriginal societies, 39
Paine, Thomas, 93
Paiute tribe, 40, 77–78, 103
Parker, Cynthia Ann, 100
patrilineal and matrilineal communities, 32, 148–151
Paul (apostle), 53
"pedagogy of the oppressed", 210
Pember, M. A., 167
Pequots, 79–80, 94
Peru, 23–24
Peter, L., 192
Pewewardy, C., 176
physical education classes, 213, 236
Piaget, 135, 199, 218
Pinkham, Jaimie A., xiv–xv
Pizzarro (Conquistador), 76
Plains Aboriginal societies, 40
Plato, 46
Plessy v. Ferguson, 122
Podolsky, A., 164
pope of the Roman Catholic Church, 62–63
population: of Aboriginal societies before conquest, 31; census information, 87–90, 89, 90, 219; of current Native Americans/Alaska Natives, xx
Portugal's first expeditions, 70–72
potlatch, 39
potlucks, community, 190, 211
poverty, 134–135, 158. *See also* socioeconomic status (SES)
Powell, J. W., 103
Pratt, Richard Henry, 104–105
prejudice, 141. *See also* racism; stereotypes
preschools, 142
Presidential executive orders, 177–178
Pretty Boy, Jason, 150, 229
private and charter schools, 185
progressive *vs.* conservative movement, 128–129
Project WILD, 236
Protestantism. *See* Christianity
Puente de Hózhǫ́ (Arizona), 176, 193
Puritans: religion and treatment of Native Americans, 79–80, 94, 95; schools established by, 101; values, 135

Qosqo (city), 29–30, 76

races of humans: Bear Heart on, 14; Human Genome Project clarifying, 69; misclassification in census, xx; only one human race, 6, 11, 13
racism: in ancient world, 46, 69–70; defined, 69, 93; Manifest Destiny and, 96–98; media's role in racism and prejudice, 93–96; prejudice in schools, xxi, 141; transfers of teachers and, 159; writers contributing to, 99–100. *See also* conquest and colonization; European explorers and early settlers; slavery
Ravitch, D., 128–129, 157–158
recognition of Native Americans, 222. *See also* righting of wrongs
Reconquista, 65, 72
Red Cloud (Lakota), 99
Red English, 210
Red Power movement, 119, 122, 123
Red Road (following), xiii, xvi, 176
Reed, Henry, 103
relational worldviews, 196–199
relationships, 211–212. *See also* families of Native Americans/Alaska Natives
religion: Islamic world, 64–65; Jewish citizens in Middle Ages, 69–70; sacredness, xiv–xv, 209; scientific knowledge *vs.* the Bible, 197–199; spirituality and, 36, 156–157, 174; "Walk in Beauty" prayer, xiii, 176. *See also* Christianity; Puritans
relocation of Native Americans: moving to reservations, 85, 98; Relocation Centers, 88; termination and, 119–120; Trail of Tears, 82, 102. *See also* boarding schools
Renaissance's Age of Discovery, 78–79
Report of the Consultations with Tribal Leaders in Indian Coutry (Duncan), 178
resilience: art and music contributing to, 176–177; balance in life and, 176; coping mechanisms, 161; culturally relevant social roles, 177–178; high school completion and, 140–141, 162–164; historical trauma and, 167, 169–173; Medicine Wheels and, 173–176, 174; Presidential executive orders and, 177–178; social and cultural capital, 165–166; socioecological factors, 164–165. *See also* Adverse Childhood Experiences (ACE) research; first-person accounts of Indigenous experiences
resources for teachers, 233–237
responses to American Indians: hatred of, 94–96; Holmberg's mistake, 22–23; rationalizing atrocities, 113–114. *See also* stereotypes
Riggs, C., 172
righting of wrongs: boarding school abuse acknowledgment, 220–221; Columbus Day

changed to Indigenous Peoples' Day, 221; genetic testing, 219–220; Indigenous representation, 223; making space, ix, xiii; for military recognition, 219; new era of equality, 222–223; reclaiming Tribal membership, 220; renewed desire to, 218; using humor in, 221
right to sovereignty, 118–119, 206–207. *See also* civil rights
Rogers, Will, 115–116
Roman Empire: about, 50–51; accomplishments before the fall of, 55–57; Christianity's origins in, 53–55; culmination of, 57; fall of, 58–59; role of emperor, 51; Visigoths of Europe and, 52–53, 56–58; writings about, 65
Russian doll analogy, 146
Ryan, W. Carson, Jr., 117

Sacajewea, 96
sacredness of legends, 209
Sahara migration, 9
San (formerly Bushmen), 13
Sand Creek massacre, 98
San Juan County (Utah) schools, 218
San peoples (formerly called Bushmen), 6, 13
Saunt, C., 215
scholars, American Indian, 116
school choice, 157–158
school failures: conservative movement narratives, 133–134; Cultural Deficit Theory as explanation of, 125–126; false narratives of, 185–186; poverty and, 134–135
School Lunch Indemnity Plan, 118
school reforms, 164–165. *See also* classroom practices
schools, boarding. *See* boarding schools
science, technology, engineering, and mathematics (STEM) studies, 217–218
scientific method, 197–198
segregation, 108, 118. *See also* racism; stereotypes
self-made man mythology, 212–214
Seneca, D., xx
Senese, G., 127, 184
SES. *See* socioeconomic status (SES)
settlements of early Aboriginal societies, 36–37
sharing of food, 211
Shoshone tribe: education and, 103, 104, 176, 218; language of, 192; massacre of, 85; Sacajewea, 96; Steward's racism and, 109; Twain writing about, 99
Siberian Clan, 10, 17
silence in the classroom, 194
Simms, C. P., 192
Sirionó Indians, 23
Skinner, B. F., 135

slavery: of Africans, xx, 70, 72; in ancient history, 46, 47, 48, 51; in early Europe, 47, 55–56, 57, 58; of Native Americans, xx, 47, 71–72, 74–75; revolts against, 50
smallpox, 79
Smith, Frank, 136
social exchange theories, 165–166
social media, 143
socioecological systems, 144–148, 145, 147, 151, 164–165
socioeconomic status (SES): Cultural Deficit Theory and, 125–126; high school dropout rates and, 162; in microsystems, 142; transfers of teachers and, 159
Sotero, 167
Southeast Aboriginal societies, 40–41
Southwest Aboriginal societies, 33
Spain: early settlements in America, 76–81; first expeditions in the Atlantic, 72–75; invading the Americas, 76–78; racism in Middle Ages, 69–70; territories of, 83–84. *See also* Colón, Christóbal (Christopher Columbus); early European history
special needs, education for, 122–123
spirituality, 36, 156–157, 174. *See also* religion
Squanto, 79
standardized testing: bell curves and, 216–217; false narratives about, 133–134, 185–186; folly of, 185; language and, 210. *See also* No Child Left Behind (NCLB)
Standards for Culturally Responsive Schools, 189
Stannard, D. E., 32
Stanton, C., 188
state resources, 236. *See also specific states*
STEM (science, technology, engineering, and mathematics) studies, 217–218
stereotypes: false images and narratives, 115, 214–215, 217; in school curriculum, 126, 211–212; self-made man mythology, 212–214; unlearning, xv, 115–119, 144–148, 145, 147. *See also* multicultural movement; media
sterilization without consent, 205
Steward, Julian, 109, 113
storytelling and metaphors, 95–96, 198, 215. *See also* media
Stosich, E. L., 164
substance abuse, 172
suicide rate for Native Americans, 171, 172
Suina, M., 173
survival of the fittest, 113
survivance, 222

Taino Indians, 73–75
teachers transfers, 159
technology, 66, 151
Termination Act, 119, 125

termination of Tribal nations, 119–120. *See also* relocation of Native Americans
terminology, xxiiin1
Thumpa Inka, 30
Tiwanaku (city), 28–29
tools, early appearance of, 20
toxic stress: about, xxi, 167, 169–173; epigenetics and, 167–170; overcoming. *See* resilience
Tozer, S. E., 127, 184
traditional art. *See* arts and culture
traditional ceremonies: before conquest, 31; for graduations, 210; name giving, 209; participating in, 208; powwows, 208; right to practice, 190. *See also* collaboration with communities
Trail of Tears, 82, 102
trauma. *See* toxic stress
treaties, 97, 98, 106–107
Treuer, D., 206, 221
Tribal Nations, xx. *See also* Native Americans/Alaska Natives; *specific tribes*
tricksters in legends, 209
trilingual language immersion programs, 193
Truer, A., 40
Twain, Mark, 99

Ute tribe, 40, 77, 103, 218

Vikings, 52–53, 63–64
Violas, P. C., 127, 184
violence, 65. *See also* massacres; racism
Visigoths, 52–53, 56–58, 63–64
Vizenor, Gerald, 222
voice control in classrooms, 194
voluntary minorities, 144
Vygotsky, L. S., 135, 196, 199, 218

Wabanaki Studies Commission (WSC), 188
"Walk in Beauty" prayer, xiii, 176
Warriors Circle of Honor, 219
Washington, President George, 81–82
waterways, 37–38
Wa Tha Huch (Bright Path), 115
Watson, James, 4–5, 135
wealth: conquering lands for, 76; greed and, 78–79; redistribution of, 39
Weatherford, J. M., 35
Wells, S., 7, 12
white guilt, 187
Wiggins, C., xx
Wilkins, Maurice, 4–5
Williams, Marcellus, 14
Wilson, J., 83
women: in ancient Rome, 49; in early Europe, 56; in Middle Ages, 60; Native Americans capturing, 77–78, 100
World Language Advancement and Readiness Act, 140
Wounded Knee, 99
writings: of ancient Rome, 49–50; khipu system, 76; as propaganda, 95–96; as record-keeping tool, 21. *See also* media
wrongs. *See* righting of wrongs
WSC (Wabanaki Studies Commission), 188

Xaltocan community, 27–28, 77

Zigler, Edward, 186
Zone of Proximal Development (ZPD), 196
Zull, J. E., 196, 199

About the Author

Beverly J. Klug, EdD, is professor emerita at Idaho State University. She is a well-respected author in the area of education for Indigenous students. She has taught and worked in classrooms with K–12 Indigenous students and multicultural populations for more than forty years. For thirty of those years she taught in teacher education programs, while still having the privilege of working with and teaching Native American students primarily on the Fort Hall Shoshone-Bannock Reservation.

Ms. Klug has served on the Idaho State Department of Education's American Indian Education Committee for more than twenty years, along with numerous university committees and professional association committees promoting diversity and Indigenous education. She was the primary investigator and director of a large statewide grant promoting diversity for Idaho. She has written/cowritten books, numerous journal articles, and chapters in books concerning Indigenous education, literacy, and special education. She also serves on the board of the *Journal of American Indian Education*.

Ms. Klug was on the founding board of Chief Tahgee Elementary Academy, a Shoshoni and Bannock language-immersion charter school in Fort Hall, Idaho, and served on the board of trustees for many years. On a personal level, Ms. Klug is the proud grandmother and great-grandmother of many Indigenous and non-Indigenous grandchildren, all of whom have her heart!

www.ingramcontent.com/pod-product-compliance
Lightning Source LLC
Chambersburg PA
CBHW080536300426
44111CB00017B/2750